The
Dead End
Kids of
St. Louis

The Dead End Kids of St. Louis

Homeless Boys and the People Who Tried to Save Them

Bonnie Stepenoff

University of Missouri Press
Columbia

Library of Congress Cataloging-in-Publication Data

Stepenoff, Bonnie, 1949–
  The dead end kids of St. Louis : homeless boys and the people
who tried to save them / Bonnie Stepenoff.
     p. cm.
  Includes bibliographical references and index.
  ISBN 978-0-8262-1888-9 (cloth : alk. paper); 978-0-8262-2242-8 (paperback : alk. paper)
  1. Homeless boys—Missouri—Saint·Louis—History. 2.
Homeless boys—Missouri—Saint Louis—Social conditions.
3. Street children—Missouri—Saint Louis—History. 4. Child
welfare—Missouri—Saint Louis—History. I. Title.
  HV4506.S25S74 2010
                                     362.7409778'66--dc22

♾™ This paper meets the requirements of the
American National Standard for Permanence of Paper
for Printed Library Materials, Z39.48, 1984.

Typefaces: Garamond and Myriad

FOR SYD

Contents

We may either smother the divine fire of youth or we may feed it. We may either stand stupidly staring as it sinks into a murky fire of crime and flares into the intermittent blaze of folly or we may tend it into a lambent flame with power to make clean and bright our dingy city streets.

—JANE ADDAMS

THERE ARE LOTS OF REASONS WHY WRITERS choose the topics of their books. Most of them are personal. The reason I wrote this book is personal: because my own father could easily have been a "dead end kid," a high school dropout hanging around the bowling alley and the pool hall, without a future. After his father died, he worked as a pin boy in a bowling alley. Although he had a mother and an older sister, they were grief stricken and unable to cope with a wild and angry teenage boy.

At the age of seventeen, he fathered a child and married my mother, but the marriage did not last. Still in his late teens, he headed for California with a local reprobate named Killer Cane. They had a few adventures, met a few celebrities, briefly worked in an aircraft plant, found a variety of other jobs, and then came back home. My father came back to his wife and child. Killer Cane's mother, who taught gym at my grade school, thought my father was a bad influence on her son. She never forgave me for being my father's daughter. One day, while the class was marching in line, she deliberately stomped on my foot. My great-aunt Helen, the cafeteria lady, came running out onto the playground and shouted at her, warning her never to do such a thing again. My father was in the service at the time. Uncle Sam wanted him. He was drafted into the United States Army during peacetime in the late 1950s.

In the service, my father became a bit of a star, skiing with frauleins in the Alps and traveling around Europe with the Army's bowling team. He sent me a postcard from Brussels, a doll in a little red hood, and a musical alarm clock with a ballerina that moved up and down. I still have the letters he wrote to me while my mother and I lived in a small apartment, waiting for him to come home, and when he did come home, we found out that he had fallen in love with Beethoven and Verdi. He bought a stereo and played classical music at top volume.

After his tour of duty, he got a job selling office equipment and bought us a brick ranch-style house in a subdivision. This was middle-class life. He and my mother sent me to a good public school, and they entertained neighbors at dinner parties. They even drank the stereotypical martinis, and it seemed for a while that he had overcome his hard adolescence and found a way to live the good life, but it did not last very long.

He died of lung cancer at the age of thirty-five. Yes, he smoked cigarettes, but the likely cause of his cancer was exposure to asbestos during his late teens and early twenties, when he worked in a variety of places, including the blast furnace of a steel mill. He was gone before his life really got started, before anyone could find out what he might have been or done.

My father's story is not unique or even terribly dramatic. He did not die in battle or end up in prison. As a matter of fact, he was one of the lucky ones. He got a taste, at least, of the American dream. But it is a sad story—a story of wasted potential. Nobody wanted it to happen. Nobody planned it. But it happened because people failed to nurture and protect a vulnerable growing boy. The same thing has happened time and again. That is why I wrote this book.

I OWE A DEBT OF GRATITUDE TO the Friends of the Missouri State Archives for awarding me a William E. Foley Research Fellowship in support of this project. Mike Everman, Pat Barge, and Sharon Kenny of the Missouri State Archives–St. Louis went out of their way to search for court records pertaining to the cases of George William Thornton, Michael Mark Pretto, and others. Librarians and archivists at the Missouri Historical Society in St. Louis steered me to records of the St. Louis House of Refuge. William M. Fischetti and Susan Beattie of the Western Historical Manuscripts Collection at the University of Missouri–St. Louis directed me to the Bureau for Men Collection and helped me find photographs. Seth Smith of the Newspaper Library at the State Historical Society of Missouri in Columbia located illustrations and found copies of articles from the *Missouri Republican* and other newspapers. Christine Montgomery of the State Historical Society kindly provided scanned illustrations. Southeast Missouri State University provided funding for travel and other research expenses. The microfilmed newspapers on file at the University's Kent Library kept me busy for hours and days on end. I made far too many demands on the interlibrary-loan staff, and I am grateful for their assistance. Sharon Kinney Hanson generously shared with me her memories of her father, Raymond Kinney. The staff of Father Dunne's Newsboys' Home (sometimes given as "Father Dunne's News Boys' Home"), recently located in Florissant but now closed, allowed me to look at historical files. Gloria Thomas and John Brenner of the University of Missouri Press were perceptive editors whose careful work improved the manuscript immensely.

As always, I depended on my husband, Jerry, for moral support, company on research trips, and many laughs. The birth of my grandson, Syd, made this work even more meaningful and closer to my heart.

Chapter 6 was published in slightly different form in the April 2010 issue of the *Missouri Historical Review*.

The
Dead End
Kids of
St. Louis

There's a blaze of fire crackling out of an old iron ash-can in the center of the street. The boys hover over it, roasting potatoes skewered on long sticks. Their impish faces gleam red one minute and are wiped by shadows the next as they lean over the flames.

—SIDNEY KINGSLEY, *Dead End*

FROM THE 1930s THROUGH THE 1950s, a group of fictional young toughs known as "the Dead End Kids" captivated audiences on Broadway and in the movies. Sidney Kingsley's melodramatic play, *Dead End,* which opened in New York in 1935, graphically depicted the lives and longings of a group of boys who swam in a polluted river, cooked food over outdoor fires, smoked cigarettes, gambled, swore, fought, carried weapons, and became entangled in the criminal underworld on Manhattan's Lower East Side. Kingsley's bad boys found even greater fame in a series of popular movies that toned down their antisocial behavior and diluted the playwright's message that life in urban slums was destroying the innocence of children and depriving young men of the fundamental American right to pursue a bright and happy future.[1]

For more than a century before the opening of *Dead End,* citizens in American cities had tried to address the problem of unsupervised youngsters on dangerous streets. In the early 1800s, churches and charitable organizations opened orphanages to shelter children who had no parents or whose parents failed to properly care for them. Throughout the nineteenth century, orphanages and other institutions used the indenture system, which involved placing children in the homes of families who would often act as employers demanding that the children work to earn their keep. By midcentury, philanthropic organizations such as the New York Children's Aid Society tried to place children in foster homes, without an indenture obligating them to work, in the hope that they

1

would be treated as part of the family. By the early twentieth century, Progressive Era reformers demanded governmental supervision of child placements to make the system more effective and humane. Each generation criticized and tried to improve upon the previous generation's handling of the problem, but in the mid-twentieth century the problem remained.[2]

During the early decades of the twentieth century, the problem even intensified. Boys and young men, looking for work or moving from job to job, swelled the populations of Skid Row neighborhoods in many American cities, including St. Louis. During the era of Prohibition in the 1920s, organized criminal gangs vying for control of the alcohol market turned the streets into shooting galleries. During the Great Depression, uncounted numbers of adolescents joined the ranks of frustrated and angry job seekers, wandering from city to city. With America's entry into World War II, legions of young men went off to fight in Europe or the Pacific, and many of them came home disabled or traumatized. The GI Bill of Rights (Servicemen's Readjustment Act of 1944) eventually helped millions of young men go to college and pursue the American dream in the suburbs. While the world changed around them, many urban boys struggled to reach adulthood in increasingly violent and desolate streets.[3]

The problem of endangered youth is difficult to define. Unlike race or ethnicity, boyhood is a temporary social category. No one remains a boy for a lifetime, and boys pass through a series of stages that have been labeled as infancy, childhood, and adolescence. Children and adolescents develop gradually from infants, who are completely dependent upon adult caregivers, to adults, who are able to take care of themselves. The beginning of adolescence is generally defined as the onset of puberty, somewhere between the ages of twelve and fourteen, but the end of adolescence is not easy to pinpoint. In general, within American society, the age of full adulthood is defined as falling somewhere between the ages of eighteen and twenty-one. For the purposes of this book, a boy will be defined as a young male under the age of twenty-one. A homeless boy will be defined as a male who has not reached adulthood and who lacks necessary shelter and supervision by responsible adults.[4]

There are plenty of homeless boys in popular fiction. Gavroche, the Paris gamin, challenges French authorities and stands with the revolutionaries on the barricades in Victor Hugo's monumental novel *Les Miserables*. Charles Dickens's iconic waif Oliver Twist miraculously preserves his innocence in the treacherous streets of nineteenth-century London, where, by the way, there were tens of thousands of real boys who

Young messenger in downtown St. Louis. (Photograph by Lewis Hine, May 12, 1910. Courtesy of the Library of Congress)

slept out in the cold. Sir Arthur Conan Doyle's Sherlock Holmes rounds up examples of these ragged urchins and sends them out on fact-finding missions to help solve his cases. Horatio Alger's boy-heroes struggle up from poverty to become captains of industry in Gilded Age New York. America's most famous boy-adventurer, Huckleberry Finn, runs away from an abusive father and floats down the Mississippi River with his companion, Jim, the runaway slave. On their way down the river, Huck and Jim pass the booming city of St. Louis, where real-life homeless boys, hundreds of them, were sleeping in alleyways or cellars and hiding out in caves at the time Mark Twain was writing the novel.[5]

Jane Addams, the Progressive Era reformer, called attention to the real dangers that threatened youthful wanderers in the growing city of Chicago. In her classic cry of the heart, *The Spirit of Youth and the City Streets,* first published in 1909, Addams proclaimed that every great civilization depended upon the energy, imagination, and innocence of youth for strength and renewal. With their own survival in the balance, societies had to find ways to nurture, protect, and encourage the growth of their young. Modern industrial cities, she warned, were failing miserably in this endeavor by using children as workers, not providing wholesome opportunities for their recreation, and allowing them to roam unsupervised in dangerous streets. This terrible failure posed dangers not only to individuals, but to society as a whole.[6]

Historian David Nasaw views the modernizing city as a place of opportunities, as well as dangers, for American children. In his 1985 book *Children of the City: At Work and at Play,* Nasaw paints a lively if overly optimistic portrait of the lives of youngsters growing up in the early twentieth-century American city. He expounds on children playing in their neighborhoods, working in mills, hustling newspapers, scavenging for food, and going on strike. In his final chapter, he expresses nostalgia for the pre–World War I era, when children experienced a high "degree of autonomy and freedom at work on the streets."[7] Nasaw does not ignore, but does underestimate, the negative effects of life on the street.

Homelessness, in general, has not been given enough attention in histories of American cities. In his 2002 book *Down and Out, On the Road: The Homeless in American History,* Kenneth Kusmer contends that although homelessness has been an important aspect of American social history, scholars have tended to overlook it. Homeless people do not appear in standard documentary sources, such as the United States Census or the city directories, but they are a part of urban life and history. Many histories of specific towns and cities fail even to mention homelessness as a social problem. James Neal Primm's excellent history of St. Louis discusses it only in the context of very recent times, but homeless people abounded in the city from the mid-nineteenth century through the mid-twentieth.[8]

Boys were a special category of the homeless in St. Louis and other growing cities. In grim nineteenth-century orphanages, boys tended to greatly outnumber girls, and institutions that were created to house incorrigible and delinquent children admitted many more males than females. Boys more often ran away from home and more frequently appeared on the city streets as workers, beggars, and petty thieves. From the late nineteenth through the mid-twentieth century, newsboys hawked their wares at every busy intersection. In the early twentieth century, male adolescents were drawn to the expanding Skid Row community, the domain of destitute, unattached males until the great slum-clearance efforts began after World War II. Boys vastly outnumbered girls among the juvenile delinquents, who became a pressing social concern in the 1950s.[9]

In St. Louis, as in other cities, homeless boys were the by-products of rapid industrialization, urbanization, and the westward movement. In the nineteenth century, the population of St. Louis soared, and so did the number of unsupervised children. Irish immigration peaked in the mid-1840s, and German immigration reached its height at the end of that decade. In addition to those who came to settle, thousands of travelers passed through St. Louis on their way to the California gold fields, the Texas plains, or the new lands in Oregon. Newcomers often lacked an extended family or a social-support network to care for their children in the event of disaster. Chapter 1 describes the streets of St. Louis in the nineteenth century, when thousands of boys wandered in and out of the city, struggling to grow up on their own or with little help from adults.[10]

Chapter 2 discusses orphans and the people who tried to care for them. In the 1850s, St. Louis struggled to recover from the 1849 cholera epidemic that killed 10 percent of its population, leaving thousands of children without parents. By 1860, there were more than fifteen hundred orphans in St. Louis. Catholics, Unitarians, Methodists, Lutherans, and people from other religious groups opened institutions to shelter parentless and indigent children. Most children remained in these facilities for short periods. To make room for younger children, orphanages commonly tried to "put out" the older ones by offering them to families who often took them far from St. Louis. In the nineteenth and early twentieth centuries, it was standard practice to indenture boys, often at very young ages, to employers who would use them as apprentices and teach them trades. Employers frequently overworked or abused these young boys, and many of them ran away. Twentieth-century reformers tried hard to change the system, but problems remained.[11]

Despite efforts to place boys in homes, bands of footloose youngsters nonetheless roamed the streets near the St. Louis riverfront. Some of them were the children of slaves or free black people. Some were the sons

Two small boys behind a dilapidated building in St. Louis. (Used by permission, State Historical Society of Missouri, Columbia)

of recent immigrants; others were in-migrants from rural areas. Some of them had been left behind by caravans heading to the Far West. Others lived in tenements with parents who were ill or indigent or neglectful. Some had no homes at all and lived in the streets. Observers in the 1870s described their loud gatherings in vacant lots and lumberyards. Fights often broke out, and feuds between various "tribes" or "clans" could go on for years. Owners of variety theaters and bawdy houses hired fast-talking boys as "claquers" or shills. Adult criminals used them for picking pockets or breaking into houses. Many of them had to steal to live, and some of them descended into lives of serious and violent crime.[12] Their experiences are treated in Chapter 3.

In the wild city streets, gangs of boys played games together, gambled together, got into trouble together, and searched for shelter in out-of-the-way places. One of the hallmarks of gang life, according to early twentieth-century sociologist J. Adams Puffer, is the tendency for groups of boys to spend long periods of time together in some particular spot on the landscape. This might be a street corner, an old abandoned building, or a shanty in the woods. In St. Louis, because of its peculiar geology, gangs of boys sometimes took shelter in the vast network of interconnected caves that lay just beneath the surface. Police sometimes traced outbreaks of thefts and other petty crimes to hidden dens, where boys could hole up for weeks and months at a time.[13] This phenomenon is discussed in Chapter 4.

In an effort to remove unruly and unsupervised boys from the streets, the city established the St. Louis House of Refuge. Although the name implied that it was a charitable institution, and its founders viewed it in that way, the House of Refuge was a grim and frightening prison. In 1872, the House of Refuge's superintendent, F. S. W. Gleason, was accused of extreme cruelty against the inmates. After that, the state mandated some changes, but the institution remained a prisonlike place with twenty-foot walls surrounding it. More than 80 percent of the children admitted to this facility were boys. Some were charged with crimes, principally stealing, but most were guilty of nothing more than vagrancy, destitution, or "improper exposure" (meaning they had been abandoned to a life on the streets). Boys generally stayed there from a few months to a few years before they escaped or went back to their parents or were indentured. Chapter 5 discusses the House of Refuge and the twentieth-century innovations that were made in attempts to correct its deficiencies.[14]

At the beginning of the twentieth century, a young priest made it his business to protect, and not incarcerate, homeless boys. Father Peter Joseph Dunne, who had spent his adolescence as an orphan in St. Joseph, Missouri, came to St. Louis in the 1890s. He found work as a night watchman at St. Louis University, where the Jesuit priests gave him an education. As a young priest assigned to the tenement district, Dunne encountered a homeless boy named James "Little Jimmie" Fleming. In 1906, Little Jimmie became one of the first occupants of Father Dunne's Newsboys' Home and Protectorate, a shelter for orphans, runaways, and delinquents. With an emphasis on education and training, Dunne tried to prepare young tramps for productive lives, and the Newsboys' Home continued to take in troubled and indigent boys for the next hundred years, closing its doors in 2006.[15] Chapter 6 describes the lives of newsboys and the work of the priest who tried to rescue them.

Although reformers attempted to clean up the city in the early twentieth century, rootless men and boys swelled the population of the increasingly shabby area near the Mississippi River and along Market Street.[16] The same phenomenon occurred in many other American cities, where Skid Row sections expanded rapidly despite efforts by politicians and philanthropists to improve urban environments. In preparation for the 1904 St. Louis World's Fair, planners and architects created a fabulous system of parks and boulevards, as the city's elites moved to the flourishing West End. Meanwhile, on the east side, seasonal workers, migrants, mendicants, and inexperienced farm boys, seeking work or handouts, congregated in cheap rooming houses, shelters, and even hobo camps along the river. Chapter 7 discusses the growth of Skid Row in St. Louis and the deterioration of the downtown area in the first half of the twentieth century.

The declining downtown area spawned new forms of criminal activity, especially during the 1920s, and these activities often involved boys in their teens or young men in their twenties. National Prohibition dealt a one-two punch to St. Louis by shutting down its brewery industry and opening the liquor business to violent gangs of outlaws. Boys and young men found new and dangerous opportunities to make money as runners for bootleggers, who initiated their young protégés into the seductive but dangerous world of urban mob warfare.[17] Chapter 8 describes a period when St. Louis streets became shooting galleries, while growing boys witnessed and sometimes participated in the carnage.

The Great Depression of the 1930s drew national attention to the problem of homeless and wandering boys, who could easily be drawn into lives of violence and crime. Kingsley's *Dead End* threw a spotlight on the brutal conditions affecting boys in our cities. A sociologist named Thomas Minehan followed young wanderers along the Mississippi River Valley, camped with them in hobo jungles, and reported their troubles to the wider world. New Deal programs like the Civilian Conservation Corps (CCC) and the National Youth Administration (NYA) directly addressed the issue of bringing poor and disaffected youths back into the mainstream of society. One well-known St. Louisan, Archie Moore, directly experienced the corrupting influence of urban life and the redemptive effect of the CCC.[18] Chapter 9 addresses the impact of the Depression and the New Deal on St. Louis's neglected boys.

Mobilization for World War II drew millions of young men into military service, and the GI Bill opened educational opportunities for millions of veterans, but many young men were left behind. In the years following the war, St. Louis became a divided city, with upwardly mobile families moving to the suburbs while the urban core declined. Racial segregation increased, as white families moved to the suburbs west of St. Louis, while black families streamed into the city from the rural South. Despite earnest efforts to clean up blighted neighborhoods, the inner core of St. Louis became even less hospitable to impoverished boys, and juvenile delinquency increased. Within the inner city, the federal government botched the effort to provide decent, affordable, family-friendly housing, and government planners neglected to provide access for residents there to health facilities, playgrounds, and public transportation.[19] As Chapter 10 shows, in the postwar era between 1945 and 1960, the landscape of St. Louis changed dramatically, but urban boys continued to struggle with the dark forces of violence and crime.

This is a study of homeless and neglected boys who lived and sometimes died on the streets of St. Louis. Some of them were runaways and rebels, looking for freedom. A few became dangerous outlaws. Some of them triumphed over neglect, loneliness, and a dangerous environment to become successful, sometimes famous, men. Others fell by the wayside. Whether they were winners or losers, their stories deserve to be told because they teach us something about the way Americans care for—or fail to care for—their growing boys and the effect it has on society.

Chapter One

The City Streets

The first time I ever saw St. Louis I could have bought it for six
million dollars, and it was the mistake of my life that I did not do
it. It was bitter now to look abroad over this domed and steepled
metropolis, this solid expanse of bricks and mortar stretching away
on every hand into dim, measure-defying distances, and remember
that I had allowed that opportunity to go by.

—MARK TWAIN, *Life on the Mississippi*

MARK TWAIN CAME TO ST. LOUIS as an ambitious boy, dream-
ing of becoming a pilot on the Mississippi River. In the 1850s,
he prowled the riverfront, boarding the steamboats that were
"packed together like sardines" along the levee. He achieved his ambition,
but lost his job when the Civil War interfered with river commerce. More
than twenty years later, he returned to his old haunts and found that the
steamboats had mostly disappeared, but that St. Louis had expanded west
of the riverfront to become "a great and prosperous and advancing city."[1]

Between the 1840s and the 1870s, St. Louis evolved from a bustling river port to a great industrial center. Railroads and factories
moved into the lowlands along the Mississippi River. By 1880, flour,
meat, chewing tobacco, malt liquor, paint, brick, cloth bags, and iron
topped the list of St. Louis's products. Coal-powered machinery gener-
ated clouds of black smoke that polluted the air. Breweries and other
manufacturing plants dumped waste into streets, gutters, and ponds.
Freight trains clattered through the bottoms, spewing dust, noise, and
prosperity. To escape the dirt and din and enjoy their newfound wealth,
many residents moved to the higher ground in the central and western
portions of the growing city.[2]

From a child's perspective, the story of Chouteau's Pond dramatizes
the changes that took place in the older sections of the city. In the 1760s,

French settlers dammed a creek to create power for a gristmill. After Auguste Chouteau purchased the property in 1779, the mill pond became known as Chouteau's Pond. More than two miles long and about a quarter of a mile wide, the pond was a great attraction for boys and others who enjoyed fishing, boating, and swimming in the summer and skating in the winter. After the cholera epidemic of 1849, city officials drained the pond while creating a sewer system. In the second half of the nineteenth century, Mill Creek Valley, the site of the pond, became the locus of railroad tracks and industrial development, and the city lost a great recreational resource.[3]

Parks and recreational developments bypassed the eastern part of the city, closest to the riverfront, leaving that heavily populated area without green space in which children could play. In 1868, Henry Shaw donated about two hundred acres of land to create Tower Grove Park, which he named after his home on the grounds of his nearby botanical gardens. In 1872, St. Louis purchased a thousand acres for the magnificent Forest Park, which also encompassed the zoological gardens. Unfortunately for residents of the riverfront area, both these parks were located in the western district of the city. By 1900, the western section of town contained nearly 85 percent (approximately 1,800 acres) of St. Louis's park land. The central district, with 21 percent of the city's population, had only 8 percent of the city's park area, and the eastern district, where nearly half of the city's 575,000 residents lived, had only 150 acres of park land (less than 7 percent of the total park area).[4]

Throughout the nineteenth century, immigrants and in-migrants crowded into the older sections of the city. In the 1840s, the city's population quadrupled, as Germans and Irish people fled social unrest and famine in their homelands. According to the 1850 census, nearly one-third of St. Louis residents were natives of Germany, outnumbering natives of Missouri. The Irish held second place among immigrants, although Germans outnumbered them by two to one. The Civil War slowed immigration in both the city and the nation as a whole, so that in 1870 foreign-born residents accounted for only 36 percent of the city's population. In the aftermath of the war, which brought an end to racial slavery and spurred in-migration from the rural South, the proportion of African Americans increased from 2 to 7 percent. Many African Americans moved to the drained Mill Creek Valley, where they struggled economically but created an exciting cultural life.[5]

Street improvements in the growing city increasingly divided the rich from the poor. Low-lying Mill Creek Valley formed a natural topographical division between the north and south sides of town. Railroad tracks, sheds, tanks, and other industrial structures created obstructions for pedestrians, wagons, and carriages in the valley. In the period of most rapid growth, between the 1850s and the 1870s, street crews avoided Mill Creek Valley, making virtually no improvements on the routes connecting the central and northern parts of the city with the south side. Over time, the physical division became a social barrier, as the south side descended into poverty and isolation.[6]

A variety of ethnic groups crowded into run-down housing in the densely built blocks in the south side near the downtown business district. German immigrants clustered in the vicinity of the Soulard Market, an open-air congeries of food and flower sellers. Throughout the Second Ward, a long, narrow strip of territory running from the levee to the eastern edge of fashionable Lafayette Park, the vast majority of the residents came from Germany, Switzerland, Alsace, and the Austro-Hungarian Empire, with a small percentage from Ireland. The First Ward, adjacent to and south of the Second Ward, had a nearly identical ethnic composition.[7]

On a typical street on the south side, small rectangular brick dwellings stood at the front edges of tiny lots. Narrow passageways between the buildings contained flights of wooden stairs leading to second- and third-floor apartments. Most apartments contained two rooms of roughly the same size, with no differentiation between living, eating, and sleeping spaces. Backyards, paved with stone or brick, were cluttered with privies, workshops, toolsheds, and wells. Women washed clothes in sinks on side porches, which also served as summer kitchens and sleeping areas when the heat inside the buildings became unbearable.[8]

Immigrants of various nationalities tried to make a living by opening businesses on shabby little byways scattered throughout the older sections near the central business district. A Chinese enclave known as Hop Alley occupied an area bounded by Walnut, Market, Seventh, and Ninth streets. Most of the residents were ordinary businessmen and their families, trying to survive by opening laundries, grocery stores, and restaurants. But in the public imagination, fueled by newspaper sensationalism, this was a world of opium, or "hop," sellers, drug-induced dreams, incense, and smoky rooms. Young men went there at midnight to buy hop and carry it away or lie in rattan bunks and smoke it in pipes.[9]

A gruesome murder took place in Hop Alley in 1883. The body of a Cantonese man named Lou Johnson was found in the alley, horribly slashed. His head was later found in a basket of rice. Police blamed the killing on the so-called Highbinders, which were secret societies of Chinese men who allegedly committed many murders. Consequently, the

Boys on the railing in back of tenement housing, ca. 1908. (Used by permission, State Historical Society of Missouri, Columbia)

authorities arrested and prosecuted six Chinese suspects, but without evidence or witnesses, no conviction was possible.[10]

As a bizarre sequel to this event, in April 1899, two small boys playing marbles discovered the body of a Chinese man under a large gasoline tank near the sidewalk in front of the Waters-Pierce Oil Company on Gratiot between Twelfth and Thirteenth streets. The boys, Charles McNorman and John Dutton, lived nearby. One of them flipped a marble too hard, and it rolled under the tank. In an effort to find it, he stumbled upon the corpse. The boys ran and told a passerby, who notified the police.[11]

When the city undertaker's men arrived on the scene, they found the body on its back, with the neck resting on a brick, and the hands clasped across the chest. Blood had congealed on the man's face and in his hair. Even for the hardened officials, this was a sickening sight. Police identified the murdered man as Jeu Chow and questioned the residents of Hop Alley. The investigation revealed that he had lived in a house at the rear of 719 Walnut Street, the same house where Lou Johnson had been killed.[12]

As the downtown area became more dangerous, residents moved into deteriorating neighborhoods on the near north side. African Americans occupied dwellings on Lucas and Morgan streets west of Twelfth and on Wash Street east of Twelfth. People from Ireland, Germany, Austria, Russia, Poland, Hungary, Romania, Greece, and Italy migrated into the area, mingling in the blocks between Seventh and Eleventh streets. Italians found housing between Seventh and Ninth streets, from Lucas to O'Fallon Street. Polish immigrants concentrated along O'Fallon Street and Cass Avenue.[13]

Jewish immigrants settled on Morgan, Carr, and Biddle streets in this north-side area. The popular Biddle Street Market was a hub of commerce. Merchants sold Jewish foods, literature, religious artifacts, and newspapers from storefronts along Biddle Street, O'Fallon Street, Carr Street, and Franklin Avenue. Non-Jewish residents shared in the local culture and gradually adopted a variety of the Yiddish expressions used in the area, which was sometimes called Little Jerusalem or the Ghetto.[14]

Residents of these north-side neighborhoods typically occupied apartments in two- or three-story brick or frame buildings that had two fronts, one facing the street and one facing an alley. Living conditions were similar to those on the south side. Each apartment building filled the entire width of the lot, leaving room only for a narrow passageway for access to the backyard. Yards were crowded with sheds, privies, stables, ashes, garbage, and manure. Rats infested piles of discarded mattresses, bed springs, and food waste. In most cases, six or more families shared the same yard, and no one took responsibility for keeping it clean. Children played in these yards, or else they went out into the alleys and streets.[15]

Families with children lived alongside vagrants and prostitutes. Residents tried to make their neighborhoods livable by growing flowers in tin cans on window ledges and doorsteps. Gossiping women congregated in front of grocers and butcher shops. Housewives went out to buy a single egg, three cents' worth of sugar, or enough meat for a single meal, and stopped and visited on their way to and from the store. Families carried tables out into the alleys and invited friends to eat, play cards, and relax. Peddlers sold candy and cakes from pushcarts. Old men philosophized in coffeehouses. Footloose boys and young men could find all sorts of entertainment on Franklin Avenue. Prostitutes worked in certain constantly changing areas of the district. Saloons served as banks and post offices, cashing paychecks and providing mailing addresses for people who had no permanent lodging. Tramps found shelter in basements and attics, and the shifting, anonymous population drifted into crime.[16]

Most notorious of all the enclaves on the near north side was the Irish American neighborhood known as "Kerry Patch," which was peopled by immigrants from Ireland's County Kerry. The boundaries of the Patch changed constantly as people moved in and out of flimsy dwellings on the

Residents in the littered yard and looking out the windows of a run-down building. (Used by permission, State Historical Society of Missouri, Columbia)

northern edge of the city's central corridor. Most of the residents of Kerry Patch were squatters, working men and their families who built their own shelters on land they did not own. Many of the houses were wooden structures with rags stuffed into broken windows. Within the Patch was a central common, or green, which residents used for gardening and games. The people shared the Catholic faith and participated in a variety of sports and pastimes, including cockfights, dogfights, and boxing matches. They defended their territory against trespassers, including policemen and people of other races and ethnic origins.[17]

The life histories of William Marion Reedy and his boyhood friends, Johnnie Cunningham and Jack Shea, reveal the dangers for boys growing up in Kerry Patch. Reedy's father was an Irish-born policeman who walked the beat and raised his family in the "Bloody Third District," which included Kerry Patch. His first son, William, was born in 1862, while Union troops occupied St. Louis. During William's childhood, the people of the Patch kept goats and raised vegetables in a common garden. William's best friend, Johnnie Cunningham, delivered milk from his mother's cows. Johnnie's life had a dark side. He robbed people in the streets at night and took his friend William to hideouts in haylofts, where they eluded the police. They pretended they were pirates, and William viewed their activities as boyhood fantasies and adventures. Their mutual friend Jack also played reckless games. Johnnie and Jack did jail time together after William became a reporter. Following a jailbreak, Jack shot and killed a police officer.[18]

William Reedy graduated from St. Louis University, pursued a career in journalism, and became the editor of a successful magazine called the *St. Louis Mirror*. His friend Johnnie Cunningham managed to avoid imprisonment, but died in a train wreck. Jack Shea spent many years in the penitentiary, while Reedy prospered. As a successful middle-aged man, looking back on his life, Reedy recalled that he and Cunningham and Shea were very much alike. As boys, they were "much of a piece mentally." All three were reckless and adventurous. There was no rational explanation for his good fortune and their terrible fates. The only difference between them was that Reedy had parents who kept track of him and punished him when he got out of line.[19]

Many parents in the poorer sections of the city failed, or were unable, to protect their children. Alcoholism, illness, despair, and death produced what some observers described as hordes of neglected and undisciplined young people, who darted in and out of the crowds on the levee, played games of dice in alleyways, begged, stole, picked pockets, and otherwise harassed honest citizens. J. A. Dacus and James W. Buel, who observed and wrote about the situation in the 1870s, were at a loss to explain how these rootless children eked out a living. Ragged urchins who appeared on the streets in the daytime as newsboys, messengers, beggars, shills, and shoe-shine boys vanished in the winter and at night into vacant buildings, cellars, and caves.[20]

To the eyes of impressionable boys, without parents to shield them, the city presented an ever-changing spectacle of violence. In the 1850s, although the population of free blacks was growing, St. Louis was still a slave city. Slave auctions occurred frequently on the courthouse steps. Slave-catchers pursued runaways. Newspaper advertisements threatened terrible punishment, even mutilation, for those who were caught. A public whipping post made it clear to everyone that the root of the slave system was brutal coercion.[21]

When the Civil War began in 1861, pro-slavery militias drilled in a forest at the western edge of the city. On May 10, about six thousand Union soldiers marched on this encampment and demanded unconditional surrender. Outnumbered and outgunned, the secessionists at "Camp Jackson" capitulated. As General Nathaniel Lyon, leader of the Union forces, gathered up prisoners, thousands of local citizens converged on the site. Most of them came to watch, but some came armed with rocks, sticks, brickbats, and guns. Someone opened fire; soldiers and civilians exchanged volleys. When the shooting stopped, twenty-eight people were dead, including some children, and many more were wounded. But the Union had secured the city.[22]

Men and boys worked together in James B. Eads's St. Louis shipyard, building ironclad gunboats for the War Department. Boys worked as runners, bringing hot rivets to the workers who constructed the armored vessels. When Dr. John Lauderdale of the United States Army's Medical Department visited the workplace in August 1862, he watched the blacksmith pull white-hot rivets from the forge and carelessly throw them at the gangs of boys waiting to carry them to the workmen. Far from expressing shock, Lauderdale noted that he found this dangerous behavior amusing. The blacksmith and other adult workers probably resented the boys for taking away skilled jobs. Two years later, when many of the city's workers went out on strike, ironworkers complained that their employers hired too many boys at low wages, depriving adult workers of employment.[23]

Ironworkers played a big role in St. Louis's labor protests during the weeklong general strike that electrified the city between July 22 and July 26, 1877. On Tuesday, July 24, just after dark, about fifteen hundred ironworkers, some armed with clubs, marched up Olive Street, four abreast, to the beat of a fife and drum, to join a crowd of striking and unemployed workers in a mass demonstration. Police and armed citizens came out into the streets and confronted the strikers, who were mostly unarmed. In the end, the strikers capitulated.[24]

Labor unrest again led to violence at the beginning of the twentieth century. On April 29, 1900, employees of the St. Louis and Suburban Electric Railroad went out on strike, and nine days later, workers struck the much larger and more powerful St. Louis Transit streetcar company.

In support of the strikers, many residents boycotted the streetcars in May and June. By early June, Suburban managers submitted to arbitration, and most of the company's employees returned to work, but St. Louis Transit managers refused to budge, and the strike became increasingly violent as strike sympathizers piled stones and garbage, built bonfires, and planted explosives on the tracks. On June 10, marching strikers clashed with a group of citizens, who had been mobilized to aid the police in keeping order. When members of this posse fired their weapons, three strikers were killed and fourteen wounded.[25]

Local and national leaders intervened to end the violence. Labor leader Samuel Gompers came to the city, but failed to settle the strike. Joseph W. Folk, a young lawyer, participated in negotiations that resulted in a temporary settlement in July, but the agreement broke down. Finally, in September, the union admitted defeat. One positive outcome of the strike was the election of Folk as St. Louis circuit attorney. Folk investigated corruption in the street railway corporations and went on to become a progressive governor of Missouri.[26]

Despite these ups and downs, St. Louis's downtown area provided a colorful and exciting life for residents. Every fall, beginning in 1878, the city's elite old families made a spectacular public appearance in the Veiled Prophet parade. According to historian Thomas Spencer, the Veiled Prophet (VP), or Grand Oracle, was a mysterious, princely being who received the city's debutantes at a yearly ball. Borrowing ideas and paraphernalia from New Orleans's Mardi Gras, the VP, his two high priests, and a secret organization of two hundred dignitaries produced an annual torchlight procession that provided entertainment for St. Louisans of all social classes who lined the streets. During the parade, the VP "visited" the city in the midst of a fireworks display.[27]

Throughout the nineteenth and early twentieth centuries, the St. Louis riverfront possessed a distinct, and sometimes shadowy, allure. People flocked there, looking for excitement and sometimes for trouble. In the brutally cold winter of 1899, a team of con artists conducted a shell game on folding tables set up on the ice halfway across the river. Within a short period of time, a crowd gathered around them. Three men ran the games, while another three mingled with the crowd. The men playing the games kept three walnut shells moving at a rapid pace, while keeping up a constant line of patter. Bettors had to guess which of the shells concealed a little black ball, which most likely was hidden under the shell man's thumb. The game was rigged; the bettors always lost. But the police could do nothing to stop it because it was taking place on the river, out of their jurisdiction.[28]

Local authorities consistently failed to enforce the laws, especially the laws against gambling. On October 11, 1878, the *St. Louis Evening Post* printed a letter from a concerned citizen to the St. Louis Board of Commissioners. The writer identified seventeen keno and faro houses on Sixth Street, Chestnut Street, and Washington Avenue. He further stated that a "great number of poker rooms," too numerous to mention, operated in private homes, and he begged the commissioners to break up these games and protect the public morals. A second letter, written by another citizen, Jacob S. Williams, and printed on October 12, lamented the fact that the police commissioners knew about the gambling problem, but did nothing to control it.[29]

Williams explained in his letter that he had asked a police captain why these "gilded hells," the gambling establishments, were allowed to exist. The policeman had shaken his head and said, "You must ask a higher authority." Williams believed that the police commissioners knew about the problem, but deliberately chose to "wink at this class of law-breakers." He called for the people to take action and replace corrupt officials.[30]

Williams believed that the gambling dens had enticed his son Frank to leave home and that the authorities had failed to protect him. According to Williams, Frank had been a conscientious young man until he came under the sway of vile men. In his father's words, Frank disappeared into St. Louis's streets to consort with "gamblers, thieves, who [had] lured him from the path of rectitude. O shame! O humiliation! Who will wonder that my heart is full of sorrow, overflowing with indignation toward those who have robbed him of his good name, toward those whose duty it was to protect him and his sorrow-stricken mother from the anguish their recreancy made possible?"[31]

There were other temptations for St. Louis boys. Some of them tried to follow the example of dime-novel desperadoes by heading out west. Because of its location at the confluence of two great rivers, where thousands embarked on journeys to the Far West, St. Louis was a magnet for daring and ambitious men hoping to make a fortune on the cattle ranges or in the gold fields. It is not so surprising, then, that in April 1884, the *St. Louis Globe-Democrat* reported that "the police are on the lookout for Charles Liebich, a 14-year-old boy, residing with his parents at 2515 North Market street, and two companions, named Davidson, of about the same age, who took a quantity of money from their parents and a double-barreled shotgun, and announced their intention of going to Texas."[32]

Even boys who stayed close to home could encounter deadly dangers. For example, in 1884, a nine-year-old boy named John McCarty died at the City Hospital after being run over by a streetcar at the corner of

Young boys by the outhouse behind their building. (Used by permission, State Historical Society of Missouri, Columbia)

Sixteenth Street and Cass Avenue. On the very next day, the coroner ruled that his death had been an accident. "The boy," said the coroner's report, "had been in the habit of playing in the street and jumping on and off the streetcars as they came along."[33]

Of course the boy had played in the streets. What else could he do? There were no compulsory education laws; no one forced him to go to school. In all likelihood, there was no green space behind his home, since backyards in poor neighborhoods were places for using the privy, hanging out laundry, raising a garden or a few chickens, and throwing out garbage. There were no playgrounds, no swing sets, no sliding boards, swimming pools, or trampolines. Colorful streetcars had wheels and bells and darted around corners in a way that enticed many a young boy to prove his own quickness and luck, until one day they failed him.

Jane Addams, the famous founder of Chicago's Hull House, recognized the dangerous ways in which industrializing cities both stimulated and thwarted the adolescent's quest for adventure. It was, she wrote, an "inveterate demand of youth that life shall afford a large element of excitement." This was a good thing, she said. Youthful energy and zest renewed, for every generation, the joy of living. But in industrializing cities, which

valued work above play and left no space for recreation, youthful eager-
ness could turn to restlessness, and this could lead to trouble. Where there
were no parks or sports fields, there were streets and bars, pool halls, gambling houses, variety theaters, and bordellos. In the quest for wealth, wrote
Addams, America's cities had ignored the needs, and the vulnerability, of
the "wistful, over-confident" young people emerging from childhood and
trying to take their place in the world.[34]

Theodore Dreiser, who came from Chicago to St. Louis as a young
newspaper reporter in 1892, found the street life of the two cities to be
very similar. He stayed in a seedy rooming house on Pine Street, where the
streetcars clanged all night long. On his first tour of the city, he observed
that the old mansions near the central business district were falling into
disrepair. Stores, factories, and offices, even a few tall, Chicago-style buildings, were rising in their place. Far from downtown, on the West End,
wealthy people were building magnificent homes in gated parks. Along
the waterfront, he found a mill area flanked by "wretched tenements, as
poor and grimy and dingy as any" he had seen in Chicago.[35]

St. Louis's east-side tenements earned nicknames like Fort Sumpter and
Castle Thunder for constantly drawing the attention of police. During the
sweltering summers, hundreds of men, women, and children came out
of the buildings at night to sleep on the roofs and in the courtyards and
alleyways. Drinking, gambling, sex, and illicit drug use took place out in
the open, and the noise was constant. Children living in these buildings
rarely attended school. Without supervision, they wandered the streets in
the neighborhood, finding companions who taught them how to survive
as gamblers, prostitutes, tramps, and thieves.[36]

Young people who wandered downtown to portions of Sixth, Seventh,
and Poplar streets and Almond Avenue would see women leaning from
upstairs windows, couples embracing on the sidewalks, drunkards sleeping in doorways, and men of all ages loafing and gawking at the all-night
saloons. Not only prostitutes, but thieves and predators haunted these
streets, where unsuspecting strangers could lose their money or their
lives. In other, less blighted, parts of the city, prostitutes lived in gaudily
furnished houses, and madams traveled the streets in sleek horse-drawn
carriages.[37]

The city's various houses of entertainment provided the potential for
ribald adventures. On one snowy evening in February 1891, a woman in
a scanty costume ran wildly from a theater on Market Street, followed by
a crowd of men and boys. Gunshots echoed from Doc Emerson's *musee,*
where the woman, known as Fatima, worked as a "serpentine dancer."
A prop man had brought real snakes onto the stage. When one of the

reptiles escaped from its box, Fatima ran screaming out into the street. The audience followed her. Emerson, the proprietor, took out a revolver and fired it at the snake. But the snake escaped into the street, where it froze to death. Fatima took refuge in one of the shops near the new railroad terminal, Union Station, which was under construction.[38]

Small, loosely organized bands of boys from the tenement districts wandered the city, looking for trouble, and they often found it. In the spring of 1899, six boys ranging in age from eleven to sixteen robbed a printing office and a saloon. Ira Adams, Jacob Lyons, Jake Schweiger, Ed Mullen, Rudolph Stuffon, and Joseph Daryear all lived in the vicinity of Second Street and Clark Avenue. On March 31, they broke into a print shop on Fourth Street and Clark Avenue and carried off about fifty pounds of metal type in cloth bags. As they were lugging away the stolen goods, they forced open a rear door into a saloon at 206 South Fourth Street.[39]

Apparently, the boys stole thirty-three quart bottles of whiskey and stashed it in the basement of a vacant house on Clark Avenue. After that, they returned to the saloon and consumed enough liquor to become noisily drunk. Their loud talk attracted the attention of police officers, who surrounded the saloon, pounced on the offenders, and loaded them into a patrol wagon. Police found the bags of metal type in an alley and the liquor in its basement hiding place.[40]

There was a fine line between boyhood shenanigans and lives of crime. Young William Marion Reedy played at being an outlaw, but eventually escaped from Kerry Patch and became a successful editor, while his boyhood friends Jack Shea and Johnnie Cunningham were not so lucky. For them, the adventures of boyhood led to prison and early death. Promising young men like Frank Williams left home and got lost in a seductive world of gamblers and thieves. Like Williams, many young men abandoned loving families for the excitement of life on the streets. Other young boys were themselves abandoned, by parents who were too sick, poor, or demoralized to care for them. Some had no parents at all. For these boys, the city could be a menacing place, in which the only available shelter might be an abandoned building, a dank basement, a jail cell, or an orphanage.

In the city that Mark Twain could have bought for six million dollars, the lives of these boys seemed not to be worth very much.

Chapter Two

Orphans and Orphanages

We have on hand a very fine lot of boys of all ages from one month to twelve years of age. We are putting them out in carefully selected homes. They are placed on three months trial. All it costs to get one is the transportation. References required. For terms address Rev. David Gay, 810 Olive Street, St. Louis, Mo., State Superintendent of the Children's Home Society.

—*St. Louis Globe-Democrat,* December 23, 1899

I N THE 1850s, A HARVARD-TRAINED MINISTER named Charles Loring Brace came to the conclusion that cities were dangerous to the moral development of boys and girls. To put his ideas into practice, he developed the placing-out system for transporting neglected and orphaned children from the streets of New York to more wholesome environments in the American West. Brace and his colleagues in the New York Children's Aid Society sent thousands of children on so-called orphan trains to Kansas, Ohio, Indiana, Illinois, Iowa, Missouri, and other states. On the theory that hard work was good for the soul, the society placed children on farms and in homes, where they helped with indoor and outdoor chores. Some of these children flourished and even grew up to be prominent people. Others felt they were hardly more than slaves.[1]

One of the weaknesses of Brace's plan was his romantic notion of life in the West. As Marilyn Holt has pointed out in her book *The Orphan Trains: Placing Out in America,* the advocates of the placing-out system failed to recognize the harsh conditions on the frontier or, just as importantly, the pace of urbanization in the western states. Cities like Cincinnati, Chicago, and St. Louis faced many of the same problems as New York. Even the cities of the Far West suffered from the ill effects of rapid population growth and the breakdown of the traditional rural family structure. San Francisco, for example, opened an orphan asylum in 1851.[2]

23

Three boys on the crude doorstep of a county poorhouse
in 1917. (Used by permission, State Historical Society of
Missouri, Columbia)

Nineteenth-century St. Louis had a miserably inadequate system for
housing society's cast-offs. Beginning in 1827, the St. Louis Poor House
sheltered indigent, infirm, mentally ill, and homeless adults and children
of all ages. In 1853, St. Ann's Foundling Home began taking in mothers
and babies under three years of age. After 1861, the city sent infants and
toddlers to St. Ann's, but continued sending older children to the Poor
House, where they mingled with society's most desperate, and sometimes
dangerous, outcasts.[3]

Churches, philanthropists, and concerned women in St. Louis tried to
alleviate the problem by creating institutions for the care of homeless

children. Mother Rose Philippine Duchesne, a prominent Catholic nun, opened a home for indigent and orphaned girls in 1827. A wealthy Irish businessman named John Mullanphy gave Duchesne and the Sisters of the Sacred Heart a lease on a property on Broadway and Convent streets with the stipulation that they would establish the Mullanphy Orphan Asylum and provide shelter to at least twenty orphans every year. The asylum continued to provide this service until the 1930s.[4]

In 1834, sixteen women affiliated with various Protestant churches established the St. Louis Protestant Orphan Asylum (POA). Presbyterian, Episcopal, and Methodist congregations supported the women's efforts. Initially, the women were responding to the crisis created by the cholera epidemic of 1832, which killed 5 percent of the city's population and left many children parentless. Cholera outbreaks occurred nearly every summer between 1832 and the 1860s, including the terrible epidemic of 1849. In 1850, twenty-one children in the orphanage died of this terrible disease.[5]

The managers of the POA identified the following criteria for accepting a child: poverty, illness of a parent, death of a parent, or intemperance of the parents. Historians have found that the residents of the POA were the children of boatmen, soldiers, drifters, pioneers, and immigrants. During the Civil War, the POA admitted eighteen children whose fathers were serving in the army. Another thirty-six children arrived during the war as refugees. After the war, the POA merged with the Soldiers' Orphans' Home and moved to the suburb of Webster Groves.[6]

Records show that the POA made a practice of indenturing children to families that promised to take care of them. Historian Ann Morris has explained that the indenture system applied to children from the age of ten to seventeen. Families who took in these children agreed to properly feed and clothe them and provide them with a basic education. In return, the children would help with chores or work as apprentices in tradesmen's shops. In many cases, the host families treated the children with love and kindness, but some families regarded the indentured children merely as free labor. When the children reached the age of eighteen, the families gave them each a few articles of clothing, a Bible, and a sum of money, usually fifty to one hundred dollars, and sent them out into the world.[7]

To make room for new arrivals, the POA placed children, especially boys over the age of ten, in homes in St. Louis, the surrounding countryside, or even in other states. Most children stayed in the POA for one year or less, and very few children over the age of ten remained in the orphanage. The average age of admission to the institution was six years; only 8 percent of those admitted were over eleven years of age. The majority (51 percent) of those who left the orphanage returned home to a surviving parent or another relative, but almost one third (32 percent) of the older children who left the institution were placed out as apprentices or indentured servants.[8]

At least four other new orphanages opened their doors in the 1830s and 1840s. In 1835, the Sisters of St. Joseph of Carondelet opened St. Joseph's Home for Boys. One year later, the Sisters of Charity opened a boys' orphan asylum and school near the St. Louis Cathedral on Second Street. St. Mary's Orphanage, run by the Daughters of Charity, opened in 1841. Two years later, Emiline Hough led a group of women from St. John's Episcopal Church in forming an association for the relief of orphans. In 1845, the Missouri General Assembly granted a formal charter to Hough and her colleagues to manage the Episcopal Home for Children.[9]

Life in the Episcopal Home, as in most nineteenth-century orphanages, was regimented and, in many ways, very grim. In the 1840s, the matron of the orphanage also served as the teacher of the parochial school. The matron and five of the children were the first people to die in the St. Louis cholera epidemic in 1849; outbreaks of whooping cough, scarlet fever, measles, and diphtheria also took their toll. The children attended school for six hours each day, although the older girls often missed school because they had sewing or other work to do. On Sundays, the children attended services at St. John's Church, Christ Church Cathedral, or the chapel in the Home. The early records of the orphanage say very little about recreation. In 1856 the board of directors provided a Christmas dinner, which became an annual event.[10]

Punishment for misbehavior could be severe. In 1867, the board of the Episcopal Home abolished the use of a whip made of cowhide, but corporal punishment continued to occur. In 1879, the board decided that girls older than ten and boys over twelve should not be whipped. Apparently, the older children rebelled against all sorts of disciplinary actions. The board lamented in 1874 that boys resisted being locked up and sometimes managed to break the lock or get out of the window.[11]

The Episcopal Home cared for girls through the age of eighteen, but would not keep boys past the age of twelve. Teenage girls commonly remained in the institution, cooking, cleaning, and sewing. Boys who reached the age of twelve were often indentured to rural families. Families taking children by indenture often lived outside the St. Louis area and even outside Missouri. Sometimes the families returned the children to the home because of behavior problems, health problems, or failure to adapt to life on the farm.[12]

The Episcopal Home, the POA, and the other early nineteenth-century orphanages could not cope with the influx of children after 1849, when the cholera epidemic, migration, and local disasters left many people homeless and thousands of youngsters without parents. During that sweltering summer, cholera wiped out seven thousand people, about 10 percent of St. Louis's population. The discovery of gold in California made St. Louis a center for outfitting wagon trains bound for the Far West. Mishaps and misadventures left many people stranded along the trail. In spring and summer of 1849, a series of wharf fires destroyed steamboats, cargoes, and businesses and left hundreds of people homeless.[13]

In response to these events and catastrophes, in 1850, the St. Louis German St. Vincent Orphan Society opened a home that sheltered thousands of children for the next several decades. As time passed, the German St. Vincent Orphan Home served as a temporary residence for poor and neglected children rather than strictly a home for orphans. Boys consistently outnumbered girls in the orphanage. In 1868, for instance, there were eighty boys and forty-nine girls in residence. When families became financially able to do so, they often reclaimed their children. If this was not possible, the society tried to place children with German Catholic families. Some disabled children remained in the home until they reached the age of sixteen or eighteen, when they entered the Poor House.[14]

In some cases, the indenture system removed boys from one kind of danger and placed them in another form of peril. For example, in 1880, a twelve-year-old boy named Peter Ladermann lived at the German St. Vincent Orphan Home. According to the United States Census for that year, there were seventy-nine boys and only four girls in residence, under the supervision of fifteen nuns. Sometime between 1880 and 1884, Ladermann was indentured to a man named Conrad Rehagen in Rich Fountain, Missouri. In March 1884, officials from the orphanage investigated allegations that Rehagen had sexually abused the boy.[15]

Within the same month, seven younger boys tried to burn down the orphanage. Families reclaimed four of these boys. Two of them, brothers William and Joseph Kuehls, had no parents. Another boy, August Miller, who was ten years old, had a mother who was mentally ill. Records indicate that Miller was committed to the St. Louis House of Refuge for arson on March 26, 1884. He remained incarcerated there for five years until he reached the upper age limit of fifteen, when he was released to the custody of his mother. Joseph Kuehls, thirteen, and William Kuehls, ten, were also committed to the House of Refuge for arson on March 26, 1884. Six months later, on September 19, 1884, they were both indentured to Forest L. Shelby of Lexington, Missouri.[16]

The House of Refuge had been established in 1854 as the city's first government-run institution for abandoned and delinquent children. The four-acre facility, which occupied several buildings previously used for the Poor House and smallpox hospital, had the dual purpose of caring for neglected children and reforming juvenile offenders. Girls between the ages of three and fourteen and boys between the ages of three and sixteen could be committed to the House of Refuge, but boys outnumbered girls four to one. A public scandal in 1872 revealed horrible mistreatment of the children there, but the House of Refuge continued in operation until 1912.[17]

Like the church-sponsored orphanages, the House of Refuge relied on the indenture system to relieve overcrowding. Records reveal that of all the young people released from the facility, about 40 percent returned to one or both parents and about 25 percent were indentured or apprenticed. In 1871, officers of the institution reported that every effort was being made to place inmates in good homes in the country with the object of removing them from the temptations of city life.[18] Few records have survived to document whether or not those placements were successful, although official reports claimed good results in the vast majority of cases. I discuss at greater length the conditions and practices of the House of Refuge in Chapter 5.

Private philanthropic groups continued to offer alternatives to the city-run institution. To keep abandoned and wayward girls off the streets and out of jail, a group of women from various Protestant churches got together and founded the Girls' Industrial Home and School in 1853, and the institution survived for 125 years. On average, between seventy-five and eighty-five girls occupied the home throughout the period 1854-1944. In addition to sheltering homeless girls, the facility provided a day school for industrial training and elementary education.[19]

Another institution that focused on education as well as providing a home for children was the Mission Free School and Home, founded in 1840 by William Greenleaf Eliot, the distinguished Unitarian minister and philosopher. In the latter part of the nineteenth century, the mission became a center of philanthropic efforts in St. Louis, bolstering the city's weak and ineffective system of relief for the poor. A female board of managers oversaw the operations of the mission, which housed, on average, about forty-two children at any one time. Mothers or other relatives often placed children there temporarily while they tried to get on their feet economically. The mission kept children only up to the age of fourteen.[20]

During the turbulent 1850s and 1860s, when children were displaced by epidemics and war, several religious groups founded orphanages. After the 1858 cholera outbreak, German immigrants established the German

Protestant Orphans Home, which took in thousands of children over a period of many decades. To protect young girls from exploitation, the Daughters of Charity founded the House of the Guardian Angels for girls aged seven to twelve in 1859. This institution had the capacity to shelter eighty youngsters. The Daughters of Charity also established St. Philomena's Technical School for girls aged twelve to eighteen in 1864. The Methodist Orphan Home opened in 1865 and continued in operation through the mid-twentieth century.[21]

Several orphanages, including two facilities for African American children, opened in the city between 1870 and 1890. The German General Protestant Orphans Home, established in 1877, provided homes for boys and girls regardless of religious denomination. The St. Louis Colored Orphans' Home, founded in 1888, later became Annie Malone's Children's Home in honor of one of its presidents, Annie Turnbo-Malone. St. Elizabeth's, the only black parish in the St. Louis Archdiocese, founded the St. Francis Orphan Asylum for African American girls in 1887. The Benevolent Association of the Christian Church chartered the Christian Orphan Home in 1889 as a refuge for destitute and homeless children. The Masonic Home for Children, which opened in 1889, also accepted both orphans and children of destitute parents.[22]

The Missouri Baptist Children's Home was founded in 1886 and endured multiple disasters before the turn of the century. Women from several Baptist churches began raising funds for the home in 1882. After a slow start, the group was able to open the home in April 1886. During its first year, the home received seventy-six children, and twenty-six of them died. Epidemics of various diseases, including whooping cough and diphtheria, continued to plague the institution at 1906 Lafayette Avenue. The deadly tornado that tore through St. Louis in 1896 and killed 300 people damaged the home. Miraculously, all the children and staff survived. The orphanage moved to temporary quarters while the building was refurbished. Ten years later, in 1906, the Missouri Baptist Children's Home moved to Pattonville, Missouri.[23]

Beginning in the 1880s, a new national organization tackled the problem of orphaned, abandoned, and neglected children. M. V. B. Van Arsdale, pastor of the Presbyterian Church in Clinton, Illinois, founded the Children's Home Society. During the subsequent decade, the interdenominational society grew into a federation of organizations in twenty-four states. Representatives of the society rescued children from city streets, brothels, poorhouses, and asylums and placed them with families. Rather than just indenturing children, the society placed them in homes where they were not necessarily expected to earn their keep.[24]

In 1891, C. W. Williams, a Methodist minister, came to St. Louis from Illinois to establish the Children's Home Society of Missouri. He approached his friend Herman Bollman, who owned a piano store at Eleventh and Olive streets. Bollman became treasurer of the statewide organization and recruited others to the cause. Associates of the society went out looking all over Missouri for needy children. By 1904, the society had established a "receiving home" in a three-story brick house at 4427 Margaretta Avenue. Children could stay there temporarily, but the society's goal was to place them in homes.[25]

Local boards of the Children's Home Society oversaw the placement of children. Families who wanted to accept a child had to prove their fitness and receive the endorsement of the board. In order to be placed in a home, children had to be legally surrendered to the society by their parents or the courts. The society placed children in homes for a three-month "trial" period, after which the families could return the children, adopt them, or indenture them. Local boards watched over the placements and could remove children from homes where they were mistreated.[26]

With limited funds and personnel, the local boards could only do so much. There was virtually no state oversight of the placing-out system. The society placed children in homes all over the country in localities where local boards could not effectively observe what went on. Families often returned children to the society if they failed to meet expectations in terms of work or domestic service. The continuing practice of indenturing or apprenticing children as servants or laborers opened the way for exploitation. Many families treated the children with affection, but the system allowed abuse to go undetected and unchecked.[27]

Families requested girls rather than boys by a ratio of nearly two to one. Most desired of all were blonde, blue-eyed girls under the age of three. This fact indicated that most of the families were looking for children to nurture rather than workers to help with chores. It also meant that boys were harder to place than girls. For this reason, the St. Louis branch of the society placed advertisements in newspapers offering boys on a trial basis to families willing to pay the costs of transportation to receive them. One of these advertisements appeared on December 23, 1899, poignantly just before Christmas.[28]

Between 1897 and 1904, the St. Louis Newsboys' Home offered shelter to boys who sold daily and weekly papers on the city streets. The murder of a newsboy in 1896 may have prompted the creation of the Newsboys' Home Association by twenty members of the King's Daughters Society. After one year of fund-raising, the association opened a facility at 1108 Locust Street in November 1897. Initially, the home had ten beds, but there was room to expand. Most newsboys had homes and families, but some spent their nights at the various branch offices around the city. For those seeking shelter, the Newsboys' Home charged a small fee. Newsboys were a special category of young males, whose story will be told more fully in Chapter 6.[29]

The city's newspapers frequently carried stories of abandoned children. In one instance, eight children lived in north St. Louis in a state of complete destitution. Their father had been killed on the railroad, and their mother had also died. There was no food in the house where they were found. The Children's Home Society placed all of them—two boys and six girls, ranging in age from two to sixteen—in homes. In another case, a father and four children lived in a tent near the railroad tracks. The children, ranging in age from six to thirteen, were sick from cold, hunger, and neglect. The father, apparently with some reluctance, signed them over to the society.[30]

On April 2, 1884, the *St. Louis Globe-Democrat* quoted a police report stating that Belle Smith, a black woman living between Fourteenth and Fifteenth streets, had deserted her two children, Edgar, aged two, and Henry, aged four. Their father, Isaac Smith, was serving a term in the Work House for theft. The newspaper did not say where the authorities placed the children.[31]

On the same day, the *Globe-Democrat* reported that John Pfeiffer, a workman who lived on South Twentieth Street, had deserted his six small children. A seventh child, "a mere babe," lived with his mother in Chicago. The police turned the children over to the mayor, who had the authority to send them to the House of Refuge.[32]

In November 1897, Mayor Henry Ziegenhein decided that the City Jail needed a thorough cleaning and renovation. To convince the city council to provide funds for this project, he led a delegation of officials on a tour of the facility. What they saw was shocking. When the jailer opened some of the cells, thousands of roaches scurried into crevices. The walls were crumbling and full of holes; metal fixtures were rusting. Beds and bedding were tattered and dirty. A kitchen constructed to feed about seventy-five had to serve nearly four hundred prisoners.[33]

Most shocking of all was the discovery that seven little boys were housed in the jail. According to newspaper reports, none of the boys appeared to be more than twelve years old. Some of them had been in the lock-up for as long as four months, and all had been charged with minor offenses. The reporter for the *St. Louis Post-Dispatch* decried the situation, arguing, "Perhaps some of these little ones were almost incorrigible when they were thrust into prison. Perhaps one or two of them were dangerous to society. But the probability is that they have been more sinned against than sinning."[34]

According to the *Globe-Democrat,* the official delegation stopped and talked to the boys. One of them, identified only as Harris, wept as he insisted he was innocent of the charge of stealing a penknife. Several of the visitors expressed outrage that these children were housed in proximity to adult offenders, including Henry Clay, who was awaiting execution for shooting a newsboy. The jailer, Anton Heubler, complained that there was no system in place for separating minor offenders from hardened criminals. One of the reforms he proposed was the construction of a separate facility to house the women and children. Both Heubler and Ziegenhein stressed the need for some remedial action.[35]

Mayor Ziegenhein's indignation echoed a national movement calling for change. For four decades beginning in the 1840s, Dorothea Dix, a New England reformer, had traveled the nation trying to persuade states to provide better care for the mentally ill. In the course of this work, she also wrote articles and gave speeches condemning the cruel treatment of inmates in prisons, jails, and poorhouses. Dix's zealous crusade was a precursor to the more pragmatic reform movements of the Progressive Era, when Jane Addams and others would continue the campaign for more humane institutions for the care of unfortunate, afflicted, and dependent adults and children.[36]

In the late nineteenth and early twentieth centuries, progressive reformers embraced the idea that life in industrial cities was hazardous for children. While Charles Loring Brace had tried to remove children from this harmful environment beginning in the 1850s, several decades later progressive men and women believed it would be possible to instead create wholesome cities, in which children would be safe. In St. Louis, an affluent, well-educated, and unmarried woman named Charlotte Rumbold campaigned for political action to bring about social justice. She wanted to clean up the streets, improve sanitation, provide better housing, and create a system of parks and playgrounds. Mayor Rolla Wells, a progressive, appointed Rumbold to the city's Public Recreation Committee. Beginning in 1910, she served, along with Jane Addams, as an officer of the Playground Association of America. Like Addams, Rumbold believed that people, through rational planning, could create an urban environment where young people could grow into healthy adults.[37]

During the Progressive Era, St. Louis and the State of Missouri recognized, along with other cities and states nationally, a desperate need to supervise the care of dependent and neglected children. The St. Louis Children's Aid Society was formed in 1909 and took an active role

Drawing of Robert Brestol on his vegetable wagon. (*St. Louis Post-Dispatch,* May 8, 1910. Used by permission, State Historical Society of Missouri, Columbia)

in overseeing the placement of orphaned, abandoned, and delinquent children.[38] In 1911, the city created the Board of Children's Guardians to take the lead in placing children in foster care. The state took action in 1913, when the General Assembly authorized the State Board of Charities and Corrections to establish a Bureau of Child Welfare. This new governmental agency employed an agent whose sole responsibility was to supervise the placement of children in foster homes.[39]

Following national trends, Missouri attempted to reform and systematize laws and policies affecting the welfare of children. In 1915, Missouri became the fourth state to create a Children's Code Commission to make recommendations to the legislature. Judge Rhodes E. Cave of St. Louis took charge of this effort, relying on input from social workers, state and local officials, and attorneys. Measures proposed by the commission included regulating adoptions and establishing state oversight of orphanages and foster homes. The legislature acted on these recommendations, improving the chances for neglected and abandoned young people to grow up in safe and nurturing surroundings.[40]

Robert Brestol suffered from poverty and became an orphan during this era of reform. In the early years of the twentieth century, Robert had to get up before daylight every morning and harness his father's horses for a long drive to the Union Market from their house on Whittier Street. His father bought produce from farmers, and Robert had to help load it into the wagon. After that he drove the wagon through the northern and northwestern parts of the city, selling vegetables from door to door. Sometimes his father was with him, sometimes he was alone. Young Robert became a familiar figure in his ragged clothing and heavy boots.[41]

Robert's parents, Frank and Annie Bressler, were weavers who had worked together in a small mill in their native Austria. After immigrating to the United States, the family lived in various places, including Paterson, New Jersey, and Shreveport, Louisiana, before coming to St. Louis. Frank Bressler's alcoholism may have caused his failure to find and keep employment as a weaver, and so he began selling produce. He changed his name to Brestol, perhaps to escape his creditors.

For a short time, Robert attended Ashland School, but his father made him quit school in the fifth grade. He made some extra money selling newspapers, but he was not allowed to keep any of it for himself. In the yard behind his family's house, Robert kept a garden and raised chickens. He rarely went out except to go to the market and sell his vegetables. His father beat him, and his mother apparently did nothing to prevent it.

On May 3, 1910, Frank Brestol killed his wife and then ended his own life while their son watched. When they entered the tiny house after the tragedy, neighbors and officials found the boy dry-eyed and showing no emotion. He was now an orphan at the age of fourteen.

Robert's story has a better ending than might be expected. An uncle of whose existence the boy was vaguely aware came to claim him, promising to treat him as his own son, dress him decently, and teach him the shoe business. Mrs. Charles Knittel, the boy's court-appointed guardian, approved of this plan. Robert told a reporter for the *Post-Dispatch*, "Maybe I'll want to learn a trade, or maybe I'll like the shoe store and want to stay in there, or maybe I'll want to go to school some more." He said he could not make up his mind, but he was sure of two things: "I'm not going to use tobacco anymore, and when I get some decent clothes I'll try to keep them looking good."

For children who had no relatives to claim them, foster care provided an alternative to institutionalization. In 1921, St. Louis policeman Joseph A. Schneider and his wife, Louisa, cared for ten foster children in their home on Goodfellow Avenue. Three foster children had already grown up and left the Schneider home. Louisa Schneider explained to a reporter from the *Post-Dispatch* that she had never had any children of her own, but she had always wanted to have a dozen. She said she would never willingly allow one of her foster children to be sent to an institution, where they would be "raised by the clock and come out as if they had been trained in a penitentiary."[42]

Schneider decided to adopt her youngest foster child, Alfred, who had "a most pathetic history." Two of his brothers and three sisters had died in the same week of diphtheria, and soon after that, his mother had also died. Alfred's father, who had tried to take care of him alone, had contracted measles and then scarlet fever. All this was too much for the grief-stricken man, who had ended up in an asylum. Alfred was a lovable child, but strong willed. Schneider feared that he might not do well if the Board of Children's Guardians moved him out of her home. Her husband agreed, and the couple adopted the boy. He was a special child, she declared, "and he just must not be cast adrift."[43]

Schneider's fear for Alfred was not misplaced. Despite all the efforts of private charities and governmental agencies, many boys in St. Louis continued to be "cast adrift." Government action would gradually result in the transition from orphanages to foster care, but the system would never adequately address the needs of all the city's neglected children. Many young boys would elude well-meaning authority figures, run away, and slip into lives of petty crime, descend into violence, or simply keep struggling to survive on the city streets.

Chapter Three

Drifters in the City Streets

The Bad Boy as a Highwayman—Youthful Lawlessness in Every
Quarter of the Land—The Effect of Dime Novel Literature . . . Boy
Burglars—Gangs of Bad Boys—Sad Juvenile Depravity

—*St. Louis Globe-Democrat* headline, March 28, 1884

TATTERED BANDS OF WANDERING BOYS haunted the streets of industrializing cities, where they sometimes strayed into lives of crime. British historian E. Royston Pike observed that, although there have been homeless children in all times and places, the middle years of the nineteenth century produced an especially large number of unsupervised boys. The industrial revolution undermined traditional family life and cast vast numbers of juveniles out into the teeming streets. Belief in a capitalist ideology of "self-made men" allowed many people to turn a blind eye to the plight of the ragged, barefoot youngsters, who struggled to support themselves as street sellers, bootblacks, and newsboys. Boys who turned in desperation to beggary and larceny faced punishment rather than pity in the bustling urban centers of England and the United States.[1]

Charles Dickens's *Oliver Twist* awakened the reading public to the tragedy of endangered innocence and corrupted youth. Born in a workhouse to an unwed mother, young Oliver survives abuse and exploitation in London before a fortunate chain of circumstances brings him back into the fold of his well-to-do family. Other characters in Dickens's novel, including the Artful Dodger, do not have a family to claim them and so have to learn to survive on the streets by picking rich men's pockets. Corrupt adults like Fagin instruct them in the ins and outs of petty crime.

Nineteenth-century journalist Henry Mayhew wandered the byways of London, observing the blighted lives of chimney sweeps, lurkers, thieves, and runaways. Parents, he discovered, sometimes sold their sons for pitifully small sums to adults who wanted apprentices or helpers for nasty and

36

dangerous jobs. Chimney sweeps, in particular, suffered sores, bruises, and injuries to their spines, eyes, and lungs. When they were too old to climb into narrow chimneys, they often went jobless and resorted to life in the streets. Other young boys pushed or pulled wheelbarrows and called out wares for costermongers (men who sold vegetables from wagons). In summer, the boys were up before dawn, worked in the marketplace until noon, and were still awake at midnight, drinking pints in the public house in the company of grown men.[2]

In America, popular novelist Horatio Alger idealized New York street boys as plucky young heroes. From the 1860s until his retirement in 1896, Alger wrote more than a hundred juvenile books, mostly about teenage boys struggling to make something of themselves in the big city. His formula was simple, effective, and popular with the reading public. In each novel, a brave and honest boy finds himself alone in a dazzling, but also menacing, urban environment. Criminals and tricksters try to fleece him, but other people help him along his way to riches. Through a combination of luck, persistence, and integrity, the boy eventually finds his way into the good graces of a wealthy patron, who rewards him with a good job, social status, and material possessions.[3]

Although his plots were formulaic and his endings saccharine, Alger tried to expose some of the real problems boys encountered in urban environments. *Oliver Twist* had a great influence on his fiction. Shamelessly borrowing from Dickens, Alger transformed the Artful Dodger to his Tom Dodger, a character who evolved from a thief into a respectable citizen. But Alger also emulated Dickens's compassion for the poor and sensitivity to the dangers of city life. Influential in Alger's work, too, were Dorothea Dix's revelations about the horrid conditions in asylums and prisons.[4]

Much more recently, historian Timothy Gilfoyle has called attention to the real New York street boys, who often followed a darker path than Alger's plucky heroes. Gilfoyle's book *A Pickpocket's Tale,* based on the autobiography of former street boy George Appo, traces a boy's descent from a street urchin in the Five Points district to an adult criminal, who spent more than ten years in prisons and jails. Growing up, Appo never attended school, but supported himself as a newsboy, a pickpocket, and a con artist. With other young street boys, he learned his way around the theaters, saloons, and opium dens of the city. By the time he reached adulthood, he had become a "good fellow" with a wide network of criminal associations. But his friends could not protect him from abuse in prison or from violence on the streets, where he was shot, stabbed, and assaulted numerous times. Finally, after a stint in an institution for the criminally insane, Appo decided to go straight and share his story with the world. The city streets produced many boys like Appo, who followed a tortuous path. Some of them eventually found redemption; others did not.[5]

The stories of most of these wandering boys have been lost to history, but some firsthand accounts have been recorded. In December 1877, a reporter for the St. Louis Globe-Democrat followed one "homeless waif" on his first night in St. Louis, seeking shelter from an icy wind. At the door of a police station, the young man (name and age undisclosed) in tattered clothing shivered "like a man in an ague." The reporter followed him into the bright, warm station, where he asked for shelter for the night. In accordance with the rules, the sergeant on duty sent him to the "Soup House," the official shelter for transients, located in an old tobacco factory near City Hall.[6]

Inside the Soup House, a long, narrow brick-and-frame building, more than a hundred men, women, and children slept in their street clothes, two to a bunk, with one person's head next to the other person's feet. There were no sheets or blankets, and the sleepers used their boots or hats for pillows. At each end of the room, a large stove emitted coal smoke and heat. As the reporter told it, "The smell of bad whiskey was certainly manifest and struggled with the odor of unwashed underclothing—principally socks."

A bouncer armed with a club kept order and expelled the most obvious drunks. While the reporter was there, a doctor came and inoculated forty-two of the transients for smallpox. One man insisted that he had already been vaccinated. The doctor demanded to see the scar, but the man displayed an empty sleeve and said he had lost the scar when he lost his arm. The doctor vaccinated his remaining arm.

A policeman who happened to be present that night explained to the reporter that the icy weather drove many people in from the streets. In the summer, only the ill and infirm came into the Soup House. Those who were able to care for themselves went out into the countryside as tramps or stayed in the city, picking up a living in whatever way they could, sleeping in the open air or under any slight shelter they could find. On that particular night in December, the homeless waif hesitated for a moment before stretching out on the floor in the midst of the overflow crowd that "slept as soundly in the noisome surroundings as if in an inviting bed." The reporter did not say what became of him after that night.

In 1878, authors J. A. Dacus and James Buel observed the sad condition of the street boys and girls of St. Louis. These young vagrants, they noted, inhabited certain well-defined areas of the city. In South St. Louis, unsupervised children congregated in the bottomlands east of Fourth Street.

Lost children also haunted the riverfront in the central part of the city, east of Broadway and north of Cherry Street. On the near north side, vagabonds mingled along Sixth, Seventh, Eighth, Ninth, and Tenth streets, from Lucas Avenue to Cass Avenue, in the area known as the Ghetto. Kerry Patch, with its flimsy dwellings and shifting population of squatters, had a large contingent of rootless youngsters. On the western edge of the downtown area, youngsters camped out in Mill Creek Valley.[7]

There was no single path to a life on the streets. Some youngsters ran away from parents or guardians in smaller towns and villages in rural Missouri or across the river in Illinois. Others escaped from orphanages, jails, poorhouses, or apprenticeships. Within the poorer neighborhoods of St. Louis, children became the victims of heartless, neglectful, and alcoholic parents. There were other parents who simply could not care for their offspring. Among immigrant families, both mothers and fathers had to go out to work, leaving their children to fend for themselves.[8]

In the natural course of events, these unattended youngsters came into contact with streetwise girls and boys, who introduced them to rough language, bad habits, and basic survival skills. Ragged, uncombed, and uneducated boys sometimes became expert sneak-thieves. Adventurous young souls found their way to gambling dens, theaters, and bordellos, where they could find work as errand boys or "claquers," loudly applauding and singing the praises of the games and entertainers. Others found more legitimate work as bootblacks, newsboys, messengers, and peddlers.[9]

In St. Louis, as in other cities, hungry children went rummaging for food early in the morning and late in the evening at open-air markets. Operators of pushcarts, fruit stands, and produce wagons often left litter behind them in the alleys and streets, and youngsters picked it up before the street cleaners did their work. Children also scavenged in the city dumps and alleyways for food, fuel, and items of value that could be sold to junk dealers. This activity, called "junking," shocked social reformers, but provided youngsters with a bare subsistence, including a few nickels and dimes to spend on luxuries.[10]

St. Louis residents were aware of the dangers posed by desperate young drifters. In 1884, the *Post-Dispatch* printed a collection of news stories from various cities and states under the headline "The Bad Boy—Astonishing Record of One Week's Crimes and Plots—The Bad Boy as a Highwayman—Youthful Lawlessness in Every Quarter of the Land." Under this banner, the paper printed stories from New York City, Boston, and other urban areas where male adolescents behaved like desperadoes. Three eleven-year-old boys in New York knocked another boy down and stole his watch and chain. In Boston, a larcenous gang of boys between the ages of ten and sixteen holed up in a cellar and called their leader "Billy the Kid." On a playground at a school in Camden, New Jersey, ten-year-old Harry Farrell pulled out a pistol and shot eleven-year-old Charles McGovern. The headline raved, "Gangs of Bad Boys—Sad Juvenile Depravity."[11]

The newspaper blamed the problem on the unwholesome influence of cheap fiction. Eighty years later, historian Lewis Atherton would agree that dime novels, including many cheap yarns about Jesse James, could incite impressionable youths to violence. In Millersburg, Pennsylvania, according to the newspaper, masked teenage gunslingers robbed peddlers in true "dime-novel" fashion. Stories of outlaws sometimes induced boys to leave home. For example, fourteen-year-old Arthur Cookson ran away from Brooklyn, New York, and was apprehended in Baltimore. When authorities questioned him, he said he was heading for the West. "The perusal of pernicious literature, dime novels, etc., is assigned as the cause of the boy's peregrinations," the newspaper said. A group of seven young boys in Quincy, Illinois, committed burglaries and called themselves "the Jesse James Gang."[12]

The papers carried stories of runaway boys who came to St. Louis and quickly landed in trouble. In November 1897, sixteen-year-old William Dunlap pleaded guilty to arson and was sent to the State Reform School. Allegedly, he set fire to a summer kitchen in the rear of Charlotte Illig's residence at 5617 Virginia Avenue. According to the newspaper, he had been in St. Louis only about two months, having run away from Alton, Illinois, where he worked on a farm.[13]

In some cases, the adventures of runaway boys had happy endings. For example, in the winter of 1898, a pair of runaways came to St. Louis from Cobden, Illinois. Police arrested them when they jumped from a boxcar at the Wabash Railway yards. Robert Frawley, thirteen, and Fred Townsend, fourteen, said they had left home because they were treated badly in school. They had hoped to find jobs in St. Louis. A railroad brakeman had taken all the money they had. For several nights, they had slept in stables. During the daytime, they begged for food. When the police took them into custody, they were thoroughly tired of their adventure. Frawley and Townsend were lucky; their parents sent money for tickets to bring them home.[14]

Other boys headed straight down the path to violence. No event more clearly demonstrates this point than the crime that occurred on November 15, 1897. On that night, three robbers held up a saloon and grocery store at Jefferson and Scott avenues and then had a shoot-out with police. The story is worth telling in detail.

At about eight o'clock on this stormy Monday evening, Peter Heibel was reading the newspaper in his saloon. His wife and seventeen-year-old son were playing checkers at a table. Another son, aged nineteen, was standing near the door. A low wooden partition separated the brightly lit saloon from the grocery store, which was illuminated only by a dim lamp.[15]

Suddenly, three intruders wearing handkerchiefs over their faces burst into the saloon, brandishing revolvers. One of the robbers jumped up on the bar, cursed at the Heibel family, and ordered them to stick up their hands. Another intruder forced the husband, wife, and two sons to line up facing the wall. At this tense moment, a neighbor came into the grocery to buy a can of oil. Taking in the situation, she quickly left. The robber who had leaped onto the bar cleaned out the cash drawer. One of his accomplices searched Heibel and took twenty dollars and a watch from him. Another customer, H. W. Knost, entered the saloon, and the robbers took about five dollars from his pockets. After forcing the Heibels and Knost into the grocery store, the intruders exited through the saloon.[16]

Heibel ran back into the saloon, got his revolver from under the bar, ran to the door, and fired five shots. The robbers fired back at him, but all the bullets missed their targets. Patrolman Martin Delaney heard the shots, saw a man running down an alley, and chased him into a railroad yard. Both Delaney and the fugitive fired shots. Another officer, Nicholas Hunt, collared the man near the railroad tracks. He turned the man over to Delaney and then pursued the other two fugitives.[17]

One of the robbers turned and shot three times at Hunt. The last shot hit the policeman in the abdomen. The officer sank to the sidewalk in the pouring rain. While still holding the captured robber, Delaney helped Hunt to his feet and led him to a nearby saloon. Two customers carried the wounded policeman to a drugstore, where a doctor examined him and had him taken to St. Mary's Infirmary. Delaney took his prisoner to the Four Courts Building in a police wagon. At the infirmary, doctors performed surgery on Hunt. Internal hemorrhaging had filled his stomach with blood. His wife and his brother were with him at the hospital when he died early the following morning.[18]

Charles Sheldon, the fugitive captured by Delaney, turned out to be an eighteen-year-old boy, whom the *Globe-Democrat* described as "little else in appearance than a freckle-face, beardless youth." While the policeman lay dying in the hospital, other officers held Sheldon in the "sweat-box," trying to scare him into naming his accomplices. According to the newspaper, he answered questions "in a low, soft voice" and his eyes had "an innocent look."[19]

Hundreds of people paid their respects as Hunt's body lay in state in his home at 2312 Wash Street. Mayor Henry Ziegenhein and the members of the Police Board accompanied the casket from Hunt's home to St. Bridget's Church at the corner of Carr Street and Jefferson Avenue, where the funeral took place. Church bells rang as a solemn procession of policemen in uniform, dignitaries, and the dead officer's wife, mother, and children, along with many other mourners, walked the two blocks from the Hunt home to the church.[20]

In the meantime, Sheldon gave incoherent and inconsistent accounts of events leading up to the night of Hunt's death. Descriptions in the *Globe-Democrat* transformed him from a beardless youth into a shifty-eyed, cigarette-smoking wise guy. When reporters questioned him, he said that he was eighteen years old and had been born in Des Moines, Iowa. He had spent about four years in an orphan asylum in Nebraska, and then he had become a self-described hobo. He carried a revolver, he said, because sometimes railroad brakemen could be mean. Asked about his partners in crime, he claimed he had met them on a train near Kirkwood, Missouri. One of them he said was a black man named Henry, and the other one was a middle-aged white man. But these descriptions turned out to be far from the truth.[21]

Twelve days after the robbery, police took a second suspect into custody. He was neither a black man nor a middle-aged white man, but an eighteen-year-old boy named Frank Stetson, who had been traveling around the country as a hobo. The newspapers described him as slender and swarthy, smart and fairly well educated. His mother kept a boarding house in Buffalo, New York.[22]

Stetson gave a detailed, but possibly flawed, account of the days leading up to the crime. He said he had arrived in St. Louis about a week before the robbery. Soon after his arrival, he met Sheldon and another young man named George Williams (George William Thornton), who was called Tip. Sheldon and Tip invited Stetson to live with them and two other men. Those two men were out of the room when Sheldon, Stetson, and Tip planned the robbery. On the day of the crime, Tip went into the saloon, ordered a glass of beer, and looked at the layout of the place.[23]

On the night of the crime, Stetson and Sheldon ran out of the saloon and turned east, and Tip followed half a block behind them. According to Stetson, it was Tip who fired the shot that killed Hunt. Stetson said he returned to the room he had shared with Sheldon and Tip. An hour later, Tip came in, and he had been shot in the back. His wound had not bled much. One of the other men who lived in the building went to a drugstore, obtained some cotton, and bandaged the wound. Stetson and Tip

Drawing of George William Thornton, alias St. Paul Tip, that ran in the *St. Louis Post-Dispatch* on November 27, 1897. (Used by permission, State Historical Society of Missouri, Columbia)

stayed in the room that night and left town in the morning. Stetson went to Arkansas, where he was captured, and Tip went to Memphis.[24]

The police already knew Tip from a previous arrest in connection with a burglary nearly two months earlier, on September 23, 1897. He stood about five feet, eight inches in height and had a sallow complexion, a flat nose, and a missing middle finger. On the day of this earlier arrest, he did not have a gun. Reportedly, he told the police that if he had one, he would never have "stood for the pinch," meaning he would never have allowed himself to be arrested. At that time, the police held him for several days, could not make a case against him, charged him with idling, and then told him to leave town.[25]

Apparently, Tip stayed in St. Louis and soon made connections with Sheldon and Stetson. For a while, the three of them shared a room at the Emmett Hotel at Eleventh and Chestnut streets. Police believed they had committed several robberies in St. Louis and Alton, Illinois. After the November 15 robbery and murder, police had grilled Sheldon daily, until he finally told them that he had stayed one night at a lodging house on Morgan Street near Union Market. Police investigated and found three names on a blotter: *Charles Sheldon, Frank Stetson,* and *George Williams* (Tip). This gave them the names of Sheldon's accomplices, which were later confirmed in their interrogations of Stetson.

Police connected Stetson with his mother in Buffalo and made arrangements for authorities there to intercept her mail. In one letter, her son informed her that he was in Hot Springs, Arkansas, and that he expected to go to Memphis, where Tip was recovering from a serious wound. This letter led St. Louis police to Stetson, but they were unable to find Tip, who was not in a hospital, but reportedly in a cheap boarding house. Tip, also known as Connors, St. Paul Tip, George Williams, John Little, and George William Thornton, his real name, left Memphis and eventually surfaced in Providence, Rhode Island.[26]

A grand jury indicted Stetson, Sheldon, and Thornton for first degree murder on December 18, 1897. Stetson and Sheldon stood trial in April, but staunchly maintained that Thornton was the one who actually shot Officer Hunt. Frank Stetson's mother came to St. Louis from Buffalo and paid for a lawyer to defend her son and Sheldon, whom the newspapers identified as "a friendless young tramp." Several witnesses, including policemen, maintained that it was Thornton who fired the fatal shot. After hearing the evidence, the judge instructed the jury to return a verdict of not guilty in the case of Stetson and Sheldon, who still faced charges of robbery.[27]

Police kept searching for Thornton as the real killer, although perhaps they were unaware of just how young he was. The 1900 U.S. Census for Providence, Rhode Island, listed George W. Thornton as an inmate at the State Home and Industrial School, a facility for homeless children. The census gave his birthplace as England and his birth month and year as May 1885; at the time of the robbery of Heibel's saloon and the shooting of Officer Hunt, Tip would have been twelve years old.[28]

In 1914, St. Louis policemen finally located Thornton in Rhode Island and brought him back to Missouri. On March 31, he pleaded not guilty to first degree murder, and court proceedings were set for May 12. All parties agreed to a continuance until June 30. Perhaps after seventeen years, the original witnesses were no longer available to testify. Court records are not very clear on this issue, but on July 13, 1914, prosecutors decided not to present their case against Thornton. Records bear the notation *nolle pros* (not prosecuted).[29]

It is possible, of course, that Thornton was guilty, and also that he was a thoroughly evil individual who got away with murder. But he managed to live an honest life, or at least one free from legal troubles, in Providence. The 1920 census listed him as a white single man, about thirty-three years old, living with his mother and working as a laborer in a cotton mill. According to the 1930 census, he remained in Providence, where he did odd jobs as a day laborer. At the age of about forty-four, he still lived with his sixty-seven-year-old mother, whose name was listed as Bascombe Chappellor.[30]

This was no Horatio Alger story. No wealthy patron opened the door to status and success, and yet George Thornton managed to give up his life of crime and live a quiet, apparently decent, life. Perhaps the training he received at the Rhode Island State Home and Industrial School helped him to change his ways. Perhaps his mother, to whom he apparently had an enduring attachment, provided enough stability to bring him back to the world of honest, hard-working citizens.

What made Thornton go bad in his youth? Without excusing his criminal activity, it is important to remember that Thornton was one of many boys who left their homes, turned up in the big, expanding industrial cities, and found themselves in trouble. In his case, the trouble was very, very bad, resulting in the death of an honest policeman. But Thornton, apparently, was not a hopelessly evil young man. Reformers like Jane Addams correctly perceived that rapidly industrializing cities, like St. Louis, could have harmful effects on the character of growing boys. Many boys, like Thornton, had a natural desire for excitement that lured them into the shadowy recesses of an urban landscape, where no one seemed to see what they were up to, and no one knew, or cared to know, how they managed to survive.

Chapter Four

Games, Gangs, Hideouts, and Caves

The police know of more than half a dozen caves excavated in favorable situations by these street boys, which are capable of accommodating from twelve to twenty-five boys each. Into these subterranean dens the boys crawl through a small aperture, and once within the grimy cavern, the coldest weather may be defied.

—J. A. DACUS AND JAMES BUEL, *A Tour of St. Louis*

IN THE LATE NINETEENTH CENTURY, street boys coalesced into tribes or clans, the precursors of mid-twentieth-century gangs. Rebels and runaways gathered in groups for safety and companionship. In many cases, the boys in these groups were of the same race or ethnicity and had ties to a particular neighborhood. History has not recorded names for most of these tribes or gangs, but a few of them evolved into adult criminal organizations. Fights between rival gangs were common, and feuds could go on for years. In most cases, the conflict involved words or fists, but sometimes the young warriors used weapons. Often they competed with each other in innocent games, but just as often they engaged in drinking, gambling, vandalism, or stealing. In summer they slept in the open air in lumberyards and vacant lots, where they disturbed the peace with yelling matches. When winter came, they bunked together in vacant buildings, cellars, or caves.[1]

According to J. Adams Puffer, a social worker in Boston in the late nineteenth and early twentieth centuries, same-sex groups or gangs were "the basis of the social life of the boy." During the years between the ages of ten and sixteen, boys passed through what Puffer called "the gang age," when ties to the family loosened and boys learned how to be men by observing and imitating the behavior of their peers. Gangs, he argued, were "instinctive human groupings, formed like pack and hive, in response to deep-seated but unconscious need."[2]

Boys shooting craps in a St. Louis street on a school day, May 5, 1910. (Photograph by Lewis Hine. Courtesy of the Library of Congress)

Boys' gangs originated in urban neighborhoods, where young children learned to play in the streets. Older boys taught the younger ones the rules of various games, including marbles, kick the can, and many types of baseball, using sticks for bats and garbage-can lids for bases. As boys grew up, they spent less time playing ball games and more time on street corners, pitching pennies or shooting craps. When eventually they became bored with these pastimes, groups or gangs would spread through the city, searching for fun, invading the neighborhoods of rival gangs, and getting into trouble.[3]

During her long career of social work in Chicago, Jane Addams found that many boys ended up in court on a variety of minor and major charges that stemmed from gang activity. Common crimes included stealing horse-and-buggy rigs, knocking down signs, cutting Western Union cable, building fires along railroad tracks, flagging trains, throwing stones at moving train windows, jumping on freight cars, harassing railroad employees, stealing cargo, and breaking signal lights on the railroad. Most of these crimes, Addams concluded, even if they involved petty theft, arose from the desire for adventure and not from malice or greed.[4]

In St. Louis in the late nineteenth century, one particular gang became notorious for a steady string of crimes. The Ashley Street gang originated in Kerry Patch and included a saloon-keeper's son named Thomas Egan. After the death of his mother, Egan became incorrigible and began running with a group of boys who picked pockets, snatched purses, and stole alcohol, cigars, jewelry, geese, chickens, and horses and carriages. Gang members wore ragged clothes, slouched hats, and fingerless gloves. At some point in his adolescence, Egan got into a knife fight and came out of it with a scar across his forehead. After he turned eighteen in 1893, he served a term in the Work House. As a grown man, he would emerge as the leader of one of St. Louis's most active criminal organizations, which would become known as Egan's Rats.[5]

For boys like Tom Egan, gang membership fulfilled two strong and conflicting desires: the impulse to leave home and the need to belong somewhere. According to Addams, boys in Chicago sometimes ended up in court for no other crime than sleeping in barns, staying out at night, or simply wandering. For these boys, the four walls of home, especially in stifling tenements, had become insufferable, and they needed to escape into the wider world. Puffer found that gangs of boys often sought out and identified with some place on the landscape, such as a particular corner or clubhouse of some kind. Often, a group of boys would leave the city or town to find a shanty in the woods—the rougher, the better. For long or short periods of time, the group of boys who occupied this hideaway would share a sense of ownership of it, spend many hours a day in it, and defend it from outsiders.[6]

Gangs looking for hideouts in St. Louis sometimes found them in the twisting system of interconnected caves that lay beneath the city's streets. These caves dated back millions of years, as surface water had seeped into the ground, percolated through the limestone bedrock, and created a vast network of underground streams. By 1764, when Pierre Laclede and his stepson, Auguste Chouteau, landed on the west bank of the Mississippi River, the subterranean streams had run dry, leaving a network of chambers and tunnels. Laclede and Chouteau founded the settlement of St. Louis on land that rested above a honeycomb of limestone caves.[7]

In the nineteenth century, beer makers used these underground caverns as a natural source of refrigeration. By 1860, forty breweries had opened up shop in the city partly because of its subterranean vaults, which could be used for storage. Lyon Park Cave near the Anheuser-Busch Brewery served as an ammunition storage area during the Civil War. Glasgow Cave under the intersection of Cass and Garrison was a wine cellar as well as a vault for storing beer. Schneider Beer Cave, Chouteau and Mississippi streets, became an underground beer garden.[8]

Uhrig's Cave, beneath the intersection of Jefferson and Washington streets, became an entertainment center in the latter half of the nineteenth century. Brothers Joseph and Ignatz Uhrig purchased the tract above the cave in 1849. Using a natural fissure as a core, the brothers dug out a chamber that measured 210 feet long and 20 feet wide 42 feet below street level. Cold beer, good food, and a variety of musical entertainment attracted prominent businessmen to this underground pleasure dome.[9]

Beginning in 1876, Uhrig's Cave offered lavish stage shows with professional actors and complete orchestras. Both men and women attended these events, which ranged from vaudeville acts to Gilbert and Sullivan to grand opera. Cadres of waiters brought foaming steins of beer, bottles of wine, and hearty food. Cads and gigolos reportedly trolled for unattended or compliant females. Hot weather drove pleasure-seekers into the cave in the summers throughout the 1890s. Under the ownership of Frank McNeary, Uhrig's Cave's entertainment achieved a high level of professionalism and popularity, with record-breaking crowds attending dramatic and musical productions.[10]

It was no secret, then, that the bustling streets of St. Louis concealed entrances to and exits from a subterranean world, where glamour, excitement, danger, or treasure might lurk. Mischievous boys found their way into this world, where they could avoid going to school and escape adult supervision. Some of these boys were carefree adventurers, but others were desperate outcasts seeking shelter, and some were budding young outlaws. Police occasionally traced thefts and other crimes to these "gophers," the name they gave to young boys hiding in caves.[11]

It is not hard to understand why boys would be drawn to the caves. Mark Twain provided a clear explanation of the attraction of boys to caves in *The Adventures of Tom Sawyer*, in which Tom returned several times to a cave near his hometown on the west bank of the Mississippi River. Tom was a respectable boy, but he chafed against the rules and customs that kept him that way. He admired another boy, Huckleberry Finn, because Huck was not respectable. He was "idle, and lawless, and vulgar and bad," a "pariah," the neglected son of a drunkard, and, in Tom's mind, a "romantic outcast." The cave, like Huck, stood apart from comforts and strictures of ordinary life, and Tom was fascinated by it.[12]

The cave was menacing, but enticing at the same time. It was the hideout and also the tomb of the murderous Injun Joe. Tom and his true love, Becky Thatcher, got lost in it, but found their way out and returned to their joyous families. Tom and Huck discovered buried treasure in it. By the end of the novel, Huck was no longer an outcast, but a wealthy boy who had captured the heart of a motherly widow. Tom and Huck had their adventures, but in the tradition of happy endings, they finally went back home.[13]

Real outlaws, like Jesse James, hid out in caves, and their exploits inspired the plots of cheap juvenile fiction. These legendary outlaws appealed to young male readers for the same reason that Huck appealed to Tom. Like Huck, they were idle and vulgar, lawless and bad, and they lived in defiance of legal authority. In the popular imagination, Jesse James became a kind of latter-day Robin Hood, stealing from the rich, giving to the poor, restoring a rough-and-tumble kind of social equality in an age of railroads and robber barons. The name *Jesse James* had a nice, poetic ring to it, and like the celebrities of a much later time period, James became famous just for being famous, and boys tried to emulate him.[14]

In the late 1850s, adventurous boys tunneled into an Indian mound on St. Louis's near north side by the intersection of Broadway and Brooklyn Street. One of the dens they created inside the mound measured about twenty feet square and seven feet high. On winter days, groups of boys crawled into this underground hideaway and played games by candle-light. Police searched these holes when boys were missing from school. On one occasion, a police officer reportedly tracked the boys into a narrow tunnel, tried squeezing his big body through the opening, and got stuck. When workers from a nearby brickyard came to his rescue, angry boys tried to fight them off. In spite of this resistance, the rescuers managed to pull the half-suffocated policeman out of the dirt. After that incident, the police began smoking the boys out.[15]

During the same time period, boys in Frenchtown on the south side found a hideaway in English Cave, which had a long and romantic history. Originally, the cave measured 255 feet in length and 125 feet in height, with many stalactites. Local legend held that once an Indian girl and her lover hid in the cave to escape the wrath of a jealous chief. Trapped in the cave by the chief's henchmen, the couple refused to surrender and died of starvation. Years later, so the story goes, their bones were discovered locked in an embrace.[16]

Brewers Isaac McHose and Ezra English had enlarged English Cave in the 1830s, removing the stalactites to make room for vats and kegs of ale. The business partners also constructed a staircase into the cave, so that customers could enjoy a nice cool brew in a place secluded from the hustle of everyday business. After the brewery went out of business in 1849, boys used the crevice as a gathering place where they could gamble and avoid adult supervision.[17]

A group of boys called the Gopher Club built a den under a vacant lot on Olive Street near Washington University in the 1860s. Grass and weeds hid a small opening that led to a cone-shaped enclosure. Using a ladder stolen from the university, the boys could climb down into a room that measured about fifteen feet square. There was carpet on the floor, and the occupants hung newspaper pictures on the walls. The boys stole a small stove and piped it out through a hole that led to the surface. Each boy in the group promised to steal food and fuel from homes or stores.[18]

Eventually, the boys' thefts and strange disappearances drew the attention of the police. One Sunday, a four-year-old boy vanished into the hole. His parents retrieved him unharmed, but neighbors informed the authorities of the incident. Suspecting the existence of a cave, police searched the neighborhood and destroyed the hideaway.

By the 1870s, police had become exasperated with these subterranean shenanigans and began to take aggressive action. In 1873, police made a systematic search for caves in which they thought tramps were hiding. On the south side, they discovered a long, narrow excavation near the river, which opened into a large cavern. Occupants had shored up the walls with heavy timbers and installed doors with padlocks. Police watched the place for several nights and found that at least twenty men lived there and ran a gambling den. Authorities demolished the cave with gunpowder. When they found a small cave at La Beaume and Tenth streets, in which the floor was covered with wood shavings, police lit a fire. A can of coal oil exploded and reduced the place to rubble.

In 1874, police suspected gophers of committing numerous petty thefts in the city and began to investigate the problem. On winter nights, policemen walking the beat noticed a large number of children lurking around an iron grating on Washington Street. A detective spent two nights hiding in a pile of rubbish, observing bootblacks and newsboys between the ages of seven and thirteen going in and out of the opening in the sidewalk. During the night, the boys came out of their hole and raided the wagons and stalls of Union Market for small amounts of fresh meat and vegetables. Some of the boys carried wood or coal into the hole, from which steam rose.

To the astonishment of the detective, two young girls came out of the hole at daybreak. The police were familiar with these girls, who were thirteen years old and made their living selling matches. After seeing the girls come out, police raided the underground hideout and found a well-organized and well-equipped domicile. Young cave dwellers had laid down wooden floors and even paneled the walls with matched boards. Around the sides of the large room were three tiers of bunk beds covered with old but warm bedding. In one corner, there was a small cookstove with a pipe that carried smoke out into the sewer opening. Near the stove were containers of coal, wood, potatoes, turnips, and onions. In another corner of the room, the occupants kept cabbages and cooking utensils. For a dining table, the children used a long board resting on piles of stones.

During the raid, police captured eleven boys, whose average age was ten. The youths explained that they had been living in this underground chamber for three months and had hired the two girls to cook for them. All of the boys were dirty and ragged, but they claimed they liked it better than living at home. When police found them, they were playing a gambling game for cigar butts (because they had no money). In the cave dwellers' pockets, police found cigar butts, cheap novels, lewd pictures, theater ticket stubs, and pawn tickets. By tracking down the pawned items, authorities were able to solve numerous thefts of small articles from stores on Franklin Avenue and in the Union Market. Eight of the boys were sent to the House of Refuge, and three went to the hospital.[19]

After this raid, police continued to put pressure on the gophers. A group of youngsters called the Vinegar Hill gang had dug a large tunnel under a stable near the corner of Twenty-third and Morgan streets. Officials found it and destroyed it. Police also uncovered and demolished a small underground storage room near Fourteenth and Spruce streets, where a gang of boys hid loot stolen from the railroads and from Centre Market.

Under an ash heap in a vacant lot at the corner of Eleventh and Webster streets, authorities found a large cave where boys gathered at night. A small shaft led down from the surface into a narrow opening that served as a vestibule. From there a ten-foot-long tunnel led into the main room, which measured twenty feet square and six feet high. On the hard clay walls, boys had carved their names and grotesque pictures. A stove provided warmth, and oil lamps gave off a smoky kind of light. In order to enter the cave, boys had to belong to a club or else pay a ten-cent admission fee. Club members and those who wanted to enter the cave foraged in the neighborhood for supplies and furniture. Older adolescents bullied, extorted, and robbed younger boys, leading to complaints from parents. Police destroyed the cave, but subsequently, boys rebuilt it, creating a secret new entrance.

Despite these aggressive tactics by the police, adventurers continued to find their way into underground lairs. A small cave in a sinkhole west of the Fifth Street horse-car stables contained a complete keno outfit. Boys in the neighborhood pretended to go to night school, but instead went down in the cave to gamble. Another cave near the river sheltered a band of young thieves, who raided the docks, the steamboats, and the railroad structures. A group of youngsters reportedly hid out in a cave under the cemetery at Grace Church, Eleventh and Warren streets. Other boys secretly drank beer in a vault under a brick-covered courtyard near Lafayette Park.

While some of these boys sought secret hideaways for mischievous reasons, others relied on caves for shelter. Dacus and Buel observed in 1878 that many homeless boys took up residence in abandoned cellars, caves, or holes they dug under vacant lots. As many as twenty-five boys would crowd into one of these dens, huddling together for warmth in the winter. In some cases, a group of boys would take a girl into the cave to keep house for them.[20]

Hard facts about St. Louis's underground world are scarce, but homeless boys (and some girls) continued to take shelter in caves there in the twentieth century, especially during the hard times of the 1930s. In 1932 and 1933, a social worker named Thomas Minehan lived among young wanderers in the Midwest and wrote a book about his experiences. On one of his nights on the road, he slept in a cave along the Mississippi River. He did not give the specific location of this cave, but it was probably north of St. Louis. Minehan provided a rare firsthand account of conditions for the young people who lived in these underground dens.[21]

A group of boys had covered the opening of this particular cave with wood and metal, leaving a small doorway and a flue for smoke. Minehan entered the cave on a winter night, when smoke curling out of the flue had melted a patch of ice and snow. Lifting a canvas flap, he entered the tunnel on his hands and knees. In the entranceway, the smoke from a wood fire nearly choked him, but the air in the main underground chamber was clear. It was warm inside, but perpetually damp.[22]

Twelve boys and two girls lived in the cave. In the evening, a girl served Minehan a cup of coffee, a roll, and an apple, while six boys played checkers on three homemade boards. When one player lost, another took his place in an elimination tournament. After an hour, a champion emerged. His prize was a large milk can, which he had to fill with snow from outside the cave. This would melt by morning and provide water for washing and shaving. Six of the fellows slept on a large billboard. Smaller billboards and straw-filled sacks provided additional beds. One of the girls slept with a slender boy, who laid down his coat for her to sleep on. The other girl slept between two boys, who put their arms around her in a protective way.[23]

Caves within the St. Louis city limits also continued to attract young inhabitants well into the twentieth century. A particularly long and sinuous network of caves underlay the old Lemp Brewery on the city's south side. William J. Lemp, a German immigrant, founded the company and an ill-starred dynasty in 1842. During the first half of the twentieth century, four members of the Lemp family committed suicide. Three of these deaths occurred in a mansion at 3322 DeMenil Place, which is still widely believed to be haunted. Under the mansion lay one part of the complex system of Lemp caves, in which the family allegedly built a swimming pool and a theater for their lavish parties.[24]

On July 15, 1941, police at the Lemp Street Station responded to a report that smoke was coming out of the ground at Thirteenth and Cherokee streets. This spot happened to overlay one of the old Lemp Brewery caves that had been closed off. Youngsters had forced their way into the old entrance, found their way to the cave sixty feet under the ground, and built a fire. The next day, workers bricked up the entrance.[25]

Closing off the entrances did not always keep people from finding their way back into these hideaways. In 1996, a reporter for the *Post-Dispatch* took a tour of the cave under the old Lemp mansion. Although he doubted reports of swimming pools and Hollywood-style parties, he had to admit the cave was "quite something." Stalactites and stalagmites projected from the ceiling, walls, and floor, and the colors, from cobalt blue to cadmium yellow, were spectacular. It was wet, of course, and empty. But the reporter saw traces of man-made improvements, including stone archways and the "ruins of a cast-iron spiral staircase." He also saw beer cans of very recent origin lining a wall in one of the cave's branches. Just how they got there remained a mystery.[26]

As Twain well knew, in the popular imagination, caves represented freedom, fun, and mischief. Underground entertainment centers, like Uhrig's Cave, gave grown-ups a temporary respite from adult responsibilities. Other caves, like the ones under the Lemp mansion, acquired an aura of mystery that attracted children of all ages. Following the example of their elders, boys went down under the ground, looking for excitement. After a brief adventure, most boys found their way back home to parents and siblings.

Twain also realized that youthful thrill-seeking could bring innocent boys into contact with danger, criminality, and tragedy. For some desperate boys, the dank shelter of St. Louis's caves was a station on the way to the orphanage, the poorhouse, the violent streets, or jail.

Chapter Five

Juvenile Delinquents and the House of Refuge

Edward Donnelly, about 13 years of age, was ordered committed to
the House of Refuge yesterday, being fined in the Second District
Police Court for stealing candy from a wagon at Twenty-third and
Biddle streets the day before.

—*St. Louis Globe-Democrat,* March 2, 1884

AS EARLY AS 1820, REFORMERS IN EASTERN CITIES took action to
rescue wayward children from the life of the streets. During that
decade, urban dwellers began using the term *juvenile delinquents* for
youngsters who ran afoul of the law. In 1823, New York City philanthropists formed the Society for the Reformation of Delinquents. Three years
later, the New York state legislature authorized construction of the House
of Refuge as the official reformatory for youthful offenders in that city.
In that same year, Boston opened its House of Reformation for Juvenile
Offenders, and in 1828 Philadelphia established its House of Refuge
to reform young miscreants while keeping them out of adult jails and
prisons.[1]

More than two decades passed before the idea moved west of these
three major cities. In 1849, facilities opened in Rochester, New York;
Westborough, Massachusetts; and Baltimore, Maryland. New Orleans
lost its first building to a fire, but erected a new one in 1850. During that
same year, Cincinnati helped carry the house of refuge idea west of the
Allegheny Mountains with the opening of its juvenile-detention facility.
In 1854, when New York City moved its House of Refuge to new quarters
on Randall's Island, similar institutions opened in many cities, including
St. Louis.[2]

Supporters and administrators of these facilities possessed, or at least
professed, the best of intentions. B. K. Pierce, who served as a chaplain

at the New York House of Refuge in the nineteenth century, asserted, "Children have a natural and civil right to be kept from the temptations of the street." Confinement in the House of Refuge served, he said, to remove impressionable young people "from the pernicious example of evil companions" and keep them away from the "haunts of sin." Within the walls of these institutions, he believed, youngsters could be schooled in the "habits of industry and the practices of virtue." Ideally, parents should guide their children, but when the parents fail to do so, society has an obligation to fill the void.[3]

Foreign observers praised these institutions. Gustave de Beaumont and Alexis de Tocqueville visited the institutions for juvenile criminals in Boston, Philadelphia, and New York in the early 1830s and recommended that France follow the American example. No one could doubt, they asserted, the value of removing young offenders from the dangerous environment of adult prisons. In some cases, boys and girls who had committed no crime at all could legitimately be placed in the House of Refuge to protect them from evil influences in their homes or on the streets. The term *house of refuge* suggested shelter and protection rather than punishment. Some young people, especially girls who had turned to prostitution and boys who had turned to thievery and drink, might resist efforts to reshape their characters. However, in the opinion of de Beaumont and de Tocqueville, America's houses of refuge provided an edifying blend of discipline and education that could turn young people away from crime and set them on the path toward honest and productive lives.[4]

Charles Dickens commented favorably on Boston's House of Reformation and New York's House of Refuge. In his *American Notes,* first published in 1842, he affirmed the importance of these facilities. The New York House of Refuge was, he said, "an Institution whose object is to reclaim youthful offenders, male and female, black and white, without distinction." If anything, he wondered if the managers of this "admirable establishment" were a little naive in their treatment of streetwise youngsters. Nevertheless, he concluded that the institution was "well conducted," and he approved of it heartily.[5]

Houses of refuge developed in the context of a widespread movement to promote the moral and physical welfare of children. In American cities, a vast number of orphanages, missions, hospitals, and schools reached out to the young and the poor. Child savers recognized that young people were physically and psychologically different from adults and that the urban environment had a deleterious effect on children's development. Historian Marion Hunt has stated the reformers' case succinctly, noting that poverty, bad air, and bad housing compromised children's health, while bad education and bad companions led to crime.[6]

In St. Louis, as in other major cities, hospitals that cared specifically for children began to appear in the second half of the nineteenth century. The first such hospital in the United States opened its doors in Philadelphia in 1855. Boston followed with a similar institution in 1869. In 1879, a group of St. Louis women opened a hospital in a small house at 2834 Franklin Street to care for the children of the poor. One of the St. Louis Children's Hospital's first subscribers was Susan E. Blow, who had founded the first public-school kindergarten in 1873.[7]

Public schools gradually made primary and secondary education available to the offspring of poor and working-class families. In St. Louis, two public elementary schools opened in 1838, and by 1854 the city had twenty-seven schools and nearly four thousand pupils. The addition of a large and well-furnished high school in 1855 inspired the middle class to send their children to public schools rather than private academies. By 1860, nearly twelve thousand students attended classes, but then the Civil War caused a drop in enrollment. After the war, the school board complied with state law, which mandated that education be made available to all children, with segregated schools for black children. Between 1868 and 1880, a dynamic school superintendent, William Torrey Harris, hired a superior group of instructors, tightened the disciplinary structure, expanded the curriculum, and created a much-admired educational system.[8]

Reformers realized, however, that many children did not attend school and that those children received their education in the streets. J. A. Dacus and James Buel noted that in the poorer neighborhoods of St. Louis many parents paid little attention to their children's education. Some of these parents were "dissipated and vicious." Others were in such dire circumstances that they had to spend all their time working, trying to make ends meet, and could not provide the supervision their children needed. Without any formal education, these young people became adept in the "language, the propensities, and the skill" of sneak-thieves and other petty criminals with whom they came in contact. No wonder many of them eventually ended up in trouble with the law.[9]

Concern for the welfare of destitute young girls prompted a group of St. Louis women affiliated with Protestant churches to establish the Girls' Industrial Home and School (GIH) in the 1850s. This was not a reformatory, but a shelter and training school for girls whose economic circumstances made it difficult for them to attend public schools. The GIH offered basic literacy and practical training in cooking, sewing, and other domestic skills.[10]

In 1851, another group of private citizens embraced the idea of establishing the St. Louis Reform School for delinquent and abandoned boys under eighteen and girls under sixteen. The idea was to create a private institution to which the courts could commit young offenders. Two years later, after this idea had failed, the municipal assembly passed an ordinance authorizing a facility for juvenile offenders on city property. The St. Louis House of Refuge opened on July 24, 1854, and the city hired F. S. W. Gleason as superintendent. One year later, the state legislature established a nine-member board of managers to oversee the facility, which was located in the southern part of the city on property between Osage Street and Meramec Street in several old buildings previously used for the City Poor House and Smallpox Hospital.[11]

The St. Louis House of Refuge got off to a very rough start. In 1856, the city began erecting a large new building, which was completed in 1858. Due to a shortage of funds, the building remained unfurnished until the early 1860s, when the city leased it to the United States government for a hospital during the Civil War. In 1864, the House of Refuge finally occupied the facility, consisting of a four-story central block and two three-story wings, situated on a hill with a panoramic view of the city and surrounding countryside. On February 14, 1865, several months after the institution opened, a young inmate set it on fire.[12]

At the time of the fire, Charles Aiken, the arsonist, was fourteen years old and had been an inmate for more than five years. Records indicate that he had committed no crime at the time of his admission to the House of Refuge. On Valentine's Day in 1865, he threw some burning coals into a pile of rags in an attic room. Superintendent Gleason discovered the fire burning through the roof. Firemen struggled for three hours before extinguishing the blaze, which destroyed the central block and east wing of the main building. After confessing to his crime, Aiken escaped and, according to authorities, "was never afterwards heard of."[13]

The fire severely damaged, but did not destroy, the new facilities. About two hundred children had to be evacuated from the burning building. Several of the older boys and girls helped get the younger ones out of harm's way and also carried furniture and other items from the scene. Guards from the City Work House took charge of about twenty of the larger boys. Students from nearby Concordia Seminary helped secure the area. No one was injured in the fire. Most of the inmates had to return to the old buildings, where they stayed for several months. In 1866, the girls remained in the older part of the facility, and the boys moved into the repaired building.[14]

Troubles like these were not unprecedented in houses of refuge. The

early years of the Philadelphia House of Refuge were marked by disturbances of various kinds. Bored and resentful young inmates tried to escape,
engaged in fights, and openly defied the authority of teachers and administrators. In the first three years of the institution's existence, children set
at least three fires. Authorities attributed these problems to the fact that
the inmates came from chaotic environments where they had received no
discipline from parents.[15]

In St. Louis, also, authorities blamed behavioral problems on the
nature of the children's home lives. According to an article in the *Missouri
Republican,* most of the inmates of the House of Refuge were "levee rats"
who issued from the poorest quarters of the city. Some were "boys of the
worst possible description." Others were merely "abandoned children,
whose chief misfortune was either being left without parents or having
parents so vicious and so poor as to be reckless about their future." City
police often came into contact with parents who taught their children
how to beg and steal. Even very young children, with this kind of home
life, could become "ungovernable in temper, mischievous, and impure in
language and thought."[16]

Many inmates of the House of Refuge were indeed very young, and
their fates were sometimes tragic. For example, a ten-year-old girl named
Mary Miller, who was found wandering alone on the streets, came to the
institution on May 10, 1856. Mary died on December 19, 1859, of an
unspecified cause after she was indentured to William B. Wilson of St.
Louis. She was about thirteen years of age. A boy named Edward Carroll
entered the House of Refuge at the age of six on May 15, 1878. Records
listed him as an abandoned child. Four years later, he died in the institution of an inflammation of the brain.[17]

Administrators of the House of Refuge allowed children as young as
nine or ten to be indentured out to farmers or businessmen who needed
extra labor. The practice continued throughout the nineteenth century.
For example, in November 1878, an abandoned eight-year-old boy named
Charles Lustenberg came to the House of Refuge. Less than a year later, he
was indentured out to W. W. Jacobs of Middle Grove, Missouri. And an
Irish American boy named Louis Garvey, age nine, arrived at the institution on November 2, 1878. On February 24, 1880, records indicate that
he was indentured to a man named B. F. Shields in Sikeston, Missouri.
Apparently, Shields did not offer Garvey a place in his home, but sent
him out to the countryside to live with a young tenant farmer. According
to census records for 1880, Garvey resided with a family in rural Scott
County, Missouri. The head of the household was twenty-three-year-old
William A. Miller, a farm laborer, who had a seventeen-year-old wife and

a seven-month-old son. Garvey, age ten, was listed in the household as a farm laborer.[18]

Throughout its history, the House of Refuge admitted both white and black children, but always housed far more boys than girls. In 1869, for instance, the average number of boys in residence each day was 102; the average number of girls was 38.[19] The following table shows the number of boys and girls among those committed to the institution[20] in five sample years:

	1855	1860	1865	1878	1897	Total	Percentage
Boys	109	147	160	146	274	836	79.6
Girls	35	22	47	30	80	214	20.4
Total	144	169	207	176	354	1,050	

Among the sad examples of the girls admitted to the House of Refuge were Annie Bains, age ten, Julia Bains, age fourteen, and Fanny Boland, age fifteen, who were all admitted on the same day in 1856. Fanny was charged with prostitution, but the other girls were simply abandoned and wandering the streets. Julia died in the City Hospital on October 9, 1857, when she would have been about fifteen years old. A small percentage of girls, like Fanny, were prostitutes, but most were guilty of no violations of the law. Boys being admitted were more likely to have committed some major or minor crime.[21]

The Journal of Commitments to the House of Refuge (the official listing of inmates admitted to the facility) recorded the names, ages, reasons for commitment, and outcomes of cases from 1854 to 1899. From the beginning, about two-thirds of the children who ended up inside the institution's walls had committed some offense, and about a third were guilty of nothing other than being left alone and unsupervised on the city streets. About one-quarter of the children sent to the House of Refuge were accused of petty larceny, and a few others were charged with more serious crimes. The following table lists the number of juveniles committed to the St. Louis House of Refuge for each of the most common reasons given in the Journal of Commitments in four sample years:

Reason	1854	1855	1860	1878	Total	Percentage
Larceny	15	59	24	38	136	25
Vagrancy	34	30	NA	NA	64	12
Improperly Exposed	NA	NA	34	NA	34	6
Abandoned	NA	NA	NA	76	76	14
Incorrigible	3	11	29	43	86	16
Destitute	2	26	37	6	71	13
Other	0	18	45	13	76	14
Total	54	144	169	176	543	

The statistics given for 1854 cover the six months after the House of Refuge opened. In 1854 and 1855, the Journal of Commitments used the term *vagrancy* to describe the condition of children left alone on the streets. In 1860, the records categorized these children as "improperly exposed." By 1878, the term had been replaced by the word *abandoned.* "Other" reasons for commitment included arson, prostitution, robbery, being a runaway, and truancy.

For its young inmates, the House of Refuge functioned as a school, a workhouse, and a prison. St. Louis followed the models of houses of refuge in New York and Philadelphia, where children worked six to eight hours a day and attended classes in the evenings. At the St. Louis House of Refuge, a staff of about forty officers, teachers, and overseers imposed strict discipline behind barred windows in buildings on a four-acre tract bounded by a tall board fence. After 1866, the facility expanded to include schoolrooms and workshops where children learned such trades as shoemaking, tailoring, baking, painting, carpentry, dressmaking, and gardening.[22]

Youngsters incarcerated in the House of Refuge worked six or seven hours a day in forced labor. In the chair-caning shop, boys wove seats for wooden chair frames. In the shoe shop, boys tended noisy machines for a local shoe manufacturer. In the bakery, the inmates made bread in huge ovens. Superintendent Gleason believed that work was the key to rehabilitating young offenders. "No institution," he wrote, "however benevolent its design may be, need entertain a hope of reforming the idle and vicious without the aid of a good system of labor adapted to the strength and capacities of its inmates."[23]

When they left the St. Louis House of Refuge, many children (about 40 percent of them) returned to the homes of their parents or other relatives, according to the Journal of Commitments. One-quarter of them were apprenticed or indentured. A surprising 8 percent of them managed to escape. Others were placed in workhouses, prisons, orphanages, and hospitals. For many of them, the journal gives no information about what happened to them after their release.

Some youths left the institution only to embark on criminal careers. The Journal of Commitments states, for example, that Patrick McDonald, age fourteen, was committed to the institution for larceny on October 23, 1855. Eighteen months later, on April 18, 1857, he escaped. Authorities captured him in June and sent him to the State Penitentiary for twelve years for highway robbery. In 1865, he was shot dead trying to escape. At that time, he would have been twenty-three years old.[24]

Milton Frame had a long history of commitments and escapes. On November 28, 1860, he came to the House of Refuge, charged with larceny, at the age of thirteen. Two weeks later, the court released him to the care of his sister. On July 30, 1861, he returned to the institution due to vagrancy and was released again to his sister's care. In January 1862 he allegedly stabbed a boy in the institution and then managed to escape. Ten months later, he returned, charged with larceny. In June 1863 he escaped again, apparently returning to a life of crime. On August 8, 1863, he went to the City Work House for grand larceny. Apparently, he escaped again. One year later, he ended up in the State Penitentiary at the age of seventeen.[25]

It is not surprising that Frame and other boys escaped—or tried to escape—from reformatories. In addition to the spirit-crushing routine of work and lessons, teachers and staff inflicted corporal punishment. At the Philadelphia House of Refuge, according to one historian, "Children were flogged, placed in dark cells, obliged to stand up at meals, and severely admonished." The Boston institution emphasized positive rewards for good behavior. But in New York, authorities leaned toward harsh penalties, including whipping. This was also true in St. Louis.[26]

In 1872, a St. Louis grand jury found convincing evidence that Superintendent Gleason and his staff had inflicted great cruelty on the inmates. The grand jury's report cited three cases in which boys had received whippings and one case in which the lash had torn pieces of flesh out of a boy's back. In addition, the report alleged that staff members had placed boys in "a dark dungeon" for up to forty-eight hours without food or drink.[27]

Records of the St. Louis Circuit Court indicate that Gleason was arrested on July 16, 1872, and charged with "willful oppression and abuse of authority." Initially, his trial was set for July 18. Prosecutors obtained several continuances, and defense lawyers filed a writ of habeas corpus on August 19. After several additional prosecutorial delays, the case was dismissed *nulle bona* (serving no good purpose). Surviving court records provide no further information about why the case ended in this way.[28]

After Gleason's departure, conditions at the House of Refuge continued to be dismal, as Dacus and Buel observed firsthand. The main problem, which they clearly identified, was that the institution functioned as a prison, although many of its unfortunate inmates had committed no crime. The buildings and the yard were enclosed by twenty-foot walls, and all the windows were grated and barred. The prison yard had a well-tended flower garden, but it was surrounded by a bare, paved, cindered enclosure. The staff continued to apply severe discipline, using corporal punishment on the boys, although not on the girls.[29]

On the positive side, Dacus and Buel observed that all the inmates

attended classes at least three hours a day. The boys' educational program offered grades one through four and also employed a music teacher.
Facilities at the House of Refuge included a theater in which boys put on
plays and a basement dining hall that seated well over one hundred boys.
With new management, headed by John D. Shaffer, the institution functioned efficiently, and there was a separate female section, supervised by
M. J. Shaffer as matron; Dacus and Buel did not describe this section in
detail.[30]

Reports of the superintendents between 1856 and 1900 complained
about overcrowding. From the beginning, construction of new facilities
lagged behind population. Average daily population increased steadily
from approximately 207 in 1865 to approximately 354 in 1897, but no
new buildings were constructed after 1885. The State Board of Charities
and Corrections reported in 1903 that the population of the House of
Refuge had ballooned to 450, and 90 of those inmates were under five
years of age.[31]

Of utmost concern to both officials and reformers was the continuing
problem of housing neglected children under the same roof as juvenile
offenders. In 1903, the Board of Charities and Corrections noted this
problem, but reported that the boys sent by police courts were kept separate from the homeless and dependent children. Still, authorities believed
the system posed a danger to innocent youngsters. By the early twentieth century, the managers of the House of Refuge actively supported the
creation of a juvenile court system and a complete reorganization of the
facilities for housing delinquent and dependent children.[32]

During the first two decades of the twentieth century, Progressive
Era reforms led to the establishment of Missouri's juvenile court system.
Beginning in 1903, only a special court that handled cases against minors
could commit delinquent children (under the age of sixteen) to the House
of Refuge. The law applied only to counties with a population of more
than 150,000, including the city of St. Louis. Important provisions of
the law established a system of probation that kept many boys out of the
institution by placing them under supervised care in their homes. A 1911
statute raised the age of minors covered by the juvenile court system to
seventeen and extended provisions of the law to counties with more than
50,000 residents.[33]

On May 4, 1903, Judge Robert M. Foster presided over the first session
of Juvenile Court in St. Louis's Four Courts Building. One year later, the
court occupied permanent quarters in the City Hall. The law prohibited
holding juvenile offenders in any jail or police station while they awaited trial. From 1903 to 1906, the House of Refuge provided a detention

room. Beginning in 1907, the city leased a three-story building on Clark Avenue near the City Hall as a juvenile detention center.[34]

The problem of wayward youth continued to trouble the city's residents after the juvenile court system was set up. In one twenty-four-hour period in spring 1903, fifteen boys, aged nine to eighteen, came to court on a variety of charges. The youngest of these, Theodore F. Adams, Jr., wept openly when a patrolman took him from his home to detention. His father declared that the boy was "absolutely incorrigible" and charged him with stealing money from his grandmother. The boy confessed to taking three dollars, but said he had given it back. Nevertheless, his father said reform school was the only place for him.[35]

On the same day, ten boys faced charges of stealing sacks of goods from freight trains. Emmett Aids, fifteen, and Thomas Gibson, eighteen, allegedly stole the contents of a mail sack thrown off a train. Both of them worked as messengers for Western Union at the time of their arrest. James Robinson, seventeen, and Joseph Nitz, fourteen, reportedly took a one-hundred-pound sack of sugar from a car on the Merchants' Terminal Railroad. Six other boys, all under sixteen years of age, faced charges of stealing three hundred pounds of sugar from freight cars in the Illinois Central Railroad yards.[36]

The list of offenders for the day continued. William Fleming, fourteen, and Arthur Lewis, eighteen, allegedly stole a pocketbook from Minnie Stamm of 4123 Donovan Avenue. The boys had brought Stamm's son's schoolbooks home for him, and when they left, the purse was missing. Upon questioning, the youths admitted to the crime. Walter Harmon, twelve, and John Donovan, fourteen, apparently vandalized machinery belonging to the Multiplex Display and Fixtures Company plant on Seventh Street. In the process, they did about two thousand dollars' worth of damage and managed to steal about ten dollars' worth of brass fittings. Officials found the brass in a junk shop near Carr Street and charged the boys with theft.[37]

In 1906, the city's probation officers handled 1,222 cases. The vast majority of cases involved boys; only 142 involved girls. Of all the children reported to the probation officers, 992 were white and 230 were black. Nearly 200 of the total number of cases involved neglected rather than delinquent children. The law defined delinquency as a violation of state law or city ordinances. However, probation officers urged the state to expand the definition to include runaways, truants, and boys who associated with criminals or frequented dangerous places.[38]

Reformers pressed for changes in the treatment of children at the House of Refuge. In 1905, St. Louis passed an ordinance changing the

A St. Louis street boy in Juvenile Court for truancy. (Photograph by Lewis Hine, May 5, 1910. Courtesy of the Library of Congress)

institution's name to the St. Louis Industrial School and placing the emphasis on vocational training rather than discipline or punishment. The Board of Education provided instructors who could conduct manual training courses in addition to classes in academic subjects. The old system of forced labor gave way to programs aimed at providing useful skills. By 1915, the bakery and the chair-caning factory had been eliminated.[39]

Advocates for child welfare urged placement of children with families rather than in institutions. Many local charitable agencies sent representatives to attend sessions of the Juvenile Court, and these agencies offered their services in helping to place children, especially those who were neglected and not delinquent, in appropriate homes. In many cases, the court sent delinquent children to live in the homes of friends or relatives under supervised probation. In 1906, about one-fourth of the cases were resolved in this way. During that year, officers of the court made 1,825 visits and reports in connection with the children under its supervision. Still, in that year, about 170 boys were sent to the St. Louis

Industrial School, and 28 of the more serious male offenders were committed to the Missouri Training School for Boys at Boonville, Missouri. Two female delinquents were sent to the State Industrial School for Girls in Chillicothe, Missouri.[40]

Reform efforts continued, and in 1910, the Municipal Assembly established a Municipal Commission on Delinquent, Dependent, and Defective Children. Based on the commission's recommendations, the city planned to phase out the St. Louis Industrial School. In 1911, the Board of Children's Guardians took charge of the dependent children who had not been convicted of any crime and placed them in foster homes. For the treatment of delinquent boys, the city planned a new facility to be known as Bellefontaine Farms.[41]

Although its construction was authorized in 1913, Bellefontaine Farms did not officially open until 1920. Located on a 359-acre site several miles west of the city, the Farms removed delinquent boys from the community, but did so without barring the windows or surrounding the inmates with high walls. Inmates lived in red brick cottages with large front porches. About twenty-five boys lived in each of the nine cottages, sharing a living room, a kitchen, a dining room, and upstairs dormitories. The living rooms were furnished with pianos, books, and study materials. Surrounding the cottages were vocational shops and farm buildings, including stables and barns.[42]

The Juvenile Court could send boys aged nine to sixteen who were not placed on probation to Bellefontaine Farms. Older boys and those considered incorrigible were sent to the Missouri Training School for Boys at Boonville. The emphasis at the Farms was on education and social skills, not punishment. Boys had to work, but on the farm or grounds, and only for four hours per day. Vocational training included carpentry, cabinetmaking, auto mechanics, agriculture, bricklaying, and shoemaking. The boys attended classes for half the day, either in the morning or in the afternoon, with a teacher provided for each cottage. Various churches conducted Sunday school services, and "cottage fathers" supervised recreational programs.[43]

By 1920, Progressive Era reformers had thoroughly discredited the House of Refuge idea, and cities across the nation sought new ways of rescuing vulnerable young people from the dangers and temptations of life on the streets. One by one, the old high-walled, prisonlike facilities gave way to less secure, but more attractive campuses, like Bellefontaine Farms, that utilized the decentralized cottage plan. In 1935, the New York House of Refuge, the first institution of its kind, closed its doors forever.[44]

The new era promised more humane treatment of juvenile offenders, but the story of the St. Louis House of Refuge serves as a reminder of the ways in which good intentions can sometimes lead to woeful results. More than a century ago, American cities in the East and the West confronted the issue of neglected and undisciplined youth, who too often turned to violence and crime. Nineteenth-century child savers clearly understood the close relationship between the urban environment and the rise of delinquency. Twentieth-century Americans developed new perspectives on this basic idea, but still were unable to solve the problem of endangered and dangerous youth in the nation's urban centers.

Chapter Six

Child Savers and St. Louis Newsboys

At 7:30 on one of the coldest nights of last winter [1909–1910] Little Cock-Eye, aged 6, was found standing on the corner with two papers [in] his hand. His stockings were down over the tops of his shoes, his overcoat open and his shirt unbuttoned. First one little hand and then another was put into his pocket to get warm as he cried, "Last edition of the . . . "

—ORA AURILLA KELLEY, "The Newsboy Problem in St. Louis"

AT THE END OF THE NINETEENTH CENTURY and the beginning of the twentieth, progressive reformers aimed to get children out of the workplace, off the streets, and into well-organized educational and recreational programs. As a highly visible presence at busy intersections, St. Louis's newsboys drew attention from child savers, who perceived them as potential victims of the city's dangers and temptations. By the turn of the century, these young salesmen had become noisy and colorful fixtures on the urban landscape. In the eyes of reformers, however, they were a daily reminder that children in the industrial city grew up too fast and joined the labor force too early.[1]

Progressives around the country tried to solve the problems of working children. Most of the reform efforts occurred at the local and state levels. In connection with this widespread movement, Missouri adopted protective legislation aimed at keeping children under age fourteen out of mines, factories, and other dangerous workplaces. In 1911, the state prohibited any child under the age of ten from selling newspapers or other kinds of merchandise in streets, hotels, railway stations, saloons, or public buildings. Between 1915 and 1919, the state created three children's-code commissions to examine and improve the state's laws relating to child welfare. Despite these efforts, however, children, parents, and employers often ignored the law, and newsboys continued to ply their trade.[2]

Selling newspapers was a common way for ambitious eleven- to fifteen-year-old boys to make money. Famous men have reminisced about their early days as "newsies." Baseball legend Yogi Berra sold newspapers on St. Louis street corners at night and practiced his sport in parks during the day. Historian David Nasaw insists that most young newspaper sellers enjoyed their experience in the "ideal workplace" of the bright and bustling city streets. These young boys, Nasaw maintains, were flesh-and-blood heroes, straight out of the pages of Horatio Alger's novels, living the American dream.[3]

At the turn of the century, the newspaper business was highly competitive, and young salesmen played an important role in it. According to Nasaw, newspaper publishers needed the children as much as the children needed their jobs. In many cases, newsboys functioned as independent contractors, setting their own hours and defining their own territories. In school, they had to obey their teachers, and at home, their parents ruled the roost, but on the streets the boys were independent. The harder they worked, the more money they made. It was a simple and effective lesson in self-reliance.[4]

Bernard "Barney" Mussman fit the American mold of the hardworking young man who lifted himself up by his own bootstraps. In 1899, he won recognition as St. Louis's top-selling north-side newsboy. Mussman worked for a news dealer named H. M. Dixon at 2141 Cass Avenue. In one week in February, he sold 1,143 copies of the *Post-Dispatch* on the corner of Nineteenth and Cass. The newspaper described him as "a fine husky lad with a fog-horn voice and a positive manner" who stood at his corner in any kind of weather.[5]

The reason Mussman worked so hard may have been that he was supporting not only himself but also his younger stepbrother. In 1900, Mussman and his sibling, James Croke, lived in a multifamily dwelling at 1852 Cass Avenue. The federal census for 1900 listed Mussman as the head of the household and reported his age as twenty-one. At that time, his stepbrother was sixteen, and both of them worked as newsboys. Ten years later, according to the 1910 federal census, Mussman had a wife named Annie and a five-year-old son named Harry. Croke still lived in his household, and both brothers worked as salesmen for a soda works.[6]

Mussman differed from the typical St. Louis newsboy, who was under sixteen and still lived at home with his parents. A Washington University student named Ora Aurilla Kelley documented the struggles of young newspaper sellers in 1912 in a thesis entitled "The Newsboy Problem in St. Louis." Kelley's survey of 507 newsboys in St. Louis revealed that most of them (377, or 74.3 percent) lived with both their parents. However, 73

BARNEY MUSSMAN.

Drawing of Bernard Mussman, top-selling newsboy, that appeared in the *St. Louis Post-Dispatch* on February 24, 1899. (Used by permission, State Historical Society of Missouri, Columbia)

(14.3 percent) lived with a widowed mother, and 13 (2.5 percent) were orphans.[7]

Many of the newsboys attended school, at least until they reached the age of fourteen, but many of these attended irregularly. More than 60 percent of the newsboys who did attend school were in a grade below their age level, and truancy rates were very high. Sixty percent of those over the age of fourteen left school entirely, but this was normal at the time in St. Louis, where only about one-third of children aged fifteen to seventeen attended school regularly. Boys who sold afternoon papers could report to work after the school day ended. Those who sold morning papers, however, had to be out on the streets long before dawn, and many of these boys lived a ragtag existence away from adult supervision.[8]

Big-city dailies aimed not to educate boys, but to sell papers. In the early twentieth century, St. Louis publishers produced two morning and three evening papers daily. All of them employed a combination of carriers, who delivered papers on regular routes from house to house, and sellers, who offered papers for sale on the streets. Carriers were mostly adult males. Adults who worked as sellers often were disabled, blind, or elderly, and sometimes combined begging with selling. Adult sellers worked only in the downtown area. Newsboys sold papers in all areas of the city.[9]

Circulation managers divided the city into four areas, designated as the northern, southern, central, and western districts. Salaried agents took charge of the districts, sending papers in bulk to various branch offices. In the southern, northern, and western districts, the branch offices tended to be connected with laundries or small stores. Newsboys in these districts generally came from homes in the vicinity. By contrast, central branch offices were likely to be located in pool rooms, coal sheds, or other unsanitary places, where grown men lounged, smoked, and drank. Boys could sometimes sleep in these places all night. "Tramp newsboys" often drifted into the city, finding temporary shelter in these offices before moving on to ply their trade somewhere else.[10]

Newsboys obtained their papers from the branch managers or from "heavy men," who drove around the downtown area in wagons. Boys paid cash for their papers and then sold them in front of office buildings, on busy corners, or on streetcars. Sunday papers came out as early as 2:30 a.m., and boys waited to obtain them for most of Saturday night. While they were waiting, they played games in the streets or, in cold weather, crouched near hot-air vents. Sometimes they slept in the central branch offices, where the heavy men and their cronies lounged around, playing cards and shooting craps.[11]

Boys of different races and ethnic groups vied for control of the business in particular neighborhoods. In the western part of the city, the newsboys tended to be native-born of American parents. Irish American boys dominated the north and northwestern sections. Mostly German American boys sold in south St. Louis. In the downtown area, Italian and Jewish boys competed for dominance. African American boys generally sold papers in their own neighborhoods. Of the 507 newsboys surveyed in 1910, 55 (about 10 percent) were black. Thirty percent were native-born of native white parents, 82 (about 16 percent) were foreign-born, and 200 (nearly 40 percent) had foreign-born parents. Of these, the most prominent ethnic groups, in descending order, were German, Irish, Jewish (with the majority coming from Russia), Italian, and Polish.[12]

Newsies used a variety of ploys to make money. Some relied on charm and persistence. Others depended on volume and persuasion. Some were little entertainers, who lured customers with humor, grins, songs, tricks, and childish grandiloquence. Creative boys yelled out false headlines to entice buyers. Older, bigger boys bullied and intimidated passersby. Young con artists scammed people out of their change. Very young newsboys could appeal to human compassion. The more pathetic they seemed, the more papers they sold. At least one St. Louis boy, known as "Red," started selling papers at the age of four, in 1910. Investigators traced him to a branch office, where he bought his papers directly from the manager. The shrill voices of very young boys attracted the attention of bustling pedestrians, who often bought papers out of sympathy.[13]

Smoking, drinking, gambling, and other risky behaviors were part of the newsboys' social lives. Zealous young salesmen jumped on and off moving streetcars to serve their customers. Of the 507 boys surveyed, 67 percent used tobacco, and many of them smoked the butts of cigars and cigarettes they found in the gutter. Branch managers turned a blind eye when boys swiped a few beers or joined in games of dice. Some of the boys went into saloons to get change or deliver papers. A few of the young carriers made regular deliveries to houses of prostitution, and others wandered into the red-light districts out of youthful curiosity. Branch managers and heavy men took it upon themselves to initiate boys into adult pleasures. As a result of this peculiar system of education, delinquency rates among newsboys were very high. More than half of the boys (58 percent) in Kelley's study had been arrested at least once, the most common violations being burglary, petty larceny, truancy, incorrigibility, disturbing the peace, and destruction of property.[14]

The true dangers newsboys faced became evident on a hot summer night in 1896. It was the first of August, and a group of newsboys idled in a room at the rear of 114 North Ninth Street, which served as a distributing point for the *St. Louis Star*. The crowd spilled out into an alley that ran from Pine Street to Chestnut Street between Eighth and Ninth streets. In the alley, a twenty-one-year-old black newspaper seller who went by the name Henry Clay, but whose real name was Tom Johnson, approached William Amend, an eighteen-year-old white newsboy. Clay's nickname was "Peggy" because he had a wooden leg. Amend, who sold the *Chronicle*, was known as "Chronicle Red." While Amend stood in a doorway, Clay walked up to him, and a deadly altercation began.[15]

A seventeen-year-old newsboy named Arthur Smith later stated that Clay engaged in crap games many times with the boys who passed their time in the alley between Pine and Chestnut. Allegedly, on the night of their fatal encounter, Clay and Amend argued over one of these games. According to some witnesses, Amend shoved Clay and knocked him down. At that point, Clay pulled a revolver from his pocket and fired a shot. Amend ran inside and tried to hide behind the door. Another newsboy tried to take the weapon from the older Clay, but he fired again. Amend fell to the floor, mortally wounded. Clay ran down the alley toward Chestnut Street. Frightened and confused, the other newsboys did not try to follow him. Police officers arrived shortly and sent Amend's body in an ambulance to the hospital and then to the morgue. Two policemen ran down the alley and found Clay hiding in a shed. He had thrown away the revolver he used, but later at the police station he did not deny the crime.[16]

Amend was the son of James and Mary Amend. In 1880, he lived with his parents and three sisters. By 1896, he had been a newsboy for several years. Apparently his parents had passed away by the time of his death, because the only family members who survived him were two sisters. Funeral services for him were held on August 4, 1896, at the home of his sister Irene and her husband, Anson W. Foot, at 4026A Kennerly Avenue. Amend was buried in Bellefontaine Cemetery.[17]

Henry Clay's short life came to an equally tragic end. He had come to St. Louis from Hot Springs, Arkansas, and sold the *Star* at the corner of Sixth and Olive streets. About five years before the fight with Amend, Clay's right leg had been sheared off at the knee by a freight train. After Amend's killing, the newspapers were quick to characterize Clay as a brutal man with a penchant for murder, but defense attorneys argued that Amend shoved Clay out of the doorway and into the alley and provoked him to uncontrollable rage. He acted, they asserted, in the grip of passion and therefore did not commit premeditated murder. Nevertheless, the jury convicted him of first-degree murder and sentenced him to death. A little more than a year after the crime, he paid the ultimate price for his transgression.[18]

At daybreak on Thursday, November 14, 1897, Clay marched from Murderers' Row in the City Jail and crossed a narrow plank called "the Bridge of Sighs" to the gallows. His sweetheart, Ella Wanza, sobbed and screamed in her cell. During the night, she had sung hymns and prayed with him, while he awaited his fate. The sheriff took him by the left arm and led him to a small soap box on top of a trap door. Clay stepped on the box, and a deputy placed a black hood over his head. The sheriff adjusted the noose. "Take your time," Clay said. "Do it right." One of the sheriff's men lifted a hatchet and cut the rope; the trap door creaked, and Clay's body shot down into the opening.[19]

Child savers in St. Louis were shocked by Amend's death. In an attempt to protect other young boys, a group of society women, the King's Daughters Society, formed the Newsboys' Home Association to establish a lodging house and social center for the young newspaper salesmen. After a year of fund-raising, the Newsboys' Home opened its doors in November 1897. The spacious home offered double parlors with a piano, games, and books, in hopes of entertaining the boys and luring them away from the gambling and other vices of the streets. Boys who had nowhere else to go could find shelter in the home for the night.[20]

To raise funds for the Newsboys' Home, a group of affluent women engaged in a very unusual event on December 8 and 9, 1897. Well-dressed and smiling matrons stood by the boot-blacking stands near several downtown buildings, selling little green tickets for ten cents that entitled the buyers to a shoe shine. Many patrons gave large tips to the ladies, although African American men in white jackets did the actual work of cleaning the shoes. The event raised more than five hundred dollars for the cause.[21]

Newsboys themselves were on display at an elaborate dinner at the new home late in December. Young representatives of St. Louis high society volunteered to serve the meal to nearly eight hundred boys, whose bright, smiling faces reportedly "formed a delightful sight to the many visitors present." According to the *Globe-Democrat,* "Newsboy guests, other visitors and hosts declared it a grand success that would long be a pleasant memory and bright spot in the lives of both givers and recipients."[22]

The St. Louis Newsboys' Home continued in operation from 1898 until 1904, and two years after that, a young priest, Father Peter Joseph Dunne, opened another facility for homeless newsboys. Dunne met a newsboy on a streetcar in the winter of 1906. James "Little Jimmie" Fleming was ten years old; his mother had passed away, and his father had abandoned him. He was trying to support himself by selling papers when he encountered Dunne. Touched by Fleming's plight, the priest convinced his church to support a residence for homeless newsboys.[23]

Dunne himself had been an orphan. Born in Chicago on June 19, 1870, Dunne moved with his Irish-born parents to Council Grove, Kansas, in 1873. Before his mother died in 1881, Dunne had a happy childhood. Early in 1882, his father sold the Kansas farm and tried to find work in Kansas City, Missouri, where he passed away on Good Friday of that year. While Dunne's brothers and sisters went to orphanages, he tried to make a living in a print shop, a blacksmith's shop, and then a dairy. As a young man, he worked as a horse trader in Kansas City and tried going to night school, but found it impossible to make a living and study at the same time. When he failed as a horse trader, he headed east to St. Louis.[24]

Although he wanted to become a priest, Dunne first found work as a laborer on the city waterworks and then became a teamster for the Mississippi Valley Glass Company. When the Panic of 1893 put an end to many construction projects, Dunne sold his team of mules and accepted a job as a night watchman at St. Louis University. The Jesuit priests at that institution gave him a basic education and then, when he was nearly thirty years old, sent him to Kenrick Seminary to study for the priesthood. After completing his education, he celebrated his first mass at St.

Margaret's Church under the supervision of Father J. J. O'Brien. On June 13, 1903, Archbishop John Glennon ordained him as a priest.[25]

Soon after his ordination, Dunne transferred to St. Patrick's Church and served as chaplain to St. Ann's Infant Asylum, working under the supervision of Father Timothy Dempsey, who was locally known as the "apostle of charity." In the vicinity of St. Patrick's were some of the city's worst slums, murky saloons, and cheap rooming houses, where thousands of homeless men and boys sought shelter. The archdiocese opened a home, known as Father Dempsey's Hotel, where a man could obtain a bed, a bath, and food for a dime. Dempsey also opened a hotel for working girls, a day nursery for children, and a convalescent home, and he encouraged Dunne to create a home for newsboys.[26]

On a cold night in February 1906, Dunne opened his Newsboys' Home and Protectorate in a rented house at 1013 Selby Place. With the house still unfurnished, three boys came in off the streets and slept on blankets loaned to them by a nearby merchant. Neighbors protested this use of the property, blaming every act of vandalism or mischief on Dunne's boys. By May of 1906, Dunne found a larger house, at 2737 Locust Street, where thirty-five boys immediately took up residence. At that time, Dunne resigned his posts at St. Patrick's and St. Ann's and devoted all his time to attending sessions of the juvenile court, feeding and clothing the boys in his care, sending the younger ones to school, helping the older ones find jobs, and supervising those who still sold newspapers. He also established a print shop and issued a monthly publication.[27]

With a constantly growing population, the house on Locust Street quickly proved too small for its purpose, and Dunne looked for new quarters. A plot of ground measuring 275 feet by 175 feet on the corner of Washington Boulevard and Garrison Avenues became available for $30,000. This amount seemed well beyond his reach, but Dunne approached local businessmen for contributions of one thousand dollars each. By November 1907, he had raised enough money to buy the property and build a three-story house. From the very first months at Selby Place and for the next three decades, a mysterious "friend of the home" sent wagonloads of provisions and cash donations but never revealed his or her identity.[28]

Father Dunne's Newsboys' Home opened its doors to a wide range of boys who had no place else to go. Some boys were too old for orphanages. Some boys who came to the home had been abandoned or turned over to the Juvenile Court by their parents. Others had parents who were ill or disabled and unable to care for them. Widows and widowers who had to go out to work turned children over to the home. Sometimes parents sent

Some boys watch as a driver from Father Dunne's Newsboys' Home polishes the home's vehicle. (Courtesy of the Western Historical Manuscripts Collection at the University of Missouri–St. Louis)

unmanageable boys to the Newsboys' Home. It sheltered runaways, victims of fires and other disasters, and "orphans of the heart," whose homes had become living hells. Boys who had to work to support themselves could also find shelter with Dunne. Within its first ten years, the home had helped about twenty-five hundred boys, and within thirty years, the number grew to about six thousand.[29]

Joseph and Tony Signorelli apparently came to the Newsboys' Home as orphans. According to the 1910 census, four-year-old Joseph and three-year-old Tony lived with their parents, Frank and Francesca Signorelli, who were Italian immigrants. Frank, who was thirty-nine years old in 1910, worked as a laborer on the streets. He and Francesca, age thirty-six, had four sons and two daughters, ranging in age from thirteen to three. Ten years later, the family had fallen apart. The parents' names did not appear in the census for St. Louis. Eldest son Antonio had also left the city. Carlo, age twenty-one, worked as a lamplighter for a gaslight company and boarded with a streetcar conductor's family. Eighteen-year-old Jennie had married a man named Steve Scimemi, and her younger sister, Anna, lived in their household. Joseph, age fourteen, and Tony, age thirteen, both lived at Dunne's home. Ten years later, when he was twenty-four years old, Joseph still lived at the Newsboys' Home and worked as a driver for Dunne.[30]

In 1920, when the census taker came to the Newsboys' Home, eighty-nine boys were in residence. Of these, thirty were more than fourteen years old and worked at various jobs. William Sexton, age fifteen, and Matthew Sweeney, age sixteen, worked as office boys for Dunne. Others worked as office boys for attorneys, factories, and railroad companies. Some had skilled jobs as linotype operators, compositors, and press men for various print shops. Fifty-nine boys, who were fourteen years old or younger, had no occupations. Of the boys in residence, the youngest was six, and the oldest was twenty-two. Two of the boys, Frederick and William Drysdale, both listed as twelve years of age, were Dunne's nephews. A twenty-six-year-old woman named Laura Bowman boarded at the home and worked as a restaurant cashier. Three women in their forties lived in the home and worked as a cook, a caretaker, and a laundress.[31]

Some boys ended up at the home not as orphans, but as half-orphans, without fathers to support their families. After losing her husband, Catherine Byington, an emigrant from England, tried to bring up three young boys while working in her home as a seamstress. Apparently, she could not manage this, because in 1920 her two youngest sons, Howard (born about 1904) and Maurice (born about 1907) both became residents of the Newsboys' Home.[32]

In 1930, Lawrence Bosing, fifteen; John Bosing, Jr., fourteen; Robert Bosing, twelve; and Carl Bosing, nine, all lived in the Newsboys' Home. They were the children of John and Frieda Bosing, who were German immigrants. In 1920, John Bosing was a shoemaker with his own shop in Rockwood, Pennsylvania. Apparently, during the next few years the family moved to St. Louis. After John passed away, Frieda had no way to make a living. Her eldest son, Henry, supported her by working as a busboy at the University Club. In 1930, Henry, twenty, and his four-year-old brother, Joseph, lived at home with their mother. Their sister Nennie, twenty-one, had probably married. With only Henry's wages to support them, the family had to send the four boys away.[33]

Raymond T. Kinney came to Father Dunne's at the age of fourteen after spending most of his young life in an orphanage. His parents, Daniel and Florence, lived in East St. Louis, Illinois, and had five children: Margaret, Agnes, Iona, Raymond, and Martin. In 1916, when Raymond was only a little more than a year old, Daniel Kinney became ill with tuberculosis and was sent away to a veterans' hospital in Chicago. Daniel's absence made life very difficult for Florence, who sent all the children to Hoyleton Orphans' Home in Hoyleton, Illinois. After six years of hospitalization, Daniel died at the age of forty-one. Raymond ran away from Hoyleton several times. At least once he managed to return to his mother, but she sent him back to the orphanage. By 1930, when he was too old to stay in an orphanage, he took up residence at the Newsboys' Home, but he ran away from there, too.[34]

The death of a mother could be just as devastating to the family as the loss of a father. As a middle-aged widower in 1910, Martin Sweeney tried to bring up three sons without a wife. Although he continued to work as a salesman, by 1920 he had moved to a rooming house. His older sons were grown men who worked as clerks, but his youngest son, Matthew T. Sweeney, became a resident of the Newsboys' Home.[35]

The city's child savers continued to support Father Dunne's home. Every year, for more than a quarter of a century, a prominent local citizen named Hugh Campbell spent more than a thousand dollars on a Thanksgiving dinner, complete with a catered feast and a string band, for the boys at the home. The famous brewer Augustus Busch funded a Christmas dinner every year. On these occasions, a boys' choir presented a program of songs. "Ireland Must Be Heaven, Since My Mother Came from There" was the all-time favorite song. Dunne gave sentimental speeches at these events, praising the boys and boasting that all of them were on the road to becoming good citizens. During World War I, he could proudly announce that 126 of his boys enlisted in the military services, and 5 of them gave their lives.[36]

When the Great Depression dealt an especially hard blow to the city's black population, Dunne recognized the need to provide shelter for African American youngsters. Although some facilities were open to both whites and blacks, St. Louis was a segregated city. In 1931, Father Dunne's Colored Orphans' Home opened at 3028 Washington Boulevard—near the Newsboys' Home, but separate from it. The church had already established a home for African American girls in the nearby town of Normandy, but this was the first home for African American boys in the diocese. At the time of its dedication on August 2, 1931, there were only two boys in residence, although there was space for thirty to forty. Archbishop Glennon gave a dedicatory address in which he spoke against discrimination.[37]

Peter Joseph Dunne died of pneumonia at the age of sixty-nine on March 16, 1939. His niece, Kathryn Drysdale, who lived at the Newsboys' Home, was present at the hospital when he passed away. Reverend John Manion, assistant at St. John Borromeo's Church, took charge of the Newsboys' Home temporarily. Within a few months, Father William F. Glynn took charge of the institution, which was by then a run-down building that had eighty-five boys in residence.[38]

Glynn refurbished the house and continued sheltering homeless boys. One improvement he made was installing showers to replace the antique bathtubs in the basement. The younger boys continued to sleep on rows of iron cots in newly painted dormitories. Older boys who made good grades in high school earned the privilege of small, private rooms. All the boys attended school or worked at some kind of job. Young boys received small allowances for helping with chores around the home. Merchants donated goods and supplies, and a group of women friends produced a "shower" of stockings, underwear, shoes, and clothing.[39]

In 1948, RKO Pictures sensationalized the Newsboys' Home in a feature film entitled *Fighting Father Dunne*. Pat O'Brien played the title character as a tough but sentimental man of the cloth who can bend pieces of steel if he needs to, to intimidate bad guys. Goons who work for competing newspapers stir up trouble in order to claim certain busy corners for their carriers. In one heart-rending scene, a fight between rival gangs of newsboys results in the death of the newsboys' beloved pony.

One of the film's main characters is a confused boy named Matt Davis, who leaves Father Dunne's, returns to his abusive father, and then turns to crime. This character was named after an actual boy of the same name who lived at the Newsboys' Home from December 1907 until December 1910. In the final scenes of the movie, Davis returns to the Newsboys' Home and begs Father Dunne to hide him from the police. The priest advises the young criminal to turn himself in to a friendly officer who happens to be visiting the home. Refusing to listen to reason, Davis shoots the kindly policeman and ends up on death row.

The real Matt Davis sued RKO Pictures for defamation of character, asking for $300,000 in damages. Matthew L. Davis said in his petition to the court that he was known as Matt Davis when he lived at the Newsboys' Home. During the three years he lived there, he alleged, he had presented no serious behavior problems, and he had never broken the law. His depiction as a desperate criminal, he said, had opened him up to ridicule and scorn. At the time of the lawsuit, Davis worked as a stereotyper for the *Post-Dispatch*. Father Glynn supported his statements and further stated that the producers of the motion picture knew that the final, melodramatic events in the film had never actually happened. Nevertheless, Davis lost his suit because the jury found that the studio had acted without malice.[40]

A product of the mid-twentieth century, the film's dark ending contrasted sharply with Horatio Alger's depictions of young men overcoming all obstacles and achieving success. Matt Davis protested because the plot-line completely misrepresented the story of his life. As a matter of fact, Davis emerged from an underprivileged childhood to become an honest and productive citizen. It would have been better, clearly, if the filmmakers had given the character a fictitious name. Perhaps they should have chosen a less melodramatic sequence of events, but they did not stray completely from the truth. There really was a dark side to the newsboys' lives.

Raymond Kinney, who ran away from Dunne's home, went on to lead a productive, but troubled, life. By 1939, he had married and started a family, but within a few years, he left his wife and two children and went on to start a second family. He had an excellent singing voice and apparently earned money during the 1930s and 1940s by singing in dance halls. Over the years he acquired skills as a pipe fitter and plumber. Eventually, he opened his own plumbing, heating, and air conditioning business. When he was in his seventies, he finally earned his high school diploma through a program at Belleville (Illinois) Area College. His daughter Sharon from his first marriage sought him out and finally reconnected with him late in his life.[41]

His daughter believed that Kinney's early experiences, especially running home to his mother and being turned away, had a significant impact on him, his first wife, and his children. "How can you learn about family," she asked, "when your family's been ripped apart?" For many years she never saw a picture of herself with her father. But when she finally reconciled with him, he opened up his wallet and pulled out two old pictures, taken in a photo booth, of himself and his daughter as a very young child. He survived his troubled childhood and youth, she said. He managed to get an education. He made a living. "But was he torn and crushed?" She asked the question aloud and answered, "Yes."[42]

Men like Raymond Kinney, Bernard Mussman, and Matt Davis overcame their rough childhood experiences and went on to live productive lives, but the dangers they faced on the streets were real. Yogi Berra achieved the American dream of fame and wealth, and he did it with honesty and talent. By contrast, the brief lives of Henry Clay and William Amend came to stark and violent ends. The image of the newsboy as a plucky young entrepreneur belied a system that placed young lives in peril.

Child-welfare reformers in the late nineteenth and early twentieth centuries recognized the vulnerability of boys and young men who lived and worked on the city streets. By investigating and writing about newsboys' lives, supporting protective legislation, and providing shelter for homeless and neglected newsboys, these concerned St. Louis citizens tried to create an urban environment that nurtured boys instead of endangering them.

Chapter Seven

City on the Skids

But what has happened to Market Street the skid row of my adolescent years? Where are the tattoo parlors, novelty stores, hock
shops—brass knucks in a dusty window—the seedy pitch men—
("This museum shows all kinds social disease and self abuse. Young
boys need it special"—Two boys standing there can't make up their
mind whether to go in or not—One said later "I wonder what was
in that lousy museum?")—Where are the old junkies hawking and
spitting on street corners under the gas lights?

—WILLIAM S. BURROUGHS, "St. Louis Return"

DESPITE THE EFFORTS OF PROGRESSIVE ERA REFORMERS, the problem of footloose and lawless men and boys continued, and in some
ways intensified, in the first three decades of the twentieth century. Recognizing the problem, the St. Louis Provident Association, the
Salvation Army, and the St. Vincent De Paul Society cooperated in 1925
to create the Central Bureau for Transient Men, which in 1926 became
the Central Bureau for Transient and Homeless Men. The Bureau for Men
offered social services to indigent men, but also tried hard to clear vagrants
from St. Louis's streets by reporting men who broke the local laws against
begging. Although its primary focus was on adult males, the Bureau for
Men developed special programs to deal with the wandering boys (under
the age of twenty-one) who joined the ranks of the homeless.[1]

In the early twentieth century, St. Louis, along with many other
American cities, including New York, Chicago, Minneapolis, and Denver,
had a well-defined section known as "Skid Row," where homeless men
and boys congregated. The term *skid row* originated in the late nineteenth
century to describe urban communities made up mostly of men and boys
who were skidding on a downhill slide of bad luck, unemployment or seasonal employment, and poverty, like the logs in a logging camp skidding

down a trail toward the sawmill: that trail was called the "skid road." There were women, including prostitutes, on Skid Row, but they were a tiny minority of the residents. In American cities, Skid Row areas were well-known places where bars, pawn shops, and seedy rooming houses catered to men and boys who wandered the country searching for work, adventure, pleasure, or a place to hide. In St. Louis, male transients turned Market Street between Union Station and the river into a shabby and menacing wasteland.[2]

Skid Row's inhabitants tended to fall into three general categories: the hobo, the tramp, and the bum. Recent social scientists have defined a hobo as a migratory worker who went from job to job across a wide geographical area. Tramps, on the other hand, were migratory nonworkers, who eked out a living by begging, stealing, or engaging in con games. Bums were stationary nonworkers, who often became permanent residents of a particular Skid Row and stereotypically suffered from alcoholism. Within Skid Row, these men helped and supported each other, forming a cohesive community and sharing a set of values and norms that defied those of mainstream society.[3]

Psychologists and sociologists have offered many explanations of why particular individuals ended up on Skid Row, but certainly the rapid growth in these areas had to be connected to social and economic conditions. Psychological explanations include chemical dependency, emotional immaturity, lack of a nurturing and supportive family, and failure to adjust to the demands of "normal" adult life. Sociological explanations include unemployment and poor housing. The primary factor in the growth of Skid Row communities in the years leading up to the Great Depression was the enormous demand for temporary male labor in fields, orchards, construction sites, railroad yards, and lumber camps around the nation.[4]

The expansion of Skid Row in St. Louis came at a time when the city was trying hard to beautify its streets and clean up its image. In 1901, Mayor Rolla Wells supported a group of amendments to the city's charter with the purpose of sprucing up the city for the Louisiana Purchase Exposition, originally planned for 1903, but held in 1904. During this feverish period, a distinguished group of planners and architects created a wide boulevard connecting several of the city's parks with Forest Park, the site of the elaborate fair. On a single day, September 15, 1904, more than four hundred thousand people came through the turnstiles to view the spectacle of lights, amusements, pavilions, and entertainment. The Palace of Arts became a permanent structure for the St. Louis Art Museum, and gracious homes on wooded streets sprang up along the fair's perimeter.[5]

While the city's elites moved west to the flourishing area around Forest Park, reformers tried to improve the conditions of life on the east side. Labor unions, socialists, the Civic League, and women's clubs joined forces to provide places for children to play and to reduce juvenile crime. By 1903, the Civic League had established six playgrounds in the run-down area between Sixth and Tenth streets, and by 1909, the city had created at least sixteen additional parks and playgrounds. A wealthy philanthropist named Philip Scanlan installed baseball diamonds and tennis courts in several parks. These improvements did provide recreational opportunities, but as a result of the movement of men in search of work or pleasure or shelter or trouble, the eastern part of the city continued its downhill slide.[6]

New populations of immigrants and in-migrants, including many unattached males, challenged the reformers' efforts. Each year in the early twentieth century, thousands of boys and young men arrived at Union Station, hoping to make connections with labor agents. These agents hired crews for the railroads under construction in the West and the Southwest. Every year, they recruited an estimated one hundred thousand men, sending them north in the springtime and south in the wintertime to grade railroad beds, lay tracks, and do all kinds of other manual labor. Recruiters worked at Union Station or visited the Greek and Italian neighborhoods on the near north side.[7]

St. Louis was a stopping point for a vast national army of itinerant, seasonal, and migratory workers who moved back and forth between the city and the countryside in response to layoffs, wage cuts, strikes, personal misfortunes, and economic downturns. Some were recent immigrants, who traveled in groups, and each of these groups was led by a "padrone," or gang boss. Many came from European countries, including Norway, Sweden, Denmark, Greece, and Italy, but many were American-born. Some had previous occupations as clerks, mechanics, or even professional men, but ran into trouble with the bottle or the law. During the Great Depression, close to two million men and about two hundred thousand boys joined the ranks of the hoboes.[8]

For some young men, the hobo life was a rite of passage that led them through youthful adventures into settled adulthood. Even college students sometimes became "tramp laborers" in the summer. Rural youngsters, leaving the farms, found their way into the hobo life. Generally, the farm boys were strong, hardworking, and heavily recruited by the labor agents. Older hoboes called these youngsters "scissorbills" until they "wised up" and learned to take life a bit easier. For impressionable boys the experience could be exciting but also very dangerous because of hazardous conditions

on highways and railroads, lack of shelter from the elements, and preda-
tory older men.[9]

Hundreds of St. Louis's saloons, restaurants, and cheap lodging houses
could not have existed without this semiannual migration of single men
and boys seeking or escaping from work. Market Street, according to a
Post-Dispatch article in 1910, would have been a "wilderness" without
them. As residences and businesses moved to the West End, Market Street
became "Rue de Hobo," inhabited by footloose males, passing through
town on their way from somewhere to somewhere else. Laborers returning
from one job stayed in St. Louis until their money ran out and the recruiters signed them up for another stint. With fifty dollars in his pocket, a
man could happily spend a few days on Market Street, enjoying alcohol,
cheap food, lodging, and a respite from back-breaking work. Recruiters
often made sure the prospective employees enjoyed a good time, taking
them to ethnic restaurants for wine and feasting, until they were ready
to sign on for the next job. Men who failed to find work could become
stranded in the city.[10]

City officials struggled to cope with the problem of indigent males.
Early in the twentieth century, the city provided temporary shelter in
the Municipal Lodging House, but the place remained disorganized and
unsanitary. The Salvation Army and other missions also offered short-
term lodging. In general, stays were limited to three nights, and then the
lodger had to find a job or another place to go. Efforts to coordinate services for homeless men were notably ineffectual until the 1920s, when the
Salvation Army joined with other agencies to form the Bureau for Men.
In the 1930s, the city benefited from federal programs that addressed this
problem.[11]

As downtown streets deteriorated, violent men endangered St. Louis's
children. In February 1908, for instance, Mary Ross sued three men for
torturing her twelve-year-old son, George. Her complaint alleged that
William Holland, Whitfield Whitman, and Fred Shafer accused the boy
of stealing a pair of horse clippers. When the boy refused to confess, the
men took him to a shed at 1000 North Garrison Street, where they tied a
rope around his neck and suspended him from a crossbeam. An hour later,
they hung him by the neck again, while Holland beat him with a whip.
Holland and Whitman paid fines of forty dollars each in police court for
this crime.[12]

For many families, life was precarious, and children lived on the brink
of homelessness. The day after reporting the crime against George Ross,
the *St. Louis Globe-Democrat* carried the story of a four-year-old boy who
saved his baby brother from a burning house. The boys' mother had left

Drawing of Tommie and Sylvester Gleason that ran in the *St. Louis Globe-Democrat* on February 21, 1908. (Used by permission, State Historical Society of Missouri, Columbia)

them alone while she went to the grocery store. Their father had gone to New Orleans to find work. Tommie Gleason was playing in the front room when the fire broke out in the back room, where fifteen-month-old Sylvester was sleeping. The four-year-old ran into the back room, picked the baby up out of his bed, and carried him outside to a chicken coop. Then he went looking for his mother. Every material thing the mother had, except for five cents in her pocket, went up in flames.[13]

In January 1911, neighbors asked police to help a woman whose husband had died in a traffic accident. The *Post-Dispatch* reported that Mrs. Asbury D. Smith lived with five children in a wooden shack at 6678 West Park Avenue. Two days before Christmas in 1910, her husband died after falling from a wagon. On Christmas Eve, while her husband's body lay in the morgue, Mrs. Smith gave birth to a son. One month later, neighbors told police that the baby was wrapped in a shawl, and the other four children lacked warm clothing. The eldest child was nine years old. Apparently, this family had no one to turn to except neighbors, who appealed to the police for help.[14]

The police had limited options in dealing with desperate families and children. On February 19, 1908, officers found two boys, who had been missing for three weeks, hiding out in a bake oven at 1921 North Prairie Avenue. Thirteen-year-old Tony Rudnicka's family lived at 1404 North Twelfth Street. There are no records of what became of him after he was found. Ten-year-old Eugene Coughlin was returned to his parents at 3282 Cass Avenue, but two years later, in 1910, he was an inmate at the St. Louis Industrial School (the former House of Refuge).[15]

As authorities struggled with the sad results of poverty and social instability, the streets became more dangerous. Most of the young men who came to St. Louis or passed through the city were honestly looking for work, but a few of them were predators who hoped to make fortunes through robbery and extortion. In 1910, three young criminals named James Cipolla, Vito Giannola, and Alphonse Palazollo left Palermo, Sicily, and headed for St. Louis. All three were junior members of an underworld organization known as the Green Ones, or the Green Onions. To pay for their transatlantic voyage, they held up a wealthy theater owner. As soon as they hit St. Louis, they headed for the neighborhood surrounding Columbus Square at Tenth and Carr streets, known as Little Italy. The newcomers began terrorizing Italian merchants, collecting a "tax" on items sold in their neighborhoods. If businessmen refused to pay, the Green Ones were perfectly capable of murder.[16]

In response to increasing criminal activity in Little Italy, many law-abiding Italian American families fled the dangerous streets of downtown St. Louis and settled on the "Italian Hill," otherwise known as the Fairmount District, just west of Kingshighway. In the late nineteenth century, Italian men had settled there because they worked in the nearby brickyards and clay pits. Between 1900 and 1930, the Hill's racially mixed neighborhood evolved into an almost entirely Italian community of more than five thousand residents, of whom 40 percent were foreign-born.[17]

Many immigrants to the Hill were young males, who found jobs in local businesses and moved in with relatives who had already settled in the economically vibrant and close-knit ethnic enclave. Once there, residents tended to stay and marry, raise children, and grow old in an area with low rates of transiency. Families often moved from a small frame house to a larger brick one on a nearby street, but in many cases they stayed within the friendly confines of a familiar neighborhood. Crime did penetrate the Hill's perimeter, but churches, schools, mutual-aid societies, grocery stores, barber shops, bakeries, banks, small manufacturing plants, and clubs kept the social fabric strong.[18]

Yogi Berra and Joe Garagiola grew up on the Hill in the 1920s and 1930s and later became famous as professional baseball players. Their families lived across the street from each other, and their fathers worked as laborers at the Laclede-Christy Clay Products Company. Yogi and Joe played baseball in the streets with old broken bats and stolen balls. When the four-thirty whistle blew, they would stop their game, run home to get the beer buckets, and take them to the nearest saloon to fill them up before their fathers got home from work.[19]

National Prohibition, which criminalized alcohol production, turned many Hill residents into bootleggers, producing wine and other beverages in their basements. In many cases, people made alcohol for their own use, but some of the local bootleggers had connections with downtown wise guys and even with the growing organized-crime syndicates of Chicago and Detroit. In connection with the profitable and dangerous traffic in illegal liquor, organized street gangs emerged in the 1920s. Primarily composed of adults, the gangs also included juveniles, who worked as messengers and runners. Because they responded to the demand for illegal substances, the gangs became part of the economic, social, and political fabric of the city. The gangs also brought intensified levels of violence that threatened the stability of the Hill. Some families left the neighborhood because of this, but many stayed.[20]

The crime rate soared throughout the city, not only on the Hill. Between 1910 and 1930, the murder rate skyrocketed in St. Louis. This was a twentieth-century phenomenon. Historical statistics indicate that throughout the period from 1865 to 1910, the homicide rate remained very stable, in spite of the fact that the city's population grew from 270,000 in 1865 to nearly 700,000 in 1910. A dramatic increase in the murder rate began after 1910 and intensified after 1920 so that the homicide rate in 1927 was seven times the rate in 1912.[21]

Prime factors in this murder spree were wars between rival gangs, most of which originated in the eastern part of the city. In 1923 alone, police attributed twenty-five unsolved murders to disputes among criminals. Many gory deaths resulted from animosities between bootleggers and moonshiners. Others could be connected to drug trafficking. Two Irish American gangs, Egan's Rats and the Jellyrolls, carried on a murderous feud between 1921 and 1923. Italian and Sicilian gangs battled each other in the latter half of the 1920s, resulting in six murders during one week in the fall of 1927. At last, by the end of a bloody decade, the hostilities died down, and gang activity began to dwindle.[22]

This violent crime wave brought increased attention to the vulnerability of adolescent boys. Founded in 1914, the Big Brothers organization specifically focused on the needs of white fatherless boys, aged nine through seventeen, who lacked parental guidance and might, therefore, be drawn into criminal life. In 1930, St. Louis's Big Brothers founded the

Thomas Dunn Boys' Hotel for homeless youths, aged fourteen to nineteen. Recognizing that the vast majority of juvenile delinquents were boys in that age group, the managers of the facility took in boys from broken homes in St. Louis and the surrounding area.[23]

Beginning in the late 1920s, the Bureau for Men provided services to older adolescents who were unsupervised and susceptible to criminal influences. From February 1925 to April 1930, the bureau's clients included 475 boys between the ages of fourteen and twenty. The vast majority (more than 80 percent) of these youths were between the ages of seventeen and twenty. Most were white; less than 10 percent were black. About 70 percent of them had no more than an eighth-grade education. Most were wanderers who had been in the city less than one year. The bureau returned many of them to their homes or found them jobs in St. Louis or elsewhere.[24]

A whole range of tragic circumstances caused these young wanderers to seek help from the bureau. Many were unemployed and wanted work. Rural boys often came to the city looking for work and stayed long enough to establish residency. By the time they appealed for help, many of the boys had diseases, such as syphilis, and were in need of treatment. Some of the bureau's young clients had run away from decent two-parent homes because of wanderlust or a desire for adventure and then found themselves in trouble. Others came from families troubled by divorce or parental irresponsibility. A small minority of the boys were orphans who had grown up in institutions. Still others were products of childhood trauma or tragedy that left them emotionally or morally compromised.[25]

Case files of the Bureau for Men provide glimpses of the dangers these youngsters faced. Rules of confidentiality forbid revealing the clients' names, but notes made by bureau personnel were sometimes chilling. For example, a handwritten note on the file of Collin Doe stated, "Parents divorced when boy was 5. Boy shifted around from mother to grandmother. Boy disgusted and ready to steal what he could get." The mother of George Doe "engaged in criminal activities until her imprisonment. Children taken by C.A.S. [Children's Aid Society]. Greatest interest of son is in criminal activities." Mike Doe's "father and mother separated and boy continued with mother. Left home at age 16 because mother was a prostitute."[26]

The Great Depression compounded the troubles of these boys by adding new layers of economic misery. When national unemployment figures rose to 8.7 percent, St. Louis's jobless rate topped 9.8 percent, which meant that more than thirty-five thousand local citizens had no way to earn a living. For black citizens the jobless rate reached the distressing level of 13.2 percent. One year later, in 1931, the national unemployment rate neared 16 percent, and in St. Louis, more than ninety thousand people, more than 24 percent of the workforce, needed jobs. For black St. Louisans, the jobless rate was nearly 43 percent. In 1933, St. Louis's overall unemployment rate topped 30 percent, and the black unemployment rate neared 80 percent. The caseload of the Bureau for Men, which was less than four hundred in 1926, grew to more than eight thousand in 1933.[27]

Lucky St. Louis residents managed to hold onto jobs through the Depression. Chuck Berry's father continued to find work as a carpenter and handyman, although he earned less than white men doing the same work. Henry and Martha Berry gave their children a stable home, a thorough grounding in religion, and a love for gospel music. When Henry's bosses at a flour mill cut his hours in the 1930s, he went to work for a realty company, cleaning and refurbishing apartments, and he also sold vegetables from a truck. His son Chuck remembered using scrap pieces of wood to supplement small supplies of coal for heating their home. He also remembered listening to Gene Autry, Kate Smith, and Fats Waller on the family's Philco radio. In spite of this stable home life, Chuck Berry responded to the lure of the streets. As a teenager in the early 1940s, he rode downtown on a streetcar to peek at the girls in the burlesque shows on Skid Row. In 1944, at the age of eighteen, he was arrested and convicted of armed robbery following a joy ride across Missouri to Kansas City. He served three years in prison. At that time he could not have foreseen his future fame as a rock and roll artist and success as a St. Louis businessman.[28]

Some families came to the brink of dissolution and fought their way back. In the mid-1930s, the father of Aaron Hotchner had to go on the road as a salesman, leaving his son alone in a hotel, while his mother was in the hospital. At the age of twelve, Hotchner ate his supper at the Dew Drop Inn and slept alone in the room at night. A local delicatessen owner packed his lunch for school. Eventually, his father came home; the family was reunited, and the son became A. E. Hotchner, a successful author who wrote a memoir about growing up in St. Louis.[29]

Like the Hotchner family, the city of St. Louis tried to look beyond the Depression and plan for the future. While hard times ravaged the city, Mayor Bernard Dickmann and a group of civic-minded businessmen made ambitious plans to clean up the blighted riverfront area. In 1934, the United States Congress created the Federal Memorial Commission to build a monument to the explorers, hunters, trappers, and pioneers who passed through St. Louis on their way to the Far West. Within a year, the city had passed a bond issue to support demolition in a forty-block area

A man and his four young children in front of the family's flimsy dwelling in St. Louis's Hooverville, the largest in the nation. (Courtesy of the Western Historical Manuscripts Collection at the University of Missouri–St. Louis)

south of the Eads Bridge. Project planners saved the Old Cathedral, which dated from 1834, but destroyed warehouses and other historic buildings to clear the area that would eventually establish the Jefferson National Expansion Memorial, encompassing an underground museum and the magnificent Gateway Arch.[30]

In the meantime, homeless people settled on the levee in the area south of the central business district between the railroad tracks and the river. Between 1930 and 1936, St. Louis had the nation's largest Hooverville, named for President Herbert Hoover, who failed to help people displaced by the Depression. Individuals and families built dwellings out of local stones, railroad ties, trash, and discarded pieces of wood and metal. At its peak, St. Louis's Hooverville had an estimated three thousand residents, including more than three hundred children, living in six hundred makeshift homes. Merchants from the Soulard neighborhood donated produce to the squatters, and Pevely Dairy delivered milk. The "Welcome Inn" under the MacArthur Bridge served meals and functioned as a post office and city hall. The community came to an end in 1936, when WPA workers demolished it in connection with land clearance for the Jefferson National Expansion Memorial.[31]

While demolishing St. Louis's Hooverville, federal authorities faced the problem of providing decent housing for low-income families in the city. The Housing Act of 1937 created partnerships between the federal government and the cities to demolish substandard structures and build multifamily dwellings for people who could not afford to buy or rent housing on the private market. By 1939, after the Missouri General Assembly passed enabling legislation, the city contracted with the federal government to build two new housing developments to replace substandard buildings. After completing these projects in 1942, the city embarked upon a dramatic program of slum clearance.[32]

Urban renewal and slum clearance dramatically changed the downtown environment, virtually obliterating the old Skid Row communities. While most citizens welcomed this change, some observers believed that something valuable had been lost. Rooming houses, hotels, and cheap restaurants in these areas may have been unsightly, but they did provide lodging and food for a population that needed them. Missions and other private service agencies operated in these neighborhoods to relieve the worst of some people's suffering. While some former Skid Row residents may have found comfortable places in mainstream society, many remained homeless, becoming the "street people" of the post–World War II era.[33]

William S. Burroughs grew up in St. Louis and had a fascination with Skid Row. As a teenager in the late 1920s and early 1930s, he was thin, awkward, unpopular, and depressed. By the time he left home and went to Harvard, he had already explored the adolescent world of vandalism, con artistry, and recreational drugs. In the 1940s, he helped to launch the Beat Generation, an artistic movement that celebrated streetwise hipsters and debunked mainstream American values. His first novel, *Junky,* minutely examined the physical and mental experience of heroin addiction. His third novel, *Naked Lunch,* made him famous.[34]

Burroughs returned to St. Louis when slum clearance was in full swing and found the city distressingly altered. In 1965, the Gateway Arch was under construction, and he thought it had "an ominous look like the only landmark to survive an atomic blast." The old warehouses along the levee, the seedy shops along Market Street, and the run-down residences and businesses of Mill Creek Valley were all gone. Mid-twentieth-century apartment buildings reminded him of the ones he had seen in postwar Europe, products of modernism in architecture that made every city look like every other city, or so it seemed to him. He recognized Union Station, one important remnant of the St. Louis he had known in the 1920s, but the rest of the city seemed empty and strange.[35]

Something less tangible than buildings had been lost. In those old, shabby, chaotic streets, boys had found trouble and danger, but also inspiration. Chuck Berry captured it in rock and roll. Yogi Berra, Joe Garagiola, and thousands of anonymous boys experienced it in the thwock of a ball on a bat and the glove reaching up for the long fly ball. It cried out to people in big spray-painted letters on bridges and walls; it whispered crude suggestions in the stalls of public toilets and found expression in Burroughs's brutal, emotional prose.

When he prowled along the deserted and empty remains of Market Street in the 1960s, Burroughs was looking for his own lost boyhood. He felt nostalgic, not for his comfortable, middle-class childhood, but for his painful, solitary adolescence. In his emotions, if not in his circumstances, he belonged to the city's searching, shifting, dangerous crowd of brave and frightened, reckless and vulnerable, streetwise and callow, wandering boys.

Chapter Eight

Young Men and Criminal Gangs

In volume of fire the attack on the gangsters probably never has been equaled in St. Louis crime history. Hundreds of shots were fired and after the killers had driven away children scurried into the streets to pick up the shells ejected by the machine guns.

—*St. Louis Post-Dispatch,* November 22, 1930

THE CRIMINAL GANGS OF THE 1920s were mostly adult organizations, but they attracted boys as hangers-on, hero worshippers, messengers, and new blood. Young admirers of flamboyant outlaws sometimes joined existing networks, started gangs of their own, or ventured out on solo lives of crime. The rewards were obvious: fast cars and fast lives. The risks of dying young or spending your best years in prison may have seemed worth taking. Even for those who were not involved in gang activity, there were dangers on the street. When gun battles erupted, boys could get caught in the cross fire. Children witnessed drive-by shootings. For young people growing up in St. Louis in the 1920s, violence was ever present—as a choice or as an undeniable fact of life.

In 1927, sociologist Frederic Thrasher defined a gang as a spontaneous and unplanned grouping of individuals detached from conventional standards of morality. Urban gangs, according to Thrasher, developed naturally from crowds of boys meeting on street corners. Activities such as talking, loafing, gambling, drinking, smoking, games, or sex created lasting bonds among gang members. Cooperative enterprises, including criminal activities, further intensified feelings of solidarity. When challenged by another gang or by authority figures, a gang could become violent and vengeful, and conflict with enemy organizations tended to strengthen the bonds within the group.[1]

Groups of adolescent boys who engaged in gambling or other illegal activities could easily come under the influence of adult racketeers, who treated crimes as profit-making enterprises. Adult males who wanted to

93

have business dealings with the boys made a practice of hanging out at certain street corners or in certain restaurants, barbershops, or taverns. Would-be bosses could ingratiate themselves by forgiving a few debts, sharing winnings, helping out boys who were in trouble, or giving charity to the boys' families. This behavior inspired feelings of gratitude and a sense of obligation that bound young men to the world of organized crime.[2]

Gang leaders had opportunities to sharpen their skills and increase their power in the 1920s, when the Volstead Act and national Prohibition outlawed the consumption and sale of alcoholic beverages. As a result of this well-intended legislation, moonshining (illegally brewing beer and distilling spirits) and bootlegging (illegally importing and distributing liquor) became big, lucrative businesses. In the early years of Prohibition, a large number of small liquor dealers competed with each other. Prices fluctuated, and competitors encroached on each other's territories. Competition often led to violence.[3]

As an example of the profits and machinations involved in the sale of illegal alcohol, in September 1923, federal agents seized a local Jack Daniel's warehouse that had suspiciously changed hands to anonymous new owners. Before the raid by federal agents, bootleggers had made off with half a million dollars' worth of whiskey, filling the empty barrels with water to cover up their trickery. On the legitimate market for medicinal use only, the missing liquor was worth only about one hundred thousand dollars (one-fifth of its black-market value). By the time the federal government became aware of the shady transactions and seized the warehouse, the missing whiskey had found its way to illegal distributors all over St. Louis.[4]

Profits from the sale of illegal alcohol provided the perfect opportunity for ruthless entrepreneurs to turn small, spontaneous gangs into large, disciplined criminal organizations. Powerful bosses recruited men, women, and boys for a variety of specialized, skilled, and unskilled tasks connected with the bootlegging trade. Gang leaders acted as managers of complex organizations involving large numbers of old hands and new recruits. Research men gathered information and supplied it to the managers. Salesmen assessed markets and cultivated new customers. Lawyers negotiated complex transactions and protected the organizations from legal prosecution. Accountants, bookkeepers, and stenographers kept track of sales, profits, and losses. Less-skilled workers carried messages, loaded and drove trucks, and performed a wide variety of thankless and dangerous tasks. For these positions, at the bottom of the hierarchy, the gangs recruited and trained boys from the streets.[5]

In the early years of Prohibition, four St. Louis criminal organizations vied for control of bootlegging profits. The Green Ones (also known as the Green gang or the Green Onions), who arrived in St. Louis in 1910, recruited foreign-born Sicilians and terrorized small-time local bootleggers. Their archrivals, the Cuckoos, originated in the historically German Soulard neighborhood but cast a wide net among Sicilians, southern Italians, and Irish Americans. Better known at the time were two Irish American gangs: the Rats, headed by Tom Egan and his brother William (Willie) "Constable" Egan, and their archrival gang, the Jellyrolls, headed by Edward "Jellyroll" Hogan. The Egan and Hogan gangs had competed for power since the turn of the century.[6]

St. Louis was wide open to the bootleggers' wars. German, Irish, and Italian American residents had long-standing traditions of producing and consuming beer, wine, and spirits in their own households, and the city's economy had long depended on the brewing industry. There were plenty of local customers willing to buy illegal booze, and there were plenty of corrupt officials willing to protect lawbreakers. In some cases the officials and the lawbreakers were one and the same.[7]

Edward Hogan served in the state legislature. Born in St. Louis in 1886, he was elected as a state representative before he was thirty years old. In March 1917, he used his position in the government to obtain a parole for his brother, James B. Hogan, who had served only two months of a two-year sentence for burglary. Four years later, James, a chronic lawbreaker, was convicted of robbing a black messenger for the North St. Louis Savings Trust Company, but the conviction was overturned. While awaiting a new trial, in the 1920s, James became involved in a shooting war among St. Louis criminals. At that time, Edward reportedly never went anywhere without a revolver. After the gang war subsided, Edward Hogan became a state senator and served as a delegate to the Missouri Constitutional Convention of 1943–1944, but his past continued to haunt him.[8]

A deadly feud between Hogan's Jellyrolls and Egan's Rats erupted on Halloween night in 1921. Willie Egan, who was a member of the Democratic City Committee, died that night when assassins fired shots from an automobile in front of his saloon at 1400 Franklin Avenue. Edward Hogan was questioned about the murder, but he said he was in Rolla, not St. Louis, that night. Police never solved the case, but Egan's friends blamed Hogan's brother James for the crime. Egan's Rats set out to avenge their leader's death, and Hogan's Jellyrolls protected themselves with preemptive strikes.[9]

The Allies' Lunchroom, an all-night diner on Franklin Avenue, about a block from Egan's saloon, was a gathering place for gangsters. One of the

regulars was Willie Egan's bodyguard, George Ruloff, who bragged openly about what he would do to Egan's killers. On December 2, 1921, the
restaurant's owner, Joseph Cavasino, left Ruloff in charge of the establishment. When Cavasino returned from running errands, he found Ruloff
dying of gunshot wounds.[10]

One of the assassins involved in this gang war was an Irish American
teenager named James "Sticky" Hennessy. He was present at a roadhouse
in St. Louis County on December 27, 1921, when several of Egan's Rats
confronted Joseph "Green Onions" Cipolla, a leader of the Green Ones,
about a robbery that had gone bad. After the argument ended, Hennessy
and another young man called Little Red Powers allegedly returned to the
roadhouse and opened fire with pistols and a sawed-off shotgun, leaving
Cipolla and a heroin addict named Everett Summers dead.[11]

At the time of this double murder, Hennessy was about seventeen years
old. Fair-haired, short, and stocky, he had been in trouble with the law for
at least a decade. In 1910, his mother, Minnie, worked as a laundress and
headed a family of five children. Her eldest son, William, age eighteen,
worked in a shoe factory. Daughters Irene and Agnes, age sixteen and
fourteen, were cashiers in a dry goods store. Her youngest son, Albert,
lived at home, but her second youngest son, James, only six years old, was
an inmate at the Industrial School. Records indicate that he appeared in
the Juvenile Court in 1909.[12]

James Hennessy continued to have run-ins with the law. On March 18,
1920, he and Thomas Troutman were arrested and charged with stealing eighty-seven dollars from a man named Frank Sorin by threatening
him with violence. A man named Louis Seidel posted Hennessy's bond
of five thousand dollars on March 24. When their case came up in the
Circuit Court of the City of St. Louis on April 20, both Hennessy and
Troutman pleaded guilty to a lesser charge of larceny from the person of
less than thirty dollars. Each received a sentence of one year in the City
Work House.[13]

When Hennessy left the Work House, he stepped into the middle of
the shooting wars between the Rats and the Jellyrolls. On two occasions,
in failed attempts to kill James Hogan, unknown gunmen fired on his
parents' home. On February 21, 1923, unidentified attackers succeeded
in killing Jacob H. Mackler, the attorney for the Jellyroll gang. In the
aftermath of that event, Father Timothy Dempsey of St. Patrick's Church
negotiated a settlement between the Hogans and William P. "Dinty"
Colbeck, the volatile new leader of the Rats. The two warring gangs met
and declared a truce, which lasted about six months. However, by mid-
September, hostilities had erupted again.[14]

OUR OWN BALKANS.

Cartoon showing St. Louis's gang wars captioned "Our Own Balkans" that ran in the *St. Louis Post-Dispatch* on September 11, 1923. (By Daniel Fitzpatrick. Used by permission, State Historical Society of Missouri, Columbia)

On September 10, 1923, three men fired shots from an automobile into a saloon at 2600 Cass Avenue, instantly killing Elmer Malone, a cousin of Edward Hogan, and fatally wounding William McGee, a member of the state legislature. Their real target probably was James Hogan, who had been at the tavern earlier, but escaped the attack. Malone was not known to be a gangster. McGee, who had been elected to the General Assembly in 1922, was a farrier. In his capacity as a state legislator, he had been try- ing to obtain paroles for two St. Louis gangsters.[15]

From his hospital bed, McGee stated that he had been standing on the corner of Jefferson and Cass, talking to a group of men. According to McGee, none of the Hogans were present. A car came north on Jefferson, cut the corner, and turned west on Cass. Some men he did not recognize started shooting. He was trying to run away when he was hit. Other witnesses told police they saw James Hogan running away after the shooting; they said he was holding his right arm, as though he had been wounded.[16]

Fifteen minutes after the shooting, police found McGee lying on a bed in James Hogan's second-floor apartment at 2430-A Cass Avenue. McGee worked in a blacksmith's shop on the ground floor at the same address. A woman who said she was Hogan's wife stated that she had no idea where her husband was. The police took McGee to the City Hospital, where he lived long enough to make a statement, but died the following day. Edward Hogan attended his funeral at St. Leo's Catholic Church.[17]

Detectives followed McGee's funeral cortege to Mount Carmel Cemetery, where they stepped up to Edward Hogan's automobile and told him that he was under arrest. Without taking the cigarette out of his mouth, Hogan mumbled, "What do you want with me? I don't know nothing." The detectives said the police chief wanted to talk to him, and he went with them to headquarters. After an hour of questioning, he admitted that he had been there at the corner of Cass and Jefferson on the night of the shooting, but said he could not identify the gunmen. He would not say whether or not he believed they were members of Egan's Rats. Police released him.[18]

Colbeck, the head of the Rats, apologized for the killings and said they did not represent a renewal of the gang war. Instead, he told detectives, the spur-of-the moment shootings resulted from a moonshine party that got of hand. He claimed he knew nothing about the crime, but admitted that three of his "boys" were drunk that night and riding around in a big Stutz touring car. "They might have seen Hogan in the crowd at Jefferson and Cass and maybe took a few shots at him for fun, but it was the moonshine that was to blame and not the old gang stuff. That has been forgotten."[19]

In the meantime, police searched for the owner of the blue Stutz touring car, which turned out to be connected to James Hennessy. At four o'clock in the morning on September 16, a group of deputy sheriffs followed the trail of this car to the Green Mill Inn in Manchester, a town just west of St. Louis. Hennessy and two other men left after the officers entered the establishment. A few minutes later, a man came in and reported a series of holdups in progress on the Manchester Road. The lawmen drove up the road and found the Stutz car in a ditch with Hennessy at the wheel. Hennessy resisted arrest, and police took a loaded revolver from his pocket.[20]

By this time, the police were well aware of Hennessy's long-standing connection to Egan's Rats. Hennessy's sister Irene had married Isidore

Londe, who had been in trouble with the law since he was twelve years old and was also a member of the gang. Hennessy lived on the corner of Sarah Street and Westminster Place with his sister Agnes, who was a typesetter. Agnes was the registered owner of the Stutz. The *Globe-Democrat* reported that the nineteen-year-old Hennessy was a "gangster and gunman."[21]

On the night of the big chase and the series of robberies on the Manchester Road, David "Chippy" Robinson and John "Kink" Connell, who were thought to be affiliated with the Hogan gang, apparently were following Hennessy. When police arrested him, Robinson and Connell sat in another car near the scene. However, they were unarmed, and none of the victims identified them as robbers. St. Louis County police released them, but arrested Hennessy on charges of highway robbery and carrying a concealed revolver.[22]

Four victims of holdups identified Hennessy as one of the men who robbed them that night. One man said he had had a wallet containing fifty dollars taken from under the seat of his car. A woman told police the robbers had taken some jewelry. Two of the victims positively identified Hennessy as one of the robbers who stole from them. Police told reporters they were going to withhold the names of the victims in order to protect them from any reprisals by gangland associates of Hennessy.[23]

How did Hennessy become involved with a criminal gang? Without excusing his violent behavior, it would not be difficult to imagine the temptations of the gang life for a boy who grew up in an Irish American household with a single mother struggling to support her family as a laundress. His brothers and sisters managed to find honest jobs in factories, print shops, and dry goods stores. There is no way of knowing why young James ended up in juvenile court at such a young age (about five or six). His experiences at the Industrial School apparently did not help him to mend his ways. By his late teens he had become a stick-up man (explaining the nickname *Sticky*) with some very shady friends.

Hennessy graduated from the Industrial School to the Work House to the brutish world of gangland warfare. His criminal friends made it possible for him to lead a fast life and drive a fancy car. In all probability, he was one of the drunken "boys" who were riding around in the Stutz touring car, gunning for James Hogan and accidentally slaughtering Malone and McGee. Prosecutors did not have enough evidence to file murder charges, but word got out that Hennessy might be the next gang member to be rubbed out. He saved his enemies the trouble of killing him. In December 1923, he drove his car into a telephone pole on an icy road. His brother-in-law, Izzy Londe, survived the accident, but Hennessy did not.[24]

Police were frustrated by obstruction of justice, intimidation of witnesses, and corruption as gang wars continued to take a heavy toll. At the end of 1923, twenty-five murders remained unsolved, and in the summer of 1926, the killings of Cuckoo leader Tony Russo and his lieutenant Vincenzo Spicuzza set off another wave of violence. According to reports, the two local mobsters had gone to Chicago to kill Al Capone, but instead were shot with tommy guns. Capone sent flowers to their joint funeral. Reportedly a young Italian man who attended the ceremony turned to a friend and said it was a swell funeral. "Wonder what will happen next?"[25]

What happened next was a deadly spiral of murder and revenge among Italian gangs. One year after Russo and Spicuzza's murder, the war spread to St. Louis, where assassins murdered Benjamin Giamanco, a friend of Russo's, at Sixth and Pine streets. Aloys Beelman, an innocent bystander, also died. Next came the shooting of Alphonse Palazollo, a dangerous killer and mobster who had initially hired Russo and Spicuzza to defend his illegal liquor business. On September 9, 1927, four men fired shots at Palazollo from a moving car at the intersection of Carr and Wash streets, one block from a police station. Palazollo pulled out a pistol and fired back at the attackers. When the shooting stopped, he was dead. The four assassins fled the scene—three in the car and one on foot. One shotgun shell had wounded a nine-year-old boy named Emanuel Capraro, who was playing in the street.[26]

The wounded boy described what he saw. Palazollo was standing in front of a pool hall when a big Chrysler raced down Carr Street, then turned around and came back. A man jumped out of the vehicle and shot at Palazollo with a pistol. The three men inside the car fired at him with shotguns. Palazollo fell down on the sidewalk, and the car drove away. At the city hospital morgue, half a dozen shotgun pellets dropped from the dead man's clothes. There were about twenty wounds in his chest, arms, and feet. One slug had passed through the heel of his shoe into his left foot, indicating that the attackers had kept on firing after he fell to the ground.[27]

Two days later, gunmen shot and killed Charles Palmisano, a wealthy Italian merchant who had ties with Palazollo's enemies. On the same day, Robert and Frank Aiello, who were friends of Palazollo's and Russo's, died of shotgun blasts in a café in Springfield, Illinois. Two months after Palazollo's death, a bootlegger and fruit dealer named Nick Palazollo died of bullet wounds in the doorway of his store. His wife, the mother of his five children, said he was not related to Alphonse Palazollo. She had no idea why assassins had targeted her husband.[28]

Frank Kennebrew, a ten-year-old African American boy, witnessed Nick Palazollo's murder. The youngster said he saw a grey closed car with a man riding on the running board turn into an alley between Fairfax Avenue and West Belle Place. Two other witnesses also told police what they knew. Ben Sheppert, a black man, told police he heard five shots. Another black man, Harry Holland, said he saw a man run down the street and jump into a car that sped away.[29]

In spite of or perhaps because of the danger, boys and young men were drawn to the gangster life. During the gang wars of 1927, Girard Polito, eighteen, the son of a justice of the peace named Nicholas Polito, left his job as a police messenger and disappeared. His father reported him missing, but there was no sign of him for more than a week. On November 19, 1927, police arrested him, along with three other young men, as a participant in several holdups. Arrested with him at a rooming house were William O'Leary, seventeen; Leo Murray, nineteen; and an ex-convict named Fred Bieber, twenty-six.[30]

Witnesses identified Polito, O'Leary, and Bieber as the men who robbed the Chester Credit Clothing Company and the Singerman Candy Company. The manager of the Peters Dyeing and Cleaning Company recognized Murray as one of three men who robbed him of eighty dollars in a holdup on September 27. Polito was also implicated in a robbery at the Astor Café at Kingshighway and Shaw Avenue on November 10, while he still worked in the office of the chief of police.[31]

The proprietor and a clerk at the Chester Credit Clothing Company stated that Polito threatened them with a pistol while O'Leary and Bieber stole two topcoats and $174 in cash. The bandits locked the boss and his employee in a back room while they made their escape. At the Singerman Candy Company, the same three robbers apparently took money and boxes of candy, which they announced they would give to their girlfriends.[32]

While in jail, Polito told his father that he initially left home to pay a visit to a well-known gangster. The young man denied any connection with any crimes and said he had quit his job at police headquarters because he was bored and also because he wanted to make a trip to Jefferson City. He told his father that the reason for his trip to the state capital was to visit Humbert Costello, one of Hogan's Jellyroll gangsters, who was serving time in the penitentiary. He said Costello was his friend. His father, a member of the Republican Committee from the Fourth Ward, told reporters that his son's bad behavior resulted from the influence of his companions. His unfortunate associations led him right back to the state penitentiary, not as a visitor, but as an inmate.[33]

Some young gangsters, more fortunate than Polito, managed to avoid prison and turn their lives around. On November 25, 1927, eighteen-year-old Jerry Novey knocked on the door of a fifty-eight-year-old man named John C. Raab and, when Raab opened the door, identified himself as a member of the Cuckoo gang and threatened Raab. The victim later stated that Novey had robbed him a month earlier. When he showed up again, Raab took out a revolver and fired two shots, wounding Novey in the abdomen. Novey managed to walk to a nearby shop, where he collapsed. The shopkeeper called the police, who took the young man to the City Hospital.[34]

Raab admitted shooting the boy, but said he did it in self-defense. According to the older man, Novey had threatened him numerous times. "It worried me," he stated, "so that I moved recently and when he came to my home yesterday, I supposed he was bent on carrying out his threats." Novey refused to identify Raab as the man who shot him.[35]

Jerry Novey was the son of Bohemian immigrants Frank and Barbara Novey. Frank Novey worked in a butcher shop. His wife was a housewife who raised four sons. Three years after the shooting incident, Jerry had married a young woman named Beatrice. At the age of twenty-two, he worked as a paperhanger. His nineteen-year-old wife worked as a wrapper in a candy factory. Apparently, he had left the criminal world behind him and joined the ranks of the honestly employed.[36]

During the last few years of the 1920s, Father Dempsey again appealed to the warring criminal gangs to stop the hostilities. Although he was unable to talk with any of the top-ranking gang members, he tried to reach them through other members of the Italian community. Most people on the Hill and in Little Italy fully supported his efforts.[37]

Deadly gun battles continued through November 1930, when machine gunners attacked two extortionists. Lester Barth and Dewey Goebel, two World War I veterans, were reportedly on their way to the Hill to pick up money they had demanded from a bootlegger. Instead of meeting them with the money, the bootlegger hired a crew of assassins to kill the two criminals, who were previously implicated in the murders of several Cuckoo gang members.[38]

Barth and Goebel were driving their Ford coupe along Columbia Avenue when a Hudson sedan pulled up behind them. Witnesses heard machine-gun fire as both cars turned north on Macklind Avenue. The Ford began to wobble, swerved, and jumped a curb before coming to a stop. The Hudson turned down a side street and disappeared. Witnesses said there were either four or five men in the car that sped away. Hundreds of shots had been fired. Bystanders found Barth and Goebel slumped down in the front seat, bleeding profusely and close to death. A group of young boys helped pull them out of their car.[39]

The bootleggers' wars subsided in the early 1930s, but criminal gangs remained a fact of urban life. The Great Depression reduced the market for illegal liquor, and the changing political climate led to the repeal of Prohibition in 1933. The gangland murders in the 1920s had removed significant leaders from St. Louis's underworld, but groups of men and boys continued to gather at local haunts, drinking, gambling, socializing, and sometimes drifting into patterns of violence and crime.[40]

William Foote Whyte's famous study *Street Corner Society: The Social Structure of an Italian Slum* painted a chilling picture of the "corner boys" of the 1930s and 1940s, who could easily be drawn into criminal organizations. These were streetwise men and boys who spent very few of their waking hours at home, but conducted their social lives at a particular intersection or in a favorite lunchroom, barbershop, pool hall, gambling den, or tavern. Friends and family members who wanted to find them went to their corner or their hangout. Leaders emerged spontaneously from within groups. Loyalty developed through years of daily contact and shared activities, and some of these activities led young men down shadowy paths to violent ends.[41]

Chapter Nine

A New Deal for Homeless Youth

Next day Peg-leg goes south on the Rock Island for St. Louis. I go east. On the way I meet Blink, the one-eyed lad, wearing a patch over his vacant socket.

"It gets so damned cold if I don't," he says as we huddle in a corner of a box car creaking through the frozen night. "It gets so damn cold when the tears roll down and freeze and then the wind gives me a sharp pain in the back of the head deep inside."

—Thomas Minehan, *Boy and Girl Tramps of America*

THE GREAT DEPRESSION DREW SHARPER ATTENTION to social outcasts, including the boys who traveled the nation's railroads, highways, and streets searching for work or shelter. St. Louis's Bureau for Men and other local agencies conducted surveys of the problems of homeless boys. Throughout the nation, sociologists studied young wanderers and convinced government officials that they represented a serious social problem. Some of President Franklin Roosevelt's New Deal programs aimed to reduce the number of youthful drifters, but throughout the 1930s, the problem remained acute.[1]

Young tramps posed a danger not only to themselves, but to others. For example, on October 14, 1933, an eleven-year-old boy named James Riordan suffered a fractured skull when a piece of iron sailed off a freight car on the Wabash Railroad tracks near Natural Bridge Road in St. Louis. An unidentified thirteen-year-old boy, who was playing on the car, said he did not see anyone coming when he hurled the scrap of metal. James and some other boys were walking home from school at the time of the accident.[2]

Between 1929 and 1933, the number of illegal riders on freight trains soared, and many of the riders were boys under the age of twenty-one. Estimates varied wildly, but in January 1933, federal officials calculated that somewhere between 250,000 and 400,000 male adolescents were tramping the highways or riding the rails. C. C. Carstens, executive director of the Child Welfare League of America, told a United States Senate committee that the number of young drifters (mostly male) was somewhere between two hundred thousand and one million. Volunteers tried to count the homeless sleeping in shelters, missions, and jails around the nation, but there was no way to count them all. How many others were sleeping in the streets, riding on freight trains, or rolling along the highways?[3]

During the summer of 1933, the St. Louis Community Council's Department of Delinquency and Its Prevention tried to get a fairly accurate count of young migrants stealing rides on the trains that came through St. Louis. Men placed at strategic points along the tracks counted 1,035 visible riders on railroad cars, coming and going, during one twenty-four-hour period on July 26. The department estimated that only one-third of the riders were visible, concluding that approximately three thousand migrants were passing through St. Louis on trains on a typical summer day that year. Of these, they estimated that between 10 and 20 percent were youths under the age of twenty-one.[4]

In the Depression decade, between 1929 and 1939, reports of the Interstate Commerce Commission indicated that more than fifty thousand "trespassers" (including pedestrians as well as riders) were killed or injured on railroad property. Placing the percentage of minors at about one-fifth of the total, this would mean that more than ten thousand young people suffered death or injury connected with trains in that decade. Riders could easily be caught between cars on a train, locked into closed compartments, crushed by shifting cargo, frozen to death in refrigerated cars, or attacked by older, tougher transients.[5]

These statistics hit home in October 1933, when a train struck and killed two young men walking toward St. Louis on the Alton Railroad tracks. Witnesses told police that the boys apparently heard the train whistle at the last moment, turned to see the engine coming toward them, and tried to run away, but could not run fast enough. One of the boys was Albert Grace, a seventeen-year-old St. Louis resident who had gone to Chicago looking for work. Near the site of the accident, police found his clothing and a card with his parents' address. Grace's parents said they did not know the other boy who was killed, but he had a tattoo of the name *Clara* on his right arm.[6]

Young men who took to the rails during the Depression had few prospects for finding a job and settling down. Sociologist Nels Anderson studied migrants and found that the typical homeless man quit school at the age of thirteen and left home at the age of nineteen. About 16 percent of male migrants left home before reaching the age of fifteen. Previous generations of youths had been able to find jobs on farms in the summer and in factories in the winter. Because of the Depression, industry stagnated, while technological changes reduced the need for farm labor. There was simply no place for many able-bodied young men to find employment. This meant that many of them had to continue moving from city to town to country village, following roads or railroad lines.[7]

In St. Louis, the Bureau for Men tried to cope with the onslaught of homeless men and boys that began in 1930–1931. The Municipal Lodging House sheltered mostly older men who were limited in their ability to find work and move on because of age, disability, or alcoholism. For younger transients, the Bureau found temporary quarters in rooming houses. The Bureau made every effort to locate the parents of adolescent boys and send them home. In the single month of March 1931, the Bureau assisted 1,041 men and boys.[8]

The Bureau also campaigned aggressively to get beggars off the streets. In May, June, and July 1931, the Anti-Begging Committee worked with 231 beggars, including "moochers," who asked for alms in the street, and panhandlers, who went from door to door. Social workers and plainclothes policemen approached the beggars in public places and either took them to court or escorted them to the committee's office. Recalcitrant beggars ended up in the Work House. Tramps were asked to leave town. For others, the committee tried to find work or financial assistance.[9]

Timothy Dempsey, by this time a monsignor, opened a free lunchroom that served anyone who came to the door, no questions asked. "When a man's hungry," he said, "he doesn't need a lecture; he needs food." Local benefactors donated the food. In 1931, Dempsey operated the lunch program in a single room. Two years later, he had moved it to a large hall. By the fall of 1933, after two years of operation, he calculated that he had served more than three million meals. By that time, the Bureau for Men had also opened a free cafeteria.[10]

In summer 1932, sociologist Thomas Minehan traveled the roads and camped with homeless boys and girls in the Mississippi River Valley. While he shared their meals and sleeping quarters, he interviewed 1,377 boys and 88 girls, who hitchhiked and rode the rails between Minnesota and Louisiana. Most of them said they had left home because of hard times. Others ran away from troubles with girlfriends or boyfriends, problems in school, or personal issues. A few said they just liked to travel.[11]

Most of the young wanderers were not starving, but their diet was inadequate for the needs of adolescents. Many relief stations served only one or two meals a day, and most stations offered no second helpings. Breakfast often consisted of an Oliver Twist–like bowl of gruel. For lunch and dinner, a boy could move from bread line to bread line. Eventually, though, relief workers would recognize him and make him work for his food or send him away. In general, the bread came from bakeries, which donated day-old goods. Some agencies offered soup or stew, usually without meat, and a cheese or peanut butter sandwich. Pie was the food of the vagrants' dreams.[12]

Municipal relief agencies and charities generally reserved supplies of clothing for local people and would not give clothing to transients. Wandering boys often went door to door begging for socks, scarves, jackets, sweaters, and shoes. Occasionally, the owner of a clothing store would have a fit of generosity. When begging failed, many boys resorted to stealing clothes off the lines in people's backyards. Using a pole or a hook, a boy could easily reach over a fence and snag a pair of pants. Shoes posed a bigger problem, and many boys tramped around in old, worn-out boots patched with adhesive tape.[13]

Most of the young tramps stayed in one place no longer than a week. Missions and shelters often gave only one or two meals and a night's lodging to transients and then encouraged them to move on. During the summer, many young wanderers slept outdoors in rural areas, but winter weather drove them to the cities, where overcrowded missions often sent them packing, urging them to go home. Then the children headed back to the railroad yards, where they jumped onto moving trains, swarming, in Minehan's words, like "a cloud of locusts."[14]

While waiting for the next train, young wanderers sometimes took refuge in hobo "jungles," where they encountered an alternative form of society that challenged mainstream values. In these encampments, many old, hardened men found temporary shelter in shacks made of tin, scrap lumber, and railroad ties. Hoboes, who made a career out of wandering, tended to camp in places where other men had cleared some ground, set up campfires, and left behind some pots and utensils. Some of these "jungles" were occupied almost all the time, with someone there to keep the fires burning. Women might live in the Hoovervilles, but not in the jungles, which had 100 percent male populations. Hoboes learned to do their own laundry, sew, and cook their own food.[15]

Men and boys gathered around a campfire, talking and stirring a pot of mulligan stew. Older hoboes often asked the younger ones to go out and beg for food to throw in the pot. Sitting around the campfire, the boys got an education, but not the kind that was likely to help them on the road to success. Older hoboes often had colorful stories to tell, and some of them were talented raconteurs who appreciated a young audience. Some of the older hoboes were ragged and grizzled, sick and depressed, or in the depths of despair. Others were Fagan-like characters, eager to train new recruits in the arts of safecracking and stealing.[16]

St. Louis had several small hobo jungles along the Missouri Pacific, Frisco, Wabash, and Rock Island tracks. Men from the Department of Delinquency and Its Prevention studied the jungle on Carrie Avenue, which was associated with the Rock Island line, in 1933. There they found men and boys relaxing under trees and willing to talk about their life on the road. Some of them said they had more to eat on the road than they did at home, but they suffered from a lack of sleep. It was hard to keep clean, and they seldom stopped in one place long enough to wash and dry their clothes.[17]

Among the menaces in the hobo jungles, the St. Louis observers found, were the streetwise older men who stayed to "hold down the town." These men could be sources of useful information about finding a free meal or some shelter for the night. But many of them were panhandlers, thieves, and bootleggers, willing to teach their skills to new recruits. In the hobo jungles, boys learned to make money by selling a variety of items, including illegal liquor and obscene postcards. And some of the older men were sexual predators.[18]

For young people riding the rails, sexual morality was a vague abstraction. Boys and girls coupled when the opportunity arose, but the culture of the road was overwhelmingly male. Minehan admitted that older men sometimes tried to seduce younger boys, but he believed the boys resisted these advances. Other observers have stated that homeless boys often became the victims of sexual abuse. In the dark, closed cube of a moving boxcar, a young boy had no means of escape, and no one would hear a cry for help.[19]

Anderson reported that homosexuality was as common among the tramp population as it was among prisoners or sailors on ships. Hoboes had few contacts with women and no money to patronize prostitutes. Older hoboes often seduced young boys by telling them fascinating stories, listening to their tales of woe, giving them small presents, or acting in the role of protector. Homosexual aggressors, known as "wolves," could move from place to place anonymously, preying on submissive boys, called "lambs." If they became infected with a sexually transmitted disease, it was very difficult for them to apply for and receive treatment, and they could go on spreading the infection to others.[20]

Despite these physical and moral dangers, some social commentators viewed the vagabond life as an educational experience for young men.

John Levy, a psychiatrist at Columbia University, interviewed homeless boys in New York City in 1933 and characterized them as "rugged individualists" whose hard lives gave them character and tenacity. He concluded that most of them left home as an act of independence. They did not expect to become rich, but they had hopes of a bright future. Even months of hunger and begging did not dampen their spirits. They could be sullen, but they did not whine. They had learned that it was useless to protest; they simply had to endure hardships in order to reach their goals in life.[21]

Conditions in the 1930s, however, could defeat even the pluckiest young adventurers in their quest for economic success. Writing on youth in the Depression, Kingsley Davis maintained that, even in hard times, most young people still grew up believing they could realize their dreams. "Except for a few who are too lazy or too discouraged," he wrote in 1935, "they are ambitious to become somebody." But the doors of opportunity were closing. According to Davis, by the early 1930s, "the machinery by which young people [were] drawn into the work of the nation had broken down; and youth, bearing the burden of this breakdown, was seeking blindly for some way out."[22]

Davis painted a disturbing picture of what might happen if the situation did not change for the better. In conditions of hopelessness, youth movements might spring up. If the older generation could not fix society's problems, young people might take matters into their own hands. Desperate young men might turn to crime. Organized protests might lead to revolution. He pointed ominously to the German youth movement and the wild boys of Russia, where homeless waifs evolved into vicious bands of outlaws.[23]

In St. Louis, there were clear signs that young people had become desperate. On January 1, 1933, the *Post-Dispatch* reported that a businessman named William Glatstein shot and killed a nineteen-year-old black man who was trying to rob Abe Fine's grocery store on Dickson Street. Before passing away in the hospital, the young robber, Percy Barth, admitted his part in the crime; his accomplice got away. Explaining the shooting, Glatstein said he began carrying a revolver after his father was killed by two other black holdup men in 1931.[24]

On the afternoon of the robbery at Fine's grocery store, Glatstein was working at his uncle's butcher shop. At five o'clock, he carried an empty bucket to Fine's to borrow some coal. When he entered through a side door, he saw Fine, three customers, and two young black men. One of the young men called to him to "stick 'em up." Glatstein said he backed out of the door, dropped his bucket, and pulled out his gun. One of the robbers, later identified as Barth, followed him outside, and Glatstein "let him have it, twice." Barth was unarmed during the robbery, but he was carrying a cigarette case shaped like a pistol. His accomplice, who ran away, was also unarmed. Before Glatstein entered the store, the young men had taken six or seven dollars from two cash registers, but they had not harmed anyone.[25]

A few days later, seventeen-year-old Emil Pretto of 6049 Arthur Avenue confessed to committing seventeen robberies on St. Louis County highways. When one of his victims failed to identify Pretto as the holdup man, Pretto said to his alleged victim, in the presence of the police, "Well, I saw you. You're the man I held up that night, all right." In a statement, Pretto confessed to numerous additional robberies involving about thirty victims. The loot from the crimes totaled about three hundred dollars, but he said he worked with accomplices, and his share was much less than that. When police asked him why he turned to crime, he told them a sad but not unusual story.[26]

Pretto, a slight young man, was born in 1915, the son of Italian immigrants. His father passed away sometime before 1920, leaving his mother, Marie, with seven children ranging in age from one to fifteen. At first, their mother placed them in an orphanage, but a year later she brought them back home. By 1920, she had married a laborer named Joseph Zaratonello, with whom she would have three children. Ten years later, the two eldest sons, Frank and Victor, had left home, but eight of the Pretto and Zaratonello children (aged seven to sixteen) lived with Marie and another husband, Romeo Nardi, who was a laborer.[27]

As a teenager, Emil Pretto attended Longfellow School and worked nights setting up pins in a bowling alley. Eventually, he had to find a way to make more money, so he quit school, bought two old trucks, and started selling vegetables. When the Depression hit, the business failed. He gave one truck to his brother, who hauled ashes in it, and sold the other one. "I tried to find a job and couldn't," he said. "And so I got to be a stickup man."[28]

Police arrested Pretto and another boy, eighteen-year-old Roy Sinks, in a stolen car after a five-mile chase on county roads. After that, Pretto cooperated fully, but he would not testify against Sinks or any other partners. What about the stolen money? "It didn't amount to much," said Pretto, "mostly two or three dollars for my share on each job. I spent a little of it on myself, but most of it went to my mother to help out running the house."[29]

Pretto was not a bad boy, but the Depression pushed him to his limits. Why was he so willing to confess when his supposed victims failed to

A muddy empty lot that passed for a children's playground during
the Great Depression in St. Louis. (Photograph by Arthur Rothstein.
Courtesy of the Library of Congress)

positively identify him? Even more to the point, why did his victims have
trouble recognizing him? The answer to this question is surprising. Emil
Pretto was trying to protect his brother Michael.

It was not Emil, but Michael Mark Pretto, age eighteen, who went on
trial for grand larceny and armed robbery in 1933. On March 16, he and
his codefendant, Patrick M. "Algie" Moran, age twenty-two, a streetcar
motorman, were charged with stealing a Ford sedan and twenty dollars
from Arthur F. C. Blasé after threatening him with a revolver. Moran
pleaded guilty and was sentenced to five years' imprisonment for that
crime. Pretto pleaded not guilty because he said he had an alibi. He was
not present at the time and place where the crime occurred. The jury
apparently did not believe his story, because they found him guilty, and
the judge sentenced him to ten years in the Missouri State Penitentiary.
His motion for a new trial was denied.[30]

In a separate case, Pretto and Moran stood trial on several counts of stealing from various victims. Items they stole included two watches, a stud, and a total of about $160. For this crime, Moran received a sentence of another five years, to run concurrently with the sentence for the robbery. In the end, Pretto was not prosecuted in this case because he had already received a ten-year sentence. His brother's attempt to save him had been in vain.[31]

When the Depression began in 1930, Algie Moran was a motorman on a streetcar, and Michael Pretto was a fifteen-year-old boy living at home with his mother, stepfather, sisters, and brothers. Moran and his older brother James were roomers in the home of a young Irish American family. Possibly there was something in Pretto's and Moran's individual characters that predisposed them to commit crimes, but surely the Depression and the pressures of life in the city were additional factors that ultimately led them to spend five and ten years of their young lives in the penitentiary.[32]

Even so-called rugged individualists, including President Herbert Hoover, admitted that poverty and the harsh conditions of urban life had a bad effect on the nation's youth. In 1930, he identified rebellious youth as one of the main problems facing the nation. At the same time, he realized that young people were the only hope for the future of democracy. He believed that urban life stunted the minds and bodies of young people by denying them contact with nature and space for wholesome recreation. Although he did not formulate a specific plan, he called for action to transfer youth to the countryside or bring the advantages of rural life to the city.[33]

Roosevelt acted on these ideas when he supported the creation of the Civilian Conservation Corps (CCC) in 1933. The United States Department of Labor, working with local relief organizations, took charge of the process of recruiting jobless single men between the ages of seventeen and twenty-five to fight fires, plant trees, dig ditches, save farmland, and build recreational structures in camps around the nation. The United States Army conducted basic training for the enrollees at local bases. Army officers supervised the men in the work camps, which were located in national and state parks, wilderness areas, and distressed rural communities.[34]

New enrollees reported first to the nearest Army recruiting station for a physical examination. If they were healthy enough to do the hard work that would be required of them, they went on to the nearest Army post. In St. Louis, this was Jefferson Barracks. There they were formally enrolled, organized into companies, and clothed in brown uniforms. After several weeks of conditioning, they were sent to work camps, either in companies or in smaller groups.[35]

There were CCC camps in every state in the union. The average number of camps operating in Missouri at any given time was forty-one. Camps in the vicinity of St. Louis included those at Babler State Park and Cuivre River Recreational Demonstration Area (which became Cuivre River State Park). Upon arrival at a work camp, enrollees took shelter in tents until they could build barracks. Most of the work was manual labor, and the pay was thirty dollars a month plus three good meals a day. Every camp had an educational adviser, who provided literacy programs and other kinds of training.[36]

The American Youth Commission studied the CCC and found that the typical new recruit was a young man between seventeen and eighteen years of age, in fairly good health, but a little underweight. Of all enrollees, 90 percent were white, and 10 percent were black; the camps were segregated. More than 50 percent came from rural areas, but 28 percent came from small cities and 16 percent from large urban areas. More than 60 percent had two living parents, but 23 percent were orphans or half-orphans, and 14 percent had parents who were divorced. Two-thirds of the enrollees had fathers who were unemployed. Many of them had worked for short periods of time at unskilled jobs. Ninety percent of them came from families whose standard of living was less than average for the United States.[37]

Most young men flourished in the CCC, although about 40 percent of new enrollees reported difficulties adjusting to life in the camps. Homesickness was the number one problem. Older enrollees often teased the younger ones, short-sheeted their beds, nailed their shoes to barracks floors, harried, bullied, and even physically attacked them. Boys who failed to take baths regularly were scrubbed with stiff brushes. Camp officials often turned a blind eye to hazing incidents, although they took action against fighting and violence. Of a total of more than two and a half million recruits, the vast majority stayed at least six months, but about five hundred thousand simply walked out of the camps after a few hours or a few weeks.[38]

One young St. Louis man who benefited from the CCC experience was the boxer Archie Moore. As a teenager during the Depression, Moore was arrested for stealing change from the cash boxes on streetcars. Before his eighteenth birthday, he spent nearly two years in the Missouri Training School for Boys in Boonville and then returned to St. Louis, where he tried to find a job. His parole officer agreed to let him join the CCC, and he became an enrollee in an African American company assigned to work with the United States Forest Service at Poplar Bluff, Missouri.[39]

In the autobiography he wrote after he became a champion fighter and entertainer, Moore spoke glowingly of the CCC experience. The work he did, clearing roads and trails, was hard, but he said, "It was the kind of work I wanted to toughen up my body for my intended boxing career." The barracks at the forestry camp compared favorably with conditions in the reformatory, and the officer in charge of the camp let Moore organize a boxing team. During one match, the crowd in Poplar Bluff made racial remarks, and bullies followed the boxers back to camp. The camp officer faced down the belligerent locals, and they dispersed. Moore continued boxing in tournaments and had at least one professional fight before he left the CCC and went back to St. Louis. All in all, he concluded, the CCC "got boys off the streets and was a great juvenile delinquency deterrent."[40]

By the mid-1930s, the federal government had assumed the primary responsibility for assisting homeless men. As part of the Federal Emergency Relief Administration program, the Transient Relief Division gave money to the states to provide shelters for wanderers. Treatment centers offered meals, bathing facilities, and beds for short stays. Men who wanted to stay longer could go to work camps, where they did various jobs, including road maintenance. For thirty hours of work, a man received board, shelter, and one dollar of spending money per week. In 1935, the nation's transient program served more than two hundred thousand homeless people, most of whom were male. One-third of them were under twenty-five years old.[41]

Reorganized with a small staff and a small caseload, St. Louis's Bureau for Men concentrated on the problems of homeless youth. Following the example of the CCC, the bureau established the Henry Shaw Boys' Camp in September 1934. Located at the Missouri Botanical Gardens' Arboretum in Gray Summit, Missouri, the camp had a threefold purpose: to provide round-the-clock supervision of a group of about fifty young men, to provide conditioning and build up the health of the boys, and to accomplish useful work. The bureau converted a large barn into a dining room and bunkhouse, with kitchen facilities, showers, and a recreation room. White boys and men between the ages of seventeen and twenty-five worked on constructing roads and trails. In return, they received food, clothing, medical care, and fifty cents a week for spending money. Local high school teachers offered classes, and the campers engaged in a variety of games and activities. Stays in the camp lasted approximately three months. After the boys left the camp, the bureau helped them find jobs. In 1935, the bureau reported that the camp was very successful, but that it reached only a small number of young men.[42]

The New Deal's most comprehensive program for young people was the National Youth Administration (NYA), established on June 26, 1935, by an executive order from President Roosevelt. The NYA specifically addressed the needs of men and women between the ages of eighteen and twenty-four who were out of school and unemployed. In every state, plus Washington, D.C., and Puerto Rico, the NYA offered programs of education, recreation, employment, and community service. First, the NYA tried to find places in industry for the young people in the category it covered. Second, the agency aimed to train young people for future careers in such areas as auto repair and librarianship. Third, the NYA provided financial aid to students attending high school and college. Finally, the new program provided jobs for young people, whether they were male or female, black or white. By 1940, the NYA had assisted more than a million young workers. However, public support and funding for the NYA remained at relatively low levels, and the agency never achieved the popularity or success of the CCC.[43]

One interesting attempt by the New Deal to reach urban youth was the creation of organized group camping facilities for underprivileged urban youngsters. Beginning in 1934, the federal government bought tracts of unproductive farmland for the purpose of creating Recreational Demonstration Areas (RDAs). The National Park Service stipulated that these tracts should be close to urban centers to provide wholesome rural experiences for city dwellers. Cuivre River RDA was located near Troy, Missouri, fifty miles northwest of St. Louis. Within the RDAs, including Cuivre River, CCC and WPA (Works Progress Administration) workers built group camping facilities, complete with rustic dining lodges, snug sleeping cabins, recreational centers, and hiking trails.[44]

Camp Sherwood Forest in Cuivre River RDA opened in 1937 under the supervision of the St. Louis Park and Playground Association. Like other RDA group camps, Sherwood Forest was a decentralized camp with clusters of small cabins arranged in secluded units around central dining and recreation halls. Alfred H. Wyman, director of the Park and Playground Association, chose a name for each unit from the Robin Hood legend. One unit became Ancaster Village, another Locksley Chase. Implicit in these literary references were ideals of brotherhood and freedom among a band of men who tried to create a system of equality by stealing from the rich and giving to the poor.[45]

Camp Sherwood Forest continued to operate after 1946, when Cuivre River RDA became Cuivre River State Park. For nearly half a century, the same closing ceremony took place after every camp session. Before the ceremony, campers came from the units, and each one of them tossed a twig into the council fire on Lincoln Green. While campers sat together quietly, a green flame shot up from the fire. Three torches blazed in the nearby woods, and three voices spoke from the darkness. The flame symbolized the spirit of Robin Hood, and the voices represented the spirits of friendship, cooperation, and learning.[46]

Throughout the 1950s and 1960s, schools and social organizations sent children to the camp. Administrators allotted to each agency in St. Louis City and County a certain number of places in the Sherwood Forest program. Boys and girls attended in alternate sessions. After 1954, the camp gradually increased the number of black participants until the ratio of black to white campers reached 50 percent. Places were also set aside for children with disabilities.[47]

In a 1960 promotional film, the Missouri State Park Board reaffirmed the value of outdoor experiences for urban youth. According to the film's narration, "at camp, everyone is on an even social level. Each child is made to feel that he, or she, is a part of the group. This feeling of belonging helps many emotional difficulties." Bonding with other children was important, but equally valuable was the chance to spend time alone in a natural setting. "Dearest to the heart of most campers," the narrator said, "is the out-camp area which is but a short distance from camp-center. But its rustic and quiet beauty brings out the pioneer spirit in each boy and girl." In addition to healing emotional difficulties, camp life put each child in touch with cherished American ideals.[48]

New Deal programs like the CCC, the NYA, and the group camping programs had multiple purposes, but one of their goals was to train young men to be patriotic citizens of the republic. Boys who grew up facing poverty and unemployment during the Great Depression faced a new challenge in the early 1940s. After the attack on Pearl Harbor in December 1941, President Roosevelt called upon them to defend their country by joining the armed forces. Millions of them, including Emil Pretto, responded to the call.[49]

The struggling, disillusioned boys of the 1930s became the generation that served victoriously in World War II. After the war, the GI Bill gave many young men the boost they needed to go to college and begin successful careers. Postwar prosperity changed the urban landscape in many ways—for better and for worse. Despite the enormous changes in America's economy and society, a new generation of young people continued to grapple with many of the same, seemingly intractable problems of life on the city streets.[50]

Chapter Ten

Youth and the Changing City Streets

The place you live is awfully important. It can give you a chance to grow, or it can twist you. . . . When I was in school, they used to teach us that evolution made men out of animals. They forgot to tell us it can also make animals out of men.

—SIDNEY KINGSLEY, *Dead End*

ACCORDING TO HISTORIAN MICHAEL BENNETT, postwar prosperity and the GI Bill brought about a "relandscaping of America." With college educations and good jobs, many veterans moved their families from congested cities to suburban areas with green lawns and safe streets. Other people, many of whom were poor and black, migrated to the cities. But the flight to the suburbs gained momentum; urban populations declined, and inner-city streets became more desolate and dangerous. The story of Charles "Sonny" Liston, the well-known prize fighter, is emblematic of St. Louis in the postwar era.[1]

In 1946, Liston, a black teenager, left the Arkansas cotton fields and followed his mother, Helen Baskin, to St. Louis, where she had found work in a shoe factory. After several days of searching, he found her living in two rooms in a house at 1017 O'Fallon Street, near the waterfront. She tried sending him to school, but he felt out of place because he was so big for his age and so far behind the other students. Within a year or two, he fell in with a group of young men who committed strong-arm robberies, and by 1950, when he was seventeen years old, he was in serious trouble with the law. After a service-station robbery, during which two people were beaten up, he was sent to the Missouri State Penitentiary, where a chaplain gave him a pair of boxing gloves.[2]

Frank W. Mitchell, owner of the *St. Louis Argus,* successfully campaigned for Liston's release and financed his boxing career. Mitchell was a gifted newspaper publisher and promoter, but he also was a racketeer with a record of arrests for gambling and counterfeiting. As Liston's boxing career began to take off, his rap sheet continued to grow. Liston had just finished a stint in the Work House when he married Geraldine Chambers in 1957. One year later, he left St. Louis for good and went on to become the heavyweight champion of the world.[3]

Even at the height of his career, Liston's past weighed him down. In 1962, when he entered the ring for a championship fight, the audience booed him. In the world of boxing, he was the "bad guy," the angry outcast, the ex-convict, the gangster. Bad guys were supposed to lose, but Liston won the fight against the much more popular Floyd Patterson. The press was brutal to Liston. *Look* magazine once described him as the "King of the Beasts," and a columnist for the *New York Mirror* called him a "sinister creature, full of hatred for the world." A sympathetic biographer characterized him as the "Champ Nobody Wanted." He lost his title in 1964, when he quit in his corner before the start of the seventh round in his fight with Cassius Clay (who would later be called Muhammad Ali). In 1965, Liston went down less than two minutes into a rematch with Ali. His short life ended abruptly in 1971, when his wife returned from visiting her mother in St. Louis and found him dead at their Las Vegas home. There was marijuana in his pocket and heroin in the kitchen. Police concluded that there was no foul play and attributed his death to a drug overdose. He was thirty-eight years old.[4]

Nobody knows what would have happened to Sonny Liston if he had never come to St. Louis and never been influenced by the rough life of the inner-city slums, but by the 1940s there was a growing number of people who believed the slum could take good boys and turn them into criminals. Sidney Kingsley's play *Dead End* dramatically made this point. First Lady Eleanor Roosevelt, a great admirer of the play, persuaded her husband to bring the production to the White House. When Senator Robert Wagner proposed a slum-clearance bill in the United States Congress, he specifically mentioned the influence of Kingsley's play. By 1940, the federal government was investing in the construction of housing projects in blighted areas of major cities. The goal of these projects was to provide decent living spaces for families who were trying to bring up children in deteriorating urban cores.[5]

In St. Louis, slum-clearance efforts began in the 1930s and intensified after World War II, although housing conditions in the inner city remained dismal. A 1937 study revealed that run-down neighborhoods within approximately fifteen blocks of the downtown area housed one-third of the city's population, but produced three-fourths of the illegitimate children, half of the infant deaths, and two-thirds of the juvenile delinquency. Ten years later, the City Plan Commission reported that half of the city's residential areas remained blighted with old and deteriorated buildings, inadequate sanitation, overcrowded conditions, rats, roaches, and other vermin. In the postwar years, the city received federal funding for the removal of slums and the creation of livable housing.[6]

St. Louis's first two housing developments, Carr Square and Clinton Peabody, constructed in the early 1940s, initially seemed livable and fairly successful. Black residents occupied Carr Square on the near north side about fifteen blocks from the central business district. White occupants moved into the nearly identical units at Clinton Peabody, about an equal distance southwest of downtown. Buildings in the developments were one- and two-story apartments, townhouses, and duplexes arranged in rows around a community center. Apartments, though small, contained decent-sized kitchens, living rooms, bedrooms, and storage space. Unfortunately, the developments were surrounded by cleared land and abandoned buildings and were far removed from jobs, stores, schools, and churches. In spite of this problem, occupancy rates remained high and crime rates remained low throughout the 1940s and 1950s.[7]

In these early days of slum clearance, there was hope that the number of cases of juvenile delinquency, as well as child neglect, might be declining. Although the statistics included only fifteen states, the Children's Bureau of the Federal Security Agency reported that juvenile court cases dropped from a peak of more than seventy-one thousand in 1945 to a low of about fifty-one thousand in 1948. The average age of children involved in delinquency cases was fifteen and a half. Boys outnumbered girls in delinquency cases by four to one. After 1948, however, statistical data became more readily available, and the rate of juvenile delinquency showed signs of increasing.[8]

By the early 1950s, it became clear that juvenile delinquency was on the rise, and the *New York Times* declared that the nation was experiencing a "junior crime wave." The Children's Bureau made a concerted effort to gather statistical data, announcing in 1952 that more than one million children annually got into trouble with the law. Because of the postwar baby boom, federal officials warned that the population of children and adolescents would increase by nearly 50 percent within the next decade, and that the number of young offenders was likely to increase.[9]

In St. Louis in the 1950s, adolescent boys appeared in the newspapers almost daily as victims or victimizers. Although there was nothing really new about it, juvenile delinquency became an issue that stirred debates and heightened fears in St. Louis as well as other American cities in the postwar era. While the fears may have been exaggerated, the daily crime reports supported the popular belief that the streets of downtown St. Louis were becoming less safe.[10]

On July 2, 1955, the battered body of eighteen-year-old Kenneth Milano was found on the Mississippi River bank near the MacArthur Bridge. An autopsy revealed that he had died of a broken neck and internal bleeding. His mother, Marcella Ruloff, said her son had arrived home at four that morning, but then had gone out again and had not returned. Police questioned three young men about Milano's death but then released them. The reason for his death remained a mystery.[11]

A few weeks later, a thirteen-year-old boy and two older adolescents confessed to a series of burglaries on South Broadway. Witnesses told police the burglars stole two motorcycles from the South Broadway Motorcycle Company. The three boys also confessed to breaking into the F. W. Woolworth Store at 7501 South Broadway on July 17 and taking about one hundred dollars' worth of merchandise. They also admitted to stealing cash from a restaurant.[12]

Two boys between seventeen and twenty years of age entered the Belt Avenue Pharmacy on the evening of July 26, 1955, borrowed a cigarette from a sixteen-year-old clerk, ordered sodas, and then pulled out their guns. Gilbert Noh, the pharmacist on duty, described the holdup men as "pimply faced boys." When one of them approached him, brandishing a gun, Noh said, "It looks like a phony," and tried to keep the robber away from the cash register. The boy pulled the trigger, but the gun failed to fire. At that point, Noh headed for the back of the store to get his own gun. The second boy aimed his revolver at Noh, but the gun misfired. The two young robbers grabbed about $150 in cash and ran out of the store, followed by the clerk and the pharmacist. One of the robbers turned back and fired twice, but the shots went wild. The boys made their escape in an automobile.[13]

A few days later, an unidentified youth wielding a leather-worker's awl stabbed two women on the street. Rosemary Schuster, age nineteen, told police that a boy about fourteen or fifteen years old approached her on a bicycle as she was walking on Wherry Avenue on July 29. The boy jumped off the bicycle, stabbed her, and then sped away. About half an hour later, at 10:30 p.m., the boy stabbed Virginia Slingwein as she waited for a bus at the corner of Macklind Avenue and Eichelberger Street, four blocks from the previous attack.[14]

Narcotics became a more prominent factor in juvenile crime. On December 22, 1959, seventeen-year-old Gloster Ervin Gates robbed a beer truck driver at Clara and Easton avenues. When police caught up with Gates on a nearby street, he pointed a revolver at them and pulled the trigger twice, but the weapon failed to fire. By the time he arrived at

Portrait of a boy with the city as a backdrop that appeared in
the *St. Louis Post-Dispatch* on December 18, 1959, in a plea for
people to help the needy at Christmastime. (Drawing by Robert
Nix. Used by permission, State Historical Society of Missouri,
Columbia)

the police station, he had lost the cash he stole. While in police custody,
Gates confessed to six more holdups and said that he had committed the
crimes to get cash to buy narcotics.[15]

Youthful crimes could be brutal and deadly. Just before Christmas
in 1959, three young men pleaded guilty to manslaughter in the death
of Charles A. Simon, a sixty-one-year-old man. On December 30 of the
previous year, the three youths had met at a bar on Mary Avenue. Later in
the evening they had robbed and beaten Simon, who collapsed and subsequently died. Macer F. Allen, age nineteen, admitted in court that he
had struck Simon on the head with a baseball bat. The judge sentenced
him to eight years in prison. James P. Tucker and John J. Parker, who
were both twenty years old, received suspended sentences, but the judge
ordered them to pay ten dollars a week to the victim's widow for the rest
of her life.[16]

The perception that the inner city had become lawless and chaotic
almost certainly hastened the movement from the urban core to the suburbs. Between 1940 and 1950, the City of St. Louis regained some of the
population it had lost during the Depression, but after 1950 the city's
population began a precipitous decline. The population of St. Louis City

fell by more than one hundred thousand (12.5 percent) during the 1950s, while the population of the surrounding suburbs grew at a rapid pace. Out-migration of white residents changed the racial composition of the central city. In 1950, nonwhites accounted for 18 percent of the city's population; by 1970, the proportion of nonwhites was more than 40 percent.[17]

Paving the way for a mass exodus from the inner city was a system of divided highways radiating outward toward the western boundaries of the metropolitan area. In 1955, Missouri voters overwhelmingly approved propositions to construct three expressways. The Daniel Boone (U.S. Highway 40) would accommodate traffic from Tenth and Clark avenues downtown to the west boundary. The Mark Twain (Alternate U.S. 40) would run from Third and Locust to the northwestern edge of the city, and the Ozark (U.S. Highway 66 and later U.S. Highway 44) would carry traffic from Eleventh and Geyer streets to the southwestern limits. Voters also approved funding for streets, bridges, parks, playgrounds and other improvements within the city. It was unclear at the time, but became apparent by the 1960s that the new divided highways would lure industry and commercial enterprises away from downtown.[18]

Highway construction leveled block after block of businesses and homes. Not only slums, but middle-class neighborhoods vanished. People who had automobiles headed out to the suburbs, where retail shopping centers sprang up. Improved streets and highways, larger trucks, and lower costs of land enticed small manufacturers to move out to where the people were relocating. In the early 1950s, St. Louis's downtown was still vibrant, with three major department stores, dime stores, specialty shops, chain stores, drugstores, restaurants, hotels, and theaters. Police directed traffic at busy intersections, and colorful streetcars still rattled up and down Market, Olive, Pine, and Washington streets. Three daily newspapers competed for attention, and newsboys still plied their noisy trade. Gradually, however, most of these enterprises moved out to the western edges of the city, and the downtown area became desolate.[19]

The housing projects of the 1950s increased the desolation of the inner city. After a new Housing Act was passed in 1949, the city planned and constructed five very large high-rise housing complexes. Steel and concrete buildings reflected the latest trends in architecture, but ignored basic needs, such as space for children's recreation. Cochran Gardens, completed in 1953, contained more than seven hundred units in two six-story, two seven-story, and four twelve-story buildings a few blocks north of the central business district. Pruitt-Igoe, completed in 1954, comprised thirty-three eleven-story buildings, each of which contained eighty or ninety units. Vaughn and Darst each contained four nine-story buildings and more than 650 apartments. These high densities reflected a desire for efficiency and a terrible insensitivity to human needs.[20]

Carr Square, Vaughn, and Pruitt-Igoe filled a ninety-eight-acre tract surrounded by decaying neighborhoods. The areas around the Clinton, Peabody, Darst, and Webbe projects became increasingly bleak as the city's central core decayed. Ironically, as the city built more and more units with higher densities, occupancy rates declined. Empty buildings posed a danger as well as an enticement to children, who had little or no access to safe parks or playgrounds. As more and more people and businesses migrated out of the downtown area, the housing complexes became more and more isolated from business and social centers.[21]

Construction of these housing projects had the effect of increasing racial segregation in the inner city. In the decades preceding urban renewal, white families occupied much of the run-down housing in the central corridor, the southern, and the southwestern sections of town. The area north of Delmar was largely black. During the 1950s, almost all the public housing was built on the north side. After 1960, the flight of many white families from the inner city made the situation even worse.[22]

In 1959, the city began demolishing buildings in Mill Creek Valley, which cut the heart out of the black community. In spite of its shabby appearance, the Valley still had nearly twenty thousand residents and more than eight hundred businesses, many of which were owned by African Americans. Among the casualties of demolition were dozens of car-repair shops, barber and beauty shops, cleaners, clothing stores, bakeries, gas stations, grocery stores, liquor stores, restaurants, and taverns, not to mention churches, doctors' and dentists' offices, lodges, and clubs.[23]

Displaced by the demolition of their neighborhoods, large numbers of African American families moved north and west within the city, displacing Irish, German, and Jewish families, who left the city and moved to outlying areas. Redevelopment of Mill Creek Valley occurred very slowly, so that throughout the 1960s the area was known as "Hiroshima Flats," suggesting a postapocalyptic world in which the social order had completely broken down. This was an exaggeration that contained a disquieting amount of truth.[24]

Concerned citizens and public officials tried to reverse the trend toward racial segregation. In 1946, the Urban League encouraged the local Social Planning Council to issue a policy statement concerning nondiscrimination for all its member agencies. Community-service groups began integrating gradually—first their employees and then their clientele. The Mayor's Council on Human Relations, established in 1949, sponsored a yearly celebration of the Universal Declaration of Human Rights.[25]

In the summer of 1949, the Division of Parks and Recreation announced that city-owned outdoor swimming pools would no longer be open to whites only, but would be integrated. Newspapers and radio stations announced the news, which came as a surprise to many residents. Black children arrived at several swimming pools without incident, but at one pool in Fairgrounds Park, a group of rowdy boys and young men created a disturbance that left nearly a dozen people injured. Police ordered city pools to close while tempers cooled, and within a few days tensions had died down. A federal judge ordered discrimination in public pools to cease.[26]

In the mid-1950s, the Congress of Racial Equality (CORE) spearheaded efforts to end segregation in St. Louis's hotels, restaurants, and theaters. By 1956, most of the downtown hotels had opened their doors to black people after several national organizations threatened to boycott the city's convention facilities. Some drugstores and dime stores began integrating, but the big department stores maintained segregated eating areas. After the swimming-pool incident, public pools, parks, and recreational facilities ended their discriminatory policies.[27]

Even before the United States Supreme Court's 1954 ruling in *Brown v. Board of Education,* St. Louis educators made some attempts to end segregation in schools. In 1946, St. Louis University began accepting black students. One year later, Archbishop Joseph E. Ritter ordered all Catholic elementary and secondary schools to open their doors to African American students. A group of parents protested the order, but the Catholic hierarchy stood its ground. A few families withdrew their children from the parochial schools, but integration of the Catholic schools went forward seven years before the landmark Supreme Court ruling. By the early 1950s, the St. Louis Board of Education had begun formulating plans for integrating the public schools.[28]

In 1955, St. Louis's nine high schools and seventy-three elementary schools officially became desegregated, although, in reality, racial imbalances continued. High schools served racially segregated neighborhoods, which meant that two of the city's high schools enrolled almost exclusively black students. Three high schools underwent some change in the composition of their student bodies and became racially mixed. Three other high schools had less than 5 percent African American students, and one high school had no black students at all. A similar situation prevailed in the elementary schools.[29]

Integration of the schools faltered in St. Louis because neighborhoods became increasingly segregated. By 1960, much of the city's north side had become what Kenneth Clark termed a "dark ghetto." At that time, eleven American cities, including St. Louis, had black populations of more than 200,000. Nearly half of St. Louis's 214,377 black residents lived in neighborhoods that were at least 90 percent African American. Clark characterized these neighborhoods as ghettos where residents crowded into substandard housing. Ghettos in all major American cities shared the common problems of limited opportunities, poor schools, family instability, and high levels of drug addiction, alcoholism, crime, juvenile delinquency, and early death.[30]

As the downtown community crumbled, Pruitt-Igoe became the byword for miserable and unlivable public housing. By the time the complex opened, Supreme Court rulings demanded racial integration, but local customs and attitudes, combined with a general movement of population out of the central city, doomed this effort to failure. Throughout the 1950s, nearly all the tenants were black. Cost-cutting efforts resulted in cramped living spaces, shoddy fixtures, damp basements, exposed water pipes, and elevators that constantly broke down. Residents complained that the elevators were dangerous and that people used them as toilets. Mice and cockroaches infested the buildings. Broken glass and trash littered the area.[31]

Transients came in and out of the complex, causing trouble by drinking, quarreling, and provoking fights. Bottles were dropped from windows, injuring people. Women felt unsafe in hallways and elevators. Thieves stole clothing and attacked women in laundry rooms. Teenagers threatened and insulted adults and younger children when they stepped outside their apartments. Children saw and heard all sorts of sexual activities, thefts, violence, and rough language. Within the confines of their tiny apartments, mothers tried to protect their children from these dangerous influences, but often lost control of adolescent daughters and sons.[32]

Street gangs, which had dwindled in the 1930s and 1940s, emerged again in the 1950s. Most of the gang activity originated just north of downtown, but gangs also roamed through western and northwestern neighborhoods. Neighborhood identification was strong, as different groups staked out their territories. Gangs engaged in both legal and illegal activities, including property crimes, peace disturbances, fistfights, knife fights, and in rare instances gunfights. Among these new gangs were the Barracudas, the Counts, the Turks, the Compton Hill gang, and the Alston gang. Felt hats in specific colors—blue, brown, and burgundy—identified gang members.[33]

Many of the gangs were white, but African American gangs became common in the 1950s and 1960s. Joe Jefferson, a fifteen-year-old resident of Pruitt-Igoe, told researchers from Harvard that there were several gangs in that complex, including at least two female gangs. But most of the gangs were male, he said, and these included Big Boy's gang, Curly's gang, the Blue Dragons, the Black Cats, and the Red Devils. Another teenage boy confessed that most of the boys in Pruitt-Igoe had a gun or a knife, because they knew they had to be ready to defend themselves from a physical attack. Jefferson, who tried hard to stay in school and out of trouble, described gangs as groups of boys, "each group thinking they are the baddest and the coolest." When they challenged each other, there were fights. In the 1960s, the Harvard researchers found that most of these gangs were small, short-lived, and not highly organized, but they did create a sense of danger for other adolescents.[34]

Beyond the flimsy walls of cramped apartments in modernistic towers, the boys of St. Louis found another, more compelling, world. In this world were friends and enemies, shifting alliances, games, excitement, fights, and constant danger. Bottles, windows, and laws were made to be broken. Alcohol and drugs heightened sensation and lowered inhibitions. Language was rough and raw, but there was poetry in it. Violence, or the threat of it, pounded like a drumbeat, adding an edge to ordinary life. Weapons were essential, because a person had to be ready, at a moment's notice, to defend himself.

A team of researchers who studied the Pruitt-Igoe housing complex in the early 1960s observed that life in the ghetto placed terrible pressures on families. Marriages often failed because discrimination in employment made it difficult for black men to find and keep jobs that would allow them to support their families. Even when they managed to stay together, parents found it almost impossible to keep their children under control because the seductive life of the street drew adolescents away from the family circle and into a world of excitement and danger.[35]

For many children growing up in the inner city, the single-sex peer group was the strongest and most reliable system of social interaction. If there was tension between parents or unhappiness in the home, children, especially adolescent males, turned to street-corner companions as their primary source of emotional support. "Hanging" with a particular group gave boys a sense of acceptance. Older members of the group taught younger boys how to grow up and become men. Younger boys gave honor and respect, even adulation, to their slightly older peers. Belonging to a group saved frightened adolescents from a sense of isolation in a society that provided little in the way of comfort and security.[36]

Because their environment offered them scant hope of success in conventional careers or business, street-corner boys developed other ways of achieving status within their groups. The qualities they valued in themselves and their peers included toughness, smartness (although not in the sense of academic achievement), resistance to authority, bravery, and skill at games (including sports, cards, and pool). Status symbols generally reflected "adult" behavior, although not a grown-up sense of responsibility. A fast car, a wad of cash, and the freedom to drink, smoke, gamble, and use narcotics were signs that the boy had risen above adolescence and become a man.[37]

Some, but certainly not all, adolescent peer groups engaged in criminal behavior and became gangs. Most commonly, this behavior included theft, assault, and shoplifting. In general, boys who committed these crimes were trying to raise their status by proving that they were strong, daring, clever, and no longer children. Gang fights resulted from the same deep desires for respect and recognition. Most often, gang fights started when a member of one gang encroached on the territory of another gang, challenging its reputation for toughness. In some cases, the encroachment was accidental, but sometimes it was a deliberate affront. A gang felt honor-bound to punish the trespasser; the trespasser returned to his own neighborhood or street corner and reported what had happened, and his friends then sought to avenge him.[38]

Whether or not they belonged to a gang, inner city boys understood that they had to protect themselves from physical danger. Carrying a gun or a knife was a defensive measure, although it also could lead to unnecessary and dangerous confrontations. One St. Louis teenager named Alex, who lived in Pruitt-Igoe, told researchers how he ended up spending six months in a reformatory for assault. The incident began in a movie theater, when he asked a girl for a piece of candy. Her boyfriend jumped up and smacked Alex on the face with a cap. Alex took the cap and hit the other boy, who threatened to kill him. When the boy reached into his pocket, Alex pulled out a knife and cut his throat.[39]

Acts of brutality might arise from the dark souls of evil or deranged individuals, but they might also arise from the conditions Kingsley portrayed in *Dead End,* conditions that turn humans into animals. Sonny Liston impressed, even frightened, many people as a man in the throes of a terrible, unappeasable anger. Because he was famous, journalists speculated about where that anger came from. At least one writer, Pete Hamill, a reporter for the *New York Post,* said it came from his experiences as an adolescent. When Liston first came to the city, he was looking for his mother, and he found her, but he also found a town full of tough guys and hustlers, who spoke the common language of violence. According to Hamill, it was St. Louis that created Sonny Liston.[40]

St. Louis created a long line of young men whose destinies were fashioned in the streets.

S T. LOUIS, LIKE OTHER INDUSTRIAL CITIES, acted as a magnet, drawing young male adventurers into its vibrant and often violent center.
Their noisy, messy, and unpredictable presence made the city more
exhilarating—and more dangerous. Life in the streets could crush them
or make them stronger. They could be "dead end kids," overwhelmed by
their environment, or heroes who beat the odds and found success. But
as many reformers perceived, the cards were often stacked against them.

A few of the boys from St. Louis's rough streets became famous men and
wrote their autobiographies. William Marion Reedy became a successful
editor and wrote about his less fortunate friends who did not escape the
crime and violence of Kerry Patch, as he had done. Yogi Berra and Joe
Garagiola remembered playing baseball with cast-off or stolen balls and
bats, while growing up on the Hill during the Great Depression. Archie
Moore got into trouble with the law and credited the CCC for giving him
the chance to straighten himself out and learn the art of boxing. Chuck
Berry had his own run-ins with police and the courts before he channeled
his energy into rock and roll. Sonny Liston, with almost no education, did
not tell his own story, but sympathetic biographers told it for him. With
all his success in the boxing ring, he could not escape his troubled youth.

Some of St. Louis's "dead end kids" had brief moments of fame that
brought their stories to light. Reporters came to Robert Brestol's door after
he witnessed the murder-suicide that killed his desperate parents. Little
Jimmie Fleming met a priest named Peter Dunne and became the first
resident of Father Dunne's Newsboys' Home and Protectorate. Tommie
Gleason, at the age of four, rescued his baby brother from their burning
house, where their mother had left them alone. Bernard Mussman was the
top-selling St. Louis newsboy in 1899; he was trying to support himself
and his younger stepbrother. Emil Pretto, at the age of seventeen, tried
to save his older brother by confessing to a string of robberies and later
served his country during World War II.

Drawing of a despondent boy that ran in the *St. Louis Post-Dispatch* on December 20, 1959. (By Simone Irving. Used by permission, State Historical Society of Missouri, Columbia)

Some of St. Louis's neglected boys could communicate only in the primitive language of violence. In 1862, a fifteen-year-old boy named Milton Frame stabbed another boy in the House of Refuge and then escaped. Fifteen-year-old Charles Aiken set a fire that severely damaged the House of Refuge in 1865. Brothers Joseph and William Kuehls, aged thirteen and ten, tried to burn down an orphanage in 1884. In 1896, Henry Clay (also known as Tom Johnson) murdered a newsboy named William Amend during a fight over a game of dice. George William Thornton was twelve years old in 1897, when he participated in an armed robbery and allegedly killed a policeman. While still in his teens, James "Sticky" Hennessy joined Egan's Rats and was implicated in more than one murder in the 1920s. At the age of nineteen in 1958, Macer Allen robbed a sixty-one-year-old man and hit him in the head with a baseball bat, killing him.

Some boys were witnesses to or victims of violence. Two young boys playing marbles discovered the body of Jeu Chow under a gasoline tank in 1899. Nine-year-old Emanuel Capraro was wounded in a mob-style shooting at the corner of Carr and Wash streets in 1927. Frank Kennebrew, age ten, witnessed the gangland murder of Nick Palazollo. Kenneth Milano, age eighteen, was found dead, with a broken neck, on the Mississippi River bank near the MacArthur Bridge in 1955.

Most of St. Louis's street boys managed to grow up and live decent lives, but that does not mean that their childhood experiences left them unscathed. Raymond Kinney, who was born in 1915, spent most of his young life in orphanages and was a resident of Father Dunne's Newsboys' Home in 1930. He survived the Great Depression and went on to become a substantial businessman. But his daughter believes that his early experience of rejection and loneliness took a toll on his ability to have a stable family life. In one sense, he lived the American dream by rising from miserable circumstances and achieving financial success. Emotionally, however, according to his daughter, his early struggles crippled and bruised him in ways that caused pain to both him and his children.

Throughout the period covered by this book, private philanthropists and public officials struggled to change the urban environment and make it more nurturing for the young. The fact that they did not completely succeed should not lead to the conclusion that success is not possible. If the stories told in this book have any value at all, they should reinforce the ideas that the environment has a great impact on human behavior and that, as a society, we have an obligation to create cities that nurture rather than endanger our youth.

Epilogue

ON MOTHER'S DAY, 2005, I was trapped in an East St. Louis club called Popp's. I say "trapped" because I had a stamp on my wrist that glowed under ultraviolet light, and the doorkeeper told me and my husband that if we went outside for any reason we would not be allowed back in. My eighteen-year-old daughter was somewhere in a crowd of people her age, mingling around a stage in the bare, high-ceilinged room. One or two other parents were there, but my husband and I were easily the oldest people in the place.

We were there for a battle of the bands, in which my daughter's boy-friend and his group would be competing. The bar served alcohol and soft drinks, but no food at all. It was after five o'clock, and I was hungry. I had a large gin and tonic. We learned at some point that Daniel and his band had won the honor of playing last, so they might not take the stage until nine o'clock. My feelings about this came close to desperation.

At about six o'clock, the first musical group assembled on the stage. The crowd got very quiet, as a young man came up to the microphone and said something like, "Happy Mother's Day, you motherf------." Well, something like that.

Then the music began. It was "emo," which means loud, raw, emotional, angry, plugged-in, screaming rock (I guess). At first I understood nothing but a few screeched expletives. The crowd of young people surging around the stage bobbed their heads and moved their hands in a rhythmic, hyp-notic kind of synchronized motion. After a while, I began to respond to the music, and I looked at the faces of the musicians. They were all young and all male, and they were all expressing the most terrible, wrenching, throat-ripping rage.

When his turn finally came, Daniel amazed me. His band had cleaned up from their previous dreadlocked image. They had cut their hair, and they were dressed in white shirts, dark pants, and suit jackets. They had carefully choreographed all their moves, and they knew how to play their instruments while moving their bodies in agile, impossible, expressive ways. Daniel sang and shouted, moved all around the stage, even got up on a chair and did a kind of backflip off of it and never missed a beat. But his lyrics, what I could understand of them, were hard and anguished and full of painful shock at the ways of the world.

Harvard professor William Pollack has concluded after years of study-ing adolescent boys that anger is the emotion through which they express their vulnerability. Parents, friends, teachers—virtually everyone involved in the process of raising male children discourages them from showing other feelings, such as fear and sadness, but encourages them to vent their anger. Because they are denied expression of the full range of human feelings, some boys become depressed or hopeless. Others become hard, aggressive, rambunctious, alienated, or even violent.[1]

Pollack points out that most of the violence in American society involves boys and young men as perpetrators and victims. He notes that, statisti-cally, males are four times more likely to be murdered than females. With more and more frequency, in the 1980s and 1990s male teenagers died from the use of firearms. Most boys, of course, did not become involved in violent crimes, but they had to grow up in this culture of violence.[2]

The emo bands in that East St. Louis club found a healthful outlet for their emotions in music. Even anger can find expression in creative, and not destructive, ways. As Jane Addams observed, the passion of youth can make our cities exciting and bright, or, twisted and crushed, it can make them dangerous.

A Glossary of Names

Adams, Ira, robbed a print shop and a saloon in 1899.

Adams, Theodore F., at age nine in 1903 wept openly when a policeman removed him from his home after his father declared him incorrigible.

Aids, Emmett, at age fifteen in 1903 allegedly stole sacks of goods from freight trains. See also Thomas Gibson.

Aiken, Charles, at age fifteen in 1865 set fire to the House of Refuge.

Allen, Macer F., at age eighteen in 1958 robbed a sixty-one-year-old man and then hit him on the head with a baseball bat, killing him. See also John J. Parker and James P. Tucker.

Amend, William "Chronicle Red," an eighteen-year-old newsboy, was shot to death in 1896 by Henry Clay, also known as Tom Johnson.

Bains, Julia, at age fourteen in 1856 was one of a small minority of girls committed to the House of Refuge. See also Fanny Boland and Mary Miller.

Bannon, Francis, an alumnus of Father Dunne's Newsboys' Home, was killed in World War I.

Barth, Lester, an extortionist belonging to the Cuckoo gang, was killed by machine-gun fire in November 1930. See also Dewey Goebel.

Barth, Percy, a nineteen-year-old man, was shot and killed in 1933 while robbing a grocery store.

Berra, Yogi, sold newspapers on the street while growing up on the Hill in the 1920s and 1930s and later achieved greatness on the baseball field.

Berry, Chuck, grew up in St. Louis in the 1930s and 1940s and later became famous in the world of rock and roll music.

Bieber, Fred, was involved in a series of robberies in 1927 with Girard Polito, William O'Leary, and Leo Murray.

Boland, Fanny, at age fifteen in 1856 was charged with prostitution and committed to the House of Refuge.

Bosing, Carl, born in 1921, resided at Father Dunne's Newsboys' Home in 1930.

Bosing, John, born in 1916, resided at Father Dunne's Newsboys' Home in 1930.

Bosing, Lawrence, born in 1915, resided at Father Dunne's Newsboys' Home in 1930.

Bosing, Robert, born in 1918, resided at Father Dunne's Newsboys' Home in 1930.

Brem, Roy, an alumnus of Father Dunne's Newsboys' Home, was killed in World War I.

Brestol, Robert, at age fourteen in 1910 lost both his parents when his father killed his mother and then committed suicide.

Burroughs, William S., had a troubled adolescence in St. Louis in the 1920s and 1930s and later became famous as a writer and a member of the Beat Generation.

Byington, Howard, born in 1904, resided at Father Dunne's Newsboys' Home in 1920.

Byington, Maurice, born in 1907, resided at Father Dunne's Newsboys' Home in 1920.

Capraro, Emanuel, at age nine in 1927 was wounded in a gangland shooting at the corner of Carr and Wash streets.

Carroll, Edward, died of an inflammation of the brain at the age of ten in the St. Louis House of Refuge in 1882.

Cipolla, James, left Sicily in 1910 and came to St. Louis, where he extorted money from Italian businessmen.

Clay, Henry, was the alias of Tom Johnson.

Colbeck, William P. "Dinty," became the leader of the Rats gang after the death of William "Constable" Egan in 1921.

Connell, John "Kink," was one of the gangsters who was following James Hennessy after the murders of Elmer Malone and William McGee in 1923.

Coughlin, Eugene, at age ten in 1908 went missing for three weeks and was found hiding in a bake oven. See also Tony Rudnicka.

Croke, James, was a newsboy and the younger stepbrother of Bernard Mussman.

Cunningham, Johnnie, a boyhood friend of William Marion Reedy's, got into trouble with the law and died in a train wreck.

Daryear, Joseph, robbed a print shop and a saloon in 1899.

Davis, Matthew L., who resided at Father Dunne's Newsboys' Home from 1907 through 1910, was falsely depicted as a killer in the 1948 movie *Fighting Father Dunne.*

Dempsey, Timothy, was a priest who provided meals and shelter for homeless men in the early twentieth century.

Donnelly, Edward, at age thirteen in 1884 stole candy from a wagon at Twenty-third and Biddle streets and was sent to the St. Louis House of Refuge.

Donovan, John, at age fourteen in 1903 vandalized machinery belonging to the Multiplex Display and Fixtures Company on Seventh Street. See also Walter Harmon.

Dreiser, Theodore, came to St. Louis from Chicago in 1892 as a reporter and later became a famous novelist.

Drysdale, Frederick, nephew of Father Dunne, lived at the Newsboys' Home in 1920.

Drysdale, William, nephew of Father Dunne, lived at the Newsboys' Home in 1920.

Dunlap, William, at age sixteen in 1897 pleaded guilty to arson and was sent to the State Reform School.

Dunne, Peter Joseph, established Father Dunne's Newsboys' Home for orphaned, abandoned, and neglected boys in 1906.

Dutton, John, while playing marbles in 1899, discovered the dead body of Jeu Chow under a gasoline tank. See also Charles McNorman.

Egan, William "Constable," headed the Rats gang until his murder on Halloween night in 1921. His brother Thomas was also a gang leader.

Euge, Michael, alumnus of Father Dunne's Newsboys' Home, was killed in World War I.

Fleming, James "Little Jimmie," at age ten in 1906 met Father Dunne on a streetcar and became one of the first residents of the Newsboys' Home.

Fleming, William, at age fourteen in 1903 allegedly stole a pocketbook from Minnie Stamm. See also Arthur Lewis.

Frame, Milton, at age fifteen in 1862 stabbed another boy in the St. Louis House of Refuge and then escaped.

Frawley, Robert, at age thirteen in 1898 ran away from Cobden, Illinois, to St. Louis, where police caught him jumping off a boxcar and sent him home to his parents. See also Fred Townsend.

Garagiola, Joe, grew up on the Hill in the 1920s and 1930s and then became famous as a baseball player.

Garvey, Lewis, was admitted to the House of Refuge in 1878 at the age of nine and later was indentured to a farmer in Sikeston, Missouri.

Gates, Gloster Ervin, at age seventeen in 1959 committed several armed robberies to get cash to buy narcotics.

Giannola, Vito, left Sicily in 1910 and came to St. Louis to make money as an extortionist.

Gleason, F. S. W., was the superintendent of the House of Refuge who was charged with extreme cruelty in the 1870s.

Gleason, Sylvester, at fifteen months of age in 1980 was rescued from a burning house by his four-year-old brother.

Gleason, Tommie, at age four in 1908 rescued his baby brother from a burning house.

Goebel, Dewey, an extortionist belonging to the Cuckoo gang, was killed by machine-gun fire in November 1930. See also Lester Barth.

Grace, Albert, at age seventeen in 1933 was hit and killed by a train after he had gone to Chicago looking for work.

Gurman, Isaac, a caseworker and administrator for the Bureau for Men, wrote a thesis on treating homeless men and boys.

Harmon, Walter, at age twelve in 1903 vandalized machinery at the Multiplex Display and Fixtures Company on Seventh Street. See also John Donovan.

Harris was a little boy found living in the city jail in November 1897.

Hennessy, James "Sticky," at age nineteen in 1923, after a ten-year criminal career, was implicated in the murder of Elmer Malone and William McGee.

Hogan, Edward "Jellyroll," headed the Jellyrolls gang in the 1920s and had a long career in Missouri state politics.

Hogan, James, brother of Edward "Jellyroll" Hogan, was thought to be responsible for the death of William Egan.

Hotchner, A. E., at age twelve in the 1930s lived alone in a hotel while his father went on the road as a salesman and his mother was in the hospital; he later became a successful author.

Hunt, Nicholas, police officer shot and killed by young drifters in 1897.

Jefferson, Joe, as a fifteen-year-old resident of Pruitt-Igoe, told researchers about gang activity in the infamous housing complex.

Johnson, Tom (a.k.a. Henry Clay), was executed for the shooting of William Amend.

Kennebrew, Frank, at age ten in 1927 witnessed the gangland murder of Nick Palazollo.

Kinney, Raymond T., born in 1915, spent most of his young life in orphanages and was a resident of Father Dunne's Newsboys' Home in 1930.

Kuehls, Joseph, at age twelve in 1884 tried to burn down the German St. Vincent Orphan Home and was sent to the St. Louis House of Refuge.

Kuehls, William, at age ten in 1884 conspired with his brother to burn down the German St. Vincent Orphan Home and was sent to the St. Louis House of Refuge.

Ladermann, Peter, at age sixteen in 1884 was allegedly subjected to "unnatural treatment" by the man in whose care he had been placed by the German St. Vincent Orphan Home.

Lewis, Arthur, at age eighteen in 1903 allegedly stole a pocketbook from Minnie Stamm. See also William Fleming.

Liebich, Charles, at age fourteen in 1884 stole money and a shotgun from his parents and announced his intention of going to Texas.

Liston, Sonny, in his teens and early twenties in St. Louis in the 1940s and 1950s, got into trouble with the law, then went on to become heavyweight boxing champion of the world.

Lyons, Jacob, robbed a print shop and a saloon in 1899.

Malone, Elmer, was killed by gangsters on September 10, 1923. See James Hennessy.

McAllister, Andrew, an alumnus of Father Dunne's Newsboys' Home, was killed in World War I.

McCarty, John, died at the age of nine after being run over by a streetcar in 1884.

McDonald, Patrick, who had been sent to the House of Refuge for larceny at the age of fourteen in 1855, ended up in the State Penitentiary, where he was shot to death in 1865 while trying to escape.

McGee, William, a member of the state legislature, was killed by gangsters on September 10, 1923. See also James Hennessy.

McGrath, Francis, an alumnus of Father Dunne's Newsboys' Home, was killed in World War I.

McNorman, Charles, while playing marbles in 1899, discovered the dead body of Jeu Chow under a gasoline tank. See also John Dutton.

Milano, Kenneth, at age eighteen in 1955 was found dead, with a broken neck, on the Mississippi River bank near the MacArthur Bridge.

Miller, August, at age ten in 1884 conspired to burn down the German St. Vincent Orphan Home and was sent to the St. Louis House of Refuge.

Miller, Mary, at age ten in 1856 was one of a small minority of girls committed to the House of Refuge.

Minehan, Thomas, a social worker, traveled and camped with young tramps during the Great Depression and wrote a book about them.

Mohrle, William, born in 1907, was a resident of Father Dunne's Newsboys' Home in 1920.

Moore, Archie, left the reformatory, joined the CCC in the 1930s, and went on to achieve fame as a boxer and entertainer.

Moran, Patrick M. "Algie," a motorman on a streetcar, was convicted of armed robbery in 1933. See also Michael Pretto.

Muench, Neil Y., died in April 1933 after he slid into a sand pit with his young friend James Riordan, who survived.

Mullen, Ed, robbed a print shop and a saloon in 1899.

Murray, Leo, at age nineteen in 1927 was involved in a series of robberies with Girard Polito, William O'Leary, and Fred Bieber.

Mussman, Bernard, was the top-selling newsboy in 1899. See also James Croke.

Nitz, Joseph, at age fourteen in 1903 reportedly stole a sack of sugar from a railroad car. See also James Robinson.

Novey, Jerry, at age eighteen in 1927, claiming he was a member of the Cuckoo gang, threatened a man named John C. Raab, who shot him.

O'Leary, William, at age seventeen in 1927 was involved in a series of robberies with Girard Polito, Leo Murray, and Fred Bieber.

Palazollo, Alphonse, left Palermo, Sicily, in 1910 and came to St. Louis to make money through extortion. He was shot and killed outside a pool hall in 1927.

Parker, John J., at age nineteen in 1958 robbed and assaulted a sixty-one-year-old man, causing his death. See also Macer F. Allen and James P. Tucker.

Pfeiffer children, six in all, were deserted by their father in 1884 and sent to the St. Louis House of Refuge.

Polito, Girard, at age eighteen in 1927 ran away from his job as a police messenger and became a holdup man. He was arrested for a series of robberies with Fred Bieber, Leo Murray, and William O'Leary.

Pretto, Emil, at age seventeen in 1933 confessed to several robberies in an attempt to keep his brother Michael out of trouble.

Pretto, Michael Mark, at age eighteen in 1933 was convicted of armed robbery and sentenced to ten years in the State Penitentiary.

Reedy, William Marion, grew up in Kerry Patch and became the successful editor of the *St. Louis Mirror.*

Riordan, James, at age eleven in 1933 was hit by a piece of iron thrown from a freight car and nearly died after sliding into a sand pit with a friend, Neil Muench, who did not survive.

Robinson, David "Chippy," was one of the gangsters who followed James Hennessy after the murders of Elmer Malone and William McGee in 1923.

Robinson, James, at age seventeen in 1903 reportedly stole a sack of sugar from a railroad car. See also Joseph Nitz.

Ross, George, at age twelve in 1908 was tortured by three adult males who accused him of stealing.

Rudnicka, Tony, at age thirteen in 1908 went missing for three weeks and was found hiding in a bake oven. See also Eugene Coughlin.

Rumbold, Charlotte, campaigned for parks and playgrounds during the Progressive Era and served on the St. Louis Public Recreation Committee and as an officer of the national Playground Association of America.

Russo, Tony, was the leader of the Cuckoo gang in the 1920s.

Schneider, Alfred, at age six in 1921 was the foster child of policeman Joseph A. Schneider and his wife, Louisa, who said he "just must not be cast adrift" and adopted him.

Schweiger, Jake, robbed a print shop and a saloon in 1899.

Sexton, William, at age fifteen in 1920 worked as an office boy for Father Dunne.

Shea, Jack, a boyhood friend of William Marion Reedy's, killed a policeman and spent many years in prison.

Sheldon, Charles, at age eighteen in 1897 robbed Peter Heibel's saloon and was involved in the death of policeman Nicholas Hunt. See also Frank Stetson and George William Thornton.

Signorelli, Joseph, born in 1906, lived at Father Dunne's Newsboys' Home for at least ten years from 1910 to 1920.

Signorelli, Tony, born in 1907, lived at Father Dunne's Newsboys' Home in 1920.

Sinks, Roy, at age eighteen in 1933 was caught in a stolen car with Emil Pretto.

Smith, Arthur, at age seventeen in 1896 testified that Tom Johnson (known as Henry Clay) played dice games with newsboys including William Amend.

Smith, Edgar, at age two in 1884 was deserted by his mother.

Smith, Henry, at age four in 1884 was deserted by his mother.

Spicuzza, Vincenzo, was a prominent member of the Cuckoo gang in the 1920s.

Stetson, Frank, at age eighteen in 1897 robbed Peter Heibel's saloon and was involved in the shooting death of policeman Nicholas Hunt. See also Charles Sheldon and George William Thornton.

Stuffon, Rudolph, robbed a print shop and a saloon in 1899.

Sweeney, Matthew T., born in 1904, resided at Father Dunne's Newsboys' Home in 1920.

Thornton, George William (a.k.a. St. Paul Tip), at age twelve in 1897 was involved in a robbery and the killing of a police officer, but was never prosecuted for these crimes. See also Charles Sheldon and Frank Stetson.

Townsend, Fred, at age fourteen in 1898 ran away from Cobden, Illinois, to St. Louis, where police caught him jumping off a freight car and sent him home to his parents. See also Robert Frawley.

Troutman, Thomas, was arrested with James Hennessy in 1920 for stealing money by threatening violence.

Tucker, James P., at age nineteen in 1958 robbed and assaulted a sixty-one-year-old man, causing his death. See also Macer F. Allen and John J. Parker.

Twain, Mark, came to St. Louis in the 1850s with dreams of becoming a riverboat pilot, later became a famous author, and returned to find the city greatly changed.

Williams, Frank, became a gambler in the 1870s and was the subject of his father's letter to the editor against the evils of gambling.

INTRODUCTION

1. Jeffrey Turner, "On Boyhood and Public Swimming: Sidney Kingsley's *Dead End* and Representations of Underclass Street Kids in American Cultural Production."

2. Henry W. Thurston, *The Dependent Child: A Story of Changing Aims and Methods in the Care of Dependent Children,* 12, 42, 92, 270.

3. See Todd DePastino, *Citizen Hobo: How a Century of Homelessness Shaped America;* Samuel E. Wallace, *Skid Row as a Way of Life;* Daniel Waugh, *Egan's Rats: The Untold Story of the Prohibition-Era Gang That Ruled St. Louis;* Thomas Minehan, *Boy and Girl Tramps of America;* Mary Skinner and Alice Scott Nutt, "Adolescents Away from Home," 51; Michael J. Bennett, *When Dreams Came True: The GI Bill and the Making of Modern America,* 3, 94.

4. A lucid and concise discussion of the question of defining childhood and adolescence may be found in Kingsley Davis, "Adolescence and the Social Structure," 8–16.

5. The Baker Street Irregulars, the young street boys who help Sherlock Holmes, appear in several of Arthur Conan Doyle's works, including *A Study in Scarlet.* See Gary Scharnhorst, *Horatio Alger, Jr.*

6. Jane Addams, *The Spirit of Youth and the City Streets,* 3–5.

7. David Nasaw, *Children of the City: At Work and at Play,* 187.

8. Kenneth L. Kusmer, *Down and Out, On the Road: The Homeless in American History,* 6–7; James Neal Primm, *Lion of the Valley: St. Louis, Missouri, 1764–1980,* 528–29.

9. The academic literature on this topic is not extensive. I have relied on the following works, in addition to others that will be cited later: Douglas E. Abrams, *A Very Special Place in Life: The History of Juvenile Justice in Missouri;* Timothy J. Gilfoyle, *A Pickpocket's Tale;* Marilyn Irvin Holt, *The Orphan Trains: Placing Out in America;* Edward Olds, *Trends in Child Dependency in St. Louis, 1860–1944;* and William F. Whyte, *Street Corner Society: The Social Structure of an Italian Slum.*

10. Peggy Thomson Greenwood wrote about these issues with great insight in several articles that were published in the *St. Louis Genealogical Society Quarterly* in 1991 and 1992.

11. Two good articles on the cholera epidemic have been published in the *Missouri Historical Review.* See Linda A. Fisher, "A Summer of Terror: Cholera in St. Louis, 1849," and Patrick E. McLear, "The St. Louis Cholera Epidemic of 1849." For insight on orphans and orphanages, see Peggy Thomson Greenwood, "Beyond the Orphanage."

12. J. A. Dacus and James W. Buel, *A Tour of St. Louis; or, The Inside Life of a Great City,* 407–12. Dacus was a Baptist minister and a reporter for the *Missouri Republican.* Buel was a prolific author of travel and history books. Their book provides unique observations on the dark side of the city's life in the 1870s.

13. J. Adams Puffer, *The Boy and His Gang,* 24, 32; Hubert Rother and Charlotte Rother, *Lost Caves of St. Louis: A History of the City's Forgotten Caves,* 94–98.

14. The house of refuge idea originated in eastern cities. For information on the development of these institutions, I have relied upon Robert S. Pickett, *House of Refuge: Origins of Juvenile Reform in New York State, 1815–1857;* B. K. Pierce, *A Half Century with Juvenile Delinquents; or, The New York House of Refuge and Its Times;* and other sources. For information on the St. Louis House of Refuge, I have depended upon William Hyde and Howard L. Conard, *Encyclopedia of the History of St. Louis,* 2:1063; Dacus and Buel, *Tour of St. Louis,* 513–19; and St. Louis House of Refuge, Journal of Commitments, July 25, 1854–January 28, 1899, Missouri Historical Society, St. Louis (hereafter cited as Journal of Commitments).

15. J. W. Gormley, *History of Father Dunne's News Boys' Home and Protectorate,* 10–61, 76–83. In 2006 the home became part of Catholic Services for Children and Youth (later called Good Shepherd Children and Family Services).

16. See Wallace, *Skid Row.* For a study of the evolution of St. Louis, see Eric Sandweiss, *St. Louis: The Evolution of an American Urban Landscape.* On May 8, 1910, the *St. Louis Post-Dispatch* printed an in-depth article on the influx of male migrants into the area along Market Street.

17. For information on criminal gang activity in St. Louis's violent past, see Waugh, *Egan's Rats,* and John Auble, *A History of St. Louis Gangsters.*

18. I highly recommend Minehan, *Boy and Girl Tramps of America.* Several well-known men who grew up in St. Louis during the Great Depression later wrote autobiographies. Among these are Chuck Berry, *Autobiography;* Yogi Berra, with Ed Fitzgerald, *Yogi: The Autobiography of a Professional Baseball Player;* Joe Garagiola, *Baseball Is a Funny Game;* and Archie Moore, *Any Boy Can: The Archie Moore Story.* For information on the Depression in St. Louis, see Primm, *Lion of the Valley,* 418, 436, 439–45. I recommend Richard A. Reiman, *The New Deal and American Youth: Ideas and Ideals in a Depression Decade.* Other useful works on the topic of youth in the Depression era include Palmer O. Johnson and Oswald L. Harvey, *The National Youth Administration;* Kenneth Holland and Frank Ernest Hill, *Youth in the CCC;* and Lewis L. Lorwin, *Youth Work Programs: Problems and Policies.*

19. For first-person accounts of the war experiences of some of St. Louis's World War II veterans, see George J. Despotis, Donald E. Korte, and Matthew Lary, eds., *Victory through Valor: A Collection of World War II Memories.* For a discussion of postwar changes, see Primm, *Lion of the Valley,* 458–64. Emblematic of this period in St. Louis history is the story of Sonny Liston. See A. S. Young, *Sonny Liston: The Champ Nobody Wanted,* and Nick Tosches, *The Devil and Sonny Liston.*

CHAPTER ONE: THE CITY STREETS

1. Mark Twain, *Life on the Mississippi,* 108 (epigraph), 22, 109.

2. Andrew Hurley, "Busby's Stink Boat and the Regulation of Nuisance Trades, 1865–1918," in *Common Fields: An Environmental History of St. Louis,* 148–49.

3. William E. Foley and C. David Rice, *The First Chouteaus: River Barons of Early St. Louis,* 16; Primm, *Lion of the Valley,* 35, 145–47, 153–57.

4. Primm, *Lion of the Valley,* 306–7, 327; Harland Bartholomew, *Problems of St. Louis,* 91. In 1900, St. Louis was the fourth-largest city in the United States.

5. Walter Kamphoefner, "Learning from the Majority-Minority City: Immigration in Nineteenth Century St. Louis," 83–84; Antonio F. Holland, "African-Americans in Henry Shaw's St. Louis," 78; Ron Fagerstrom, *Mill Creek Valley: A Soul of St. Louis,* 5, 20; John A. Wright, *Discovering African-American St. Louis: A Guide to Historic Sites,* 23–27.

6. Eric Sandweiss, "Paving St. Louis's Streets: The Environmental Origins of Social Fragmentation," in Andrew Hurley, ed., *Common Fields,* 95.

7. Walter Kamphoefner, "Learning from the Majority-Minority City: Immigration in Ninteenth Century St. Louis," 84–85.

8. Eric Sandweiss, "Construction and Community in South St. Louis, 1850–1910," 97–99; Sandweiss, *St. Louis,* 101–7.

9. *St. Louis Globe-Democrat,* April 9, 1899. For a thorough discussion of Hop Alley, see Huping Ling, *Chinese St. Louis: From Enclave to Cultural Community.*

10. Ling, *Chinese St. Louis,* 31; *St. Louis Globe-Democrat,* April 6, 1899.

11. *St. Louis Globe-Democrat,* April 6, 1899.

12. Ibid.

13. Charlotte Rumbold, *Housing Conditions in St. Louis: Report of the Housing Committee of the Civic League of St. Louis,* 63–65.

14. Gary Ross Mormino, *Immigrants on the Hill: Italian-Americans in St. Louis, 1882–1982,* 16–17, 1–2; Walter Ehrlich, *Zion in the Valley: The Jewish Community of St. Louis,* vol. 2, *The Twentieth Century,* 29–30.

15. Rumbold, *Housing Conditions in St. Louis,* 8–13.

16. Ibid., 36, 68–72.

17. Primm, *Lion of the Valley,* 339, 353; Mormino, *Immigrants on the Hill,* 17; Dacus and Buel, *Tour of St. Louis,* 417–18.

18. Max Putzel, *The Man in the Mirror: William Marion Reedy and His Magazine,* 15–18.

19. Ibid., 18.

20. Dacus and Buel, *Tour of St. Louis,* 408–11.

21. Primm, *Lion of the Valley,* 179–80.

22. Ibid., 236–40.

23. Louis S. Gerteis, *Civil War St. Louis,* 236, 252, 255.

24. Primm, *Lion of the Valley,* 310–14. For a book-length treatment of the 1877 strike, see David Burbank, *Reign of the Rabble: The St. Louis General Strike of 1877.*

25. James F. Baker, "The St. Louis and Suburban Streetcar Strike of 1900," 226, 234–36; Andrew D. Young, *The St. Louis Streetcar Story,* 92–93; Steven L. Piott, "Modernization and the Anti-Monopoly Issue: The St. Louis Transit Strike of 1900," 8, 10, 12–15.

26. Young, *St. Louis Streetcar Story,* 92–93; Piott, "Modernization and the Anti-Monopoly Issue," 12–15.

27. Thomas Spencer, *The St. Louis Veiled Prophet Celebration: Power on Parade, 1877–1995,* 26–32.

28. *St. Louis Post-Dispatch,* February 12, 1899.

29. *St. Louis Evening Post,* October 11 and 12, 1878.

30. Ibid., October 12, 1878.

31. Ibid.

32. *St. Louis Globe-Democrat,* April 2, 1884.

33. Ibid., March 17 and 18, 1884.

34. Addams, *Spirit of Youth,* 68, 161. This book, first published in 1909, reflected Addams's many years of experience working with families in the poorer sections of Chicago.

35. Theodore Dreiser, *A Book about Myself,* 100–101.

36. Dacus and Buel, *Tour of St. Louis,* 406–8, 412–15.

37. Ibid., 445–46.

38. *St. Louis Post-Dispatch,* February 11, 1899.

39. *St. Louis Globe-Democrat,* April 1, 1899.

40. Ibid.

CHAPTER TWO: ORPHANS AND ORPHANAGES

1. Holt, *Orphan Trains,* 41–49.

2. Ibid., 44.

3. Gaylord E. Landau, "A History of the St. Louis Board of Children's Guardians in Relation to the Care of Dependent and Neglected Children from 1912–1938," 8–9.

4. Katharine T. Corbett, *In Her Place: A Guide to St. Louis Women's History,* 26. Olds provides a list of such institutions in *Trends in Child Dependency,* 21–24.

5. Ann N. Morris, "The History of the St. Louis Protestant Orphan Asylum," 80–83.

6. Ibid., 3; Susan Whitelaw Downs and Michael W. Sherraden, "The Orphan Asylum in the Nineteenth Century," 275–77, 283.

7. Morris, "History of the St. Louis Protestant Orphan Asylum," 85.

8. Downs and Sherraden, "The Orphan Asylum," 280.

9. Olds, *Trends in Child Dependency,* 21–24; Corbett, *In Her Place,* 38, 66; Evelyn Roberts Koenig, "The History of the Episcopal Home for Children in St. Louis, 1843–1935," 28–35.

10. Corbett, *In Her Place,* 66; Koenig, "History of the Episcopal Home," 215–57.

11. Koenig, "History of the Episcopal Home," 257–63.

12. Ibid., 292–93.

13. Genealogist Peggy Thomson Greenwood perceptively pointed out the historical effects of these 1849 events on the children of St. Louis in a 1991 article entitled "Beyond the Orphanage." See also Primm, *Lion of the Valley,* 166–68.

14. Regina M. Faden, "The German St. Vincent Orphan Home: The Institution and Its Role in the Immigrant German Catholic Community of St. Louis, 1850–1900," 1–109.

15. Ibid., 109–10, 143; United States Bureau of the Census, Tenth Census, 1880, for the City of St. Louis, Microfilm Roll T9, 721. For this and subsequent citations of the federal census, microfilm is available from the National Archives and Records Administration in Washington, D.C., or from branch locations in several cities.

16. Journal of Commitments, 142.

17. Landau, "History of the St. Louis Board of Children's Guardians," 11–28; William Clark Breckenridge, handwritten sketch of the St. Louis House of Refuge, William Clark Breckenridge Papers, 1897, Missouri Historical Society, St. Louis.

Statistics on boys/girls derived from a study of the Journal of Commitments.

18. Landau, "History of the St. Louis Board of Children's Guardians," 24–25. Statistics on indenture/apprenticeship were derived from a study of the Journal of Commitments.

19. Lisa G. Guinn, "Building Useful Women from the Depths of Poverty: A Social History of the Girls' Industrial Home and School in St. Louis, Missouri, 1853–1935," 1–6. See also Lisa G. Guinn, "Building Useful Women from the Depths of Poverty: The Founding and Establishment of the Girls' Industrial Home and School in St. Louis, 1853–1916."

20. Charlotte C. Eliot, *William Greenleaf Eliot: Minister, Educator, Philanthropist,* 62–63; Corbett, *In Her Place,* 138.

21. Greenwood, "Beyond the Orphanage," 107; Olds, *Trends in Child Dependency,* 21–24.

22. Olds, *Trends in Child Dependency,* 21–24; Corbett, *In Her Place,* 142.

23. Jo Colay Ray, *These Little Ones: The History of the Missouri Baptist Children's Home,* 12–47; Julian Curzon, *The Great Cyclone at St. Louis and East St. Louis, May 27, 1896,* 17–27, 75–205.

24. *St. Louis Globe-Democrat,* July 30, 1899.

25. Mary Kimbrough, *He Who Helps a Child: The Children's Home Society of Missouri: Its First 100 Years,* 5, 20, 41–42.

26. *St. Louis Globe-Democrat,* July 30, 1899.

27. Kimbrough, *He Who Helps a Child,* 18.

28. *St. Louis Globe-Democrat,* July 30 and December 23, 1899.

29. Olds, *Trends in Child Dependency,* 21–24; *St. Louis Globe-Democrat,* November 21, 1897.

30. *St. Louis Globe-Democrat,* July 30, 1899.

31. Ibid., April 2, 1884.

32. Ibid.

33. Ibid., November 18, 1897.

34. *St. Louis Post-Dispatch,* November 18, 1897.

35. *St. Louis Globe-Democrat,* November 18, 1897.

36. Peggy Thomson Greenwood, "The House of Refuge," 45. Interestingly, Dorothea Dix was a Unitarian and a friend of William Greenleaf Eliot's. For a discussion of the philosophical similarities and differences between Dix and Addams, see J. David Greenstone, "Dorothea Dix and Jane Addams: From Transcendentalism to Pragmatism in American Social Reform." For a book-length biography of Dix, see Thomas J. Brown, *Dorothea Dix: New England Reformer.*

37. Corbett, *In Her Place,* 170; Rumbold, *Housing Conditions in St. Louis,* 76; Primm, *Lion of the Valley,* 397.

38. In 1936 the St. Louis Children's Aid Society joined forces with the Provident Association (which had been giving relief to destitute people since 1860), and by 1941 the combined organization had changed its name to Family and Children's Services. For a complete history of this organization, see Mary Kimbrough, *125 Years of Caring: A History of Family and Children's Services of Greater St. Louis, 1860–1985.*

39. Kimbrough, *125 Years of Caring,* 56–57; D. L. Edson, "Neglected and Dependent Children in Missouri," 201–7; Greenwood, "The House of Refuge," 45.

40. Abrams, *Very Special Place in Life,* 65–67; Edson, "Neglected and Dependent Children," 208.

41. *St. Louis Post-Dispatch*, May 8, 1910. Information on Brestol in the following paragraphs is also from this source.

42. Ibid., April 10, 1921.

43. Ibid. The 1930 federal census for St. Louis (Microfilm Roll 1241, p. 5–A, Enumeration District 153) confirms that Joseph A. and Louisa Schneider had adopted Alfred, whose name was given as Alfred Schneider, born about 1914.

CHAPTER THREE: DRIFTERS IN THE CITY STREETS

1. E. Royston Pike, *Human Documents of the Victorian Golden Age, 1850–1873*, 145–46.

2. Henry Mayhew, *London Labor and the London Poor*, 1:33–39, 483–84; 2:346–54.

3. Scharnhorst, *Horatio Alger, Jr.*, 67–68.

4. Ibid., 71–73.

5. Gilfoyle, *A Pickpocket's Tale*, xiv–xvii, 18–29, 303, 315.

6. *St. Louis Globe-Democrat*, December 3, 1877. Information on the Soup House in the next three paragraphs is also from this source.

7. Dacus and Buel, *Tour of St. Louis*, 407.

8. Ibid., 406–8.

9. Ibid., 406–12.

10. Nasaw, *Children of the City*, 98–99.

11. *St. Louis Post-Dispatch*, March 28, 1884.

12. Ibid.; Lewis Atherton, *The Cattle Kings*, 32–33.

13. *St. Louis Post-Dispatch*, November 18, 1897.

14. *St. Louis Globe-Democrat*, January 6, 1898.

15. *St. Louis Post-Dispatch*, November 16, 1897.

16. Ibid.

17. Ibid.

18. Ibid.

19. *St. Louis Globe-Democrat*, November 17, 1897.

20. Ibid., November 19, 1897.

21. Ibid., November 21, 1897.

22. Ibid., November 28, 1897.

23. Ibid.

24. Ibid.

25. Ibid., November 27, 1897.

26. Ibid.; *Review of Famous Crimes Solved by St. Louis Policemen*, 53–56.

27. *State of Missouri vs. Charles Sheldon, Frank Stetson, and William C. Thornton, alias Connors, alias St. Paul Tip*, Grand Jury Indictment, December 18, 1897, Trial Record, Verdict, April 13, 1898, in Case File No. 125, Circuit Court, City of St. Louis, December Term 1897, on file at Missouri State Archives–St. Louis; *St. Louis Globe-Democrat*, April 14, 1898.

28. United States Bureau of the Census, Twelfth Census, 1900, for the City of Providence, R.I., Microfilm Roll T623, p. 221, Enumeration District 247.

29. Handwritten notations on the jacket for Case File No. 125, Circuit Court, City of St. Louis, December Term 1897.

30. The little book entitled *Review of Famous Crimes Solved by St. Louis Policemen* (pp. 53–56) alleges that Thornton spent fifteen years in prison before being pardoned by the governor of Rhode Island. However, this appears not to be true; there are no records of any such imprisonment or pardon. After 1897, Thornton made no mark on society for good or ill. However, he did continue to reside in Providence, according to the United States Bureau of the Census, Fourteenth Census, 1920, for the City of Providence, R.I., Microfilm Roll T625_1672, p. 21–A; United States Bureau of the Census, Fifteenth Census, 1930, for the City of Providence, R.I., Microfilm Roll 2171, p. 5–A.

CHAPTER FOUR: GAMES, GANGS, HIDEOUTS, AND CAVES

1. Dacus and Buel, *Tour of St. Louis,* 411–12.
2. Puffer, *Boy and His Gang,* 1–9.
3. Nasaw, *Children of the City,* 28–33.
4. Addams, *Spirit of Youth,* 55–57.
5. Waugh, *Egan's Rats,* 20–23.
6. Puffer, *Boy and His Gang,* 24, 32; Addams, *Spirit of Youth,* 56.
7. John M. McGuire, "A Morning in the Cave," 7–9.
8. Helen D. Vollmar and Joseph E. Vollmar, Jr., "Caves, Tunnels and Other Holes under St. Louis," 2; McGuire, "A Morning in the Cave," 7.
9. Vollmar and Vollmar, "Caves, Tunnels and Other Holes," 2.
10. "Summer Beer Gardens of St. Louis"; *St. Louis Post-Dispatch,* August 2, 1896.
11. Rother and Rother, *Lost Caves of St. Louis,* 94–98.
12. Mark Twain, *The Adventures of Tom Sawyer,* 73–74.
13. Ibid., 209–16, 229–28.
14. For an excellent study of why Jesse James was so famous, see William A. Settle, Jr., *Jesse James Was His Name; or, Fact and Fiction concerning the Career of the Notorious James Brothers of Missouri.*
15. *Missouri Republican,* December 9, 1877.
16. Primm, *Lion of the Valley,* 195; *Missouri Republican,* December 9, 1877; Vollmar and Vollmar, "Caves, Tunnels and Other Holes," 3.
17. Vollmar and Vollmar, "Caves, Tunnels and Other Holes," 3; Primm, *Lion of the Valley,* 195; *Missouri Republican,* December 9, 1877.
18. *Missouri Republican,* December 9, 1877. The information in the next several paragraphs about police investigations into and destruction of cave hideouts is also from this source.
19. It was not possible to identify and trace these boys.
20. Dacus and Buel, *Tour of St. Louis,* 411.
21. Minehan, *Boy and Girl Tramps of America,* 108.
22. Ibid.
23. Ibid., 109.
24. Primm, *Lion of the Valley,* 195; McGuire, "A Morning in the Cave," 7.
25. *St. Louis Post-Dispatch,* July 15, 1941; McGuire, "A Morning in the Cave," 7.
26. McGuire, "A Morning in the Cave," 7.

CHAPTER FIVE: JUVENILE DELINQUENTS AND THE HOUSE OF REFUGE

1. Negley K. Teeters, "The Early Days of the Philadelphia House of Refuge"; Pickett, *House of Refuge.*

2. Pickett, *House of Refuge,* 100–102; Homer Folks, *The Care of Destitute, Neglected, and Delinquent Children,* 111–25.

3. Pierce, *A Half Century with Juvenile Delinquents,* 286.

4. Gustave de Beaumont and Alexis de Tocqueville, *On the Penitentiary System in the United States and Its Application in France,* 136–51.

5. Charles Dickens, *American Notes: A Journey,* 94.

6. Marion Hunt, "Women and Child Saving: St. Louis Children's Hospital, 1879–1979," 68.

7. Ibid., 66–71.

8. Primm, *Lion of the Valley,* 315–26.

9. Dacus and Buel, *Tour of St. Louis,* 408–9.

10. See Guinn, "Building Useful Women from the Depths of Poverty: The Founding and Establishment of the Girls' Industrial Home."

11. Breckenridge, sketch of the House of Refuge, Breckenridge Papers; Eugene Maurice Jonquet, "A History of Bellefontaine Farms from 1853 to 1938," 13.

12. Breckenridge, sketch of the House of Refuge, Breckenridge Papers; *Missouri Republican,* May 2, 1870.

13. *Missouri Republican,* May 2, 1870; United States Bureau of the Census, Eighth Census, 1860, for the City of St. Louis, Microfilm Roll M653_656, p. O. The 1860 census lists Charles Aiken, age nine, as an inmate of the House of Refuge and indicates that he had committed "no crime." The author has not been able to trace, through the records, what might have become of him.

14. *Missouri Republican,* May 2, 1870.

15. Teeters, "Early Days of the Philadelphia House of Refuge," 182–83.

16. *Missouri Republican,* May 2, 1870.

17. Journal of Commitments, 8, 114.

18. Ibid., 8, 114, 117; United States Bureau of the Census, Tenth Census, 1880, for Richland, Scott County, Mo., Microfilm Roll T9_737, p. 285.

19. St. Louis House of Refuge, Proceedings of the Board of Managers, August 6, 1869, housed in the Vertical File, Missouri Historical Society, St. Louis. Note that an alternative for destitute girls existed in the Girls' Industrial Home and School. See Guinn, "Building Useful Women from the Depths of Poverty: The Founding and Establishment of the Girls' Industrial Home."

20. Statistical information has been derived from a close study of the Journal of Commitments. Please note that the Journal did not record the races of the people committed, so statistics on race for the sample years are not available.

21. Journal of Commitments, 8.

22. Pickett, *House of Refuge,* 177–78; Teeters, "Early Days of the Philadelphia House of Refuge," 174–80; Breckenridge, sketch of the House of Refuge, Breckenridge Papers.

23. St. Louis House of Refuge, Proceedings of the Board of Managers, August 6, 1869; Dacus and Buel, *Tour of St. Louis,* 515–16.

24. Journal of Commitments, 6.

25. Ibid., 29, 30, 33, 34, 36, 40, 44, 45, 50.

26. Teeters, "Early Days of the Philadelphia House of Refuge," 183; Pickett, *House of Refuge,* 90, 144–45.

27. *New York Times,* July 15, 1872.

28. St. Louis Criminal Court Issues Book, 1872, on file at the Missouri State Archives–St. Louis. A search for the case files uncovered no further information.

29. Dacus and Buel, *Tour of St. Louis,* 514–15, 519.

30. Ibid., 514–17.

31. Abrams, *Very Special Place in Life,* 14–15; Jonquet, "History of Bellefontaine Farms," 15, 16, 31, 75; State Board of Charities and Corrections, Second Biennial Report, bound with Appendix to the House and Senate Journals of the 42nd Missouri General Assembly, 1903, 50–51. Statistical information was derived from the Journal of Commitments.

32. Abrams, *Very Special Place in Life,* 14–15; Jonquet, "History of Bellefontaine Farms," 15, 16, 31, 75; State Board of Charities and Corrections, Second Biennial Report, 50–51.

33. *Laws of Missouri,* 42nd Missouri General Assembly, 1902–1903 (Jefferson City, Mo.: Tribune Printing Co., 1903); *Laws of Missouri,* 46th Missouri General Assembly, 1906–1907 (Jefferson City, Mo.: Hugh Stephens Printing Co., 1911); Jonquet, "History of Bellefontaine Farms," 17.

34. Juvenile Court, St. Louis, Probation Officer's Report, Appendix to the House and Senate Journals of the 44th Missouri General Assembly, 1907 (Jefferson City, Mo.: Hugh Stephens Printing Co., 1907), 53–54.

35. *St. Louis Post-Dispatch,* April 1, 1903.

36. Ibid.

37. Ibid.

38. Juvenile Court, Probation Officer's Report, 1907, 54–57.

39. Jonquet, "History of Bellefontaine Farms," 96–100.

40. Juvenile Court, Probation Officer's Report, 1907, 54–57. The Missouri Training School for Boys at Boonville has a checkered history. The state established it in 1887 for the purpose of reshaping the characters of juvenile offenders. In the 1940s, large numbers of boys escaped from the training school, and investigations revealed shocking treatment of inmates there, including corporal punishment. Two boys were murdered by other inmates in separate incidents in 1948 and 1949. After these tragedies, the state reformed the institution and banned corporal punishment. See Albert Deutsch, *Our Rejected Children,* 123–31.

41. Greenwood, "The House of Refuge," 45; Olds, *Trends in Child Dependency,* 5; Jonquet, "History of Bellefontaine Farms," 15–16.

42. Jonquet, "History of Bellefontaine Farms," 36–37.

43. Ibid., 17–18, 95–100.

44. Pickett, *House of Refuge,* v, 181–86.

CHAPTER SIX: CHILD SAVERS AND ST. LOUIS NEWSBOYS

1. Michael McGerr, *A Fierce Discontent: The Rise and Fall of the Progressive Movement in America, 1870–1920,* 107–13. See also Addams, *Spirit of Youth,* and Ora Aurilla Kelley, "The Newsboy Problem in St. Louis."

2. McGerr, *A Fierce Discontent,* 111–13; Abrams, *Very Special Place in Life,* 45–67.

See also Peter Romanofsky, "The Public Is Aroused: The Missouri Children's Code Commission, 1915–1919."

3. Berra, *Yogi,* 55; Nasaw, *Children of the City,* 62, 69–71. Nasaw notes that accurate statistical data on newsboys is difficult to obtain. Boys slipped in and out of the labor force. Parents and children often lied about their working on the street, especially when child-labor laws became stricter.

4. Nasaw, *Children of the City,* 66–68.

5. *St. Louis Post-Dispatch,* February 24, 1899.

6. United States Bureau of the Census, Twelfth Census, 1900, for the City of St. Louis, Microfilm Roll T623_895, p. 4–B, Enumeration District 246, and Thirteenth Census, 1910, Microfilm Roll T624_820, p. 13–B, Enumeration District 281.

7. Kelley, "Newsboy Problem in St. Louis," 21–29.

8. Ibid.; Nasaw, *Children of the City,* 62–63; United States Bureau of the Census, Thirteenth Census, 1910, vol. 2: *Population Reports by States* (Washington, D.C.: Government Printing Office, 1913), p. 1119. Census data for 1910 indicates that about 80 percent of St. Louis children aged six to nine and about 90 percent of St. Louis children aged ten to fourteen attended school, although these figures may be exaggerated and may reflect a tendency to lie about this to census takers.

9. Kelley, "Newsboy Problem in St. Louis," 4.

10. Ibid., 6–9.

11. Ibid., 9–11, 56–57.

12. Ibid., 12–14.

13. Ibid., 19, 17, 48, 75–76; Nasaw, *Children of the City,* 78–83. Of 507 newsboys surveyed in 1910, 42 (8 percent) were under ten years of age.

14. Kelley, "Newsboy Problem in St. Louis," 53–60.

15. *St. Louis Post-Dispatch,* August 2, 1896, and November 14, 1897; *St. Louis Globe-Democrat,* August 2, 1896.

16. *St. Louis Post-Dispatch,* August 2, 1896; *State of Missouri vs. Henry Clay,* judge's instructions to the jury, June 24, 1897, and notarized statement of Arthur Smith, July 29, 1897, St. Louis Court of Criminal Correction, Microfilmed Criminal Cases, C46920, Case Number 26, Missouri State Archives–St. Louis.

17. Grand Jury Indictment of Henry Clay for the Murder of William Amend, October 31, 1896, Case Number 26; United States Bureau of the Census, Tenth Census, 1880, for the City of St. Louis, Microfilm Roll T9_728, p. 624.1000, Enumeration District 81; *St. Louis Globe-Democrat,* August 2, 1896; *St. Louis Post-Dispatch,* August 3, 1896. Although certain court documents state that Amend lingered nearly a week before he died, the *St. Louis Post-Dispatch* carried a notice on August 3 giving the date of death as August 1 and announcing the funeral date as August 4.

18. Jury's Verdict, June 24, 1897, Record of the St. Louis Criminal Court, January 4, 1897, to February 5, 1898, Division 9, Circuit Court for Criminal Cases, p. 296, on file at the Missouri State Archives–St. Louis; *St. Louis Post-Dispatch,* August 2, 1896, and November 18, 1897.

19. *St. Louis Post-Dispatch,* November 14, 1897.

20. *St. Louis Globe-Democrat,* November 21, 1897.

21. Ibid., December 9, 1897.

22. Ibid., January 2, 1898.

23. Olds, *Trends in Child Dependency,* 21–24; Gormley, *History of Father Dunne's*

News Boys' Home, 47—48.

24. Gormley, *History of Father Dunne's News Boys' Home,* 10–24; John Rothensteiner, *History of the Archdiocese of St. Louis,* 2:653–54.

25. Gormley, *History of Father Dunne's News Boys' Home,* 37–50; Rothensteiner, *History of the Archdiocese,* 2:654; *St. Louis Globe-Democrat,* March 17, 1939. The 1900 census for St. Louis lists Dunne, age twenty-nine, as a student at Kenrick Seminary (Microfilm Roll T623_896, p. 6–B, Enumeration District 256).

26. Gormley, *History of Father Dunne's News Boys' Home,* 37–50; Rothensteiner, *History of the Archdiocese,* 2:652; *St. Louis Globe-Democrat,* March 17, 1939.

27. *St. Louis Globe-Democrat,* February 1, 1931; Rothensteiner, *History of the Archdiocese,* 2:652. Father Dunne's Home predated the much more famous Boys' Town, which was founded in Nebraska by Father Edward J. Flanagan in 1917.

28. *St. Louis Globe-Democrat,* February 1, 1931; Rothensteiner, *History of the Archdiocese,* 2:653.

29. Gormley, *History of Father Dunne's News Boys' Home,* 75–83.

30. United States Bureau of the Census, Thirteenth Census, 1910, for the City of St. Louis, Microfilm Roll T624_813, p. 11–A, Enumeration District 81. A list of the residents of Father Dunne's Newsboys' Home is found in the United States Bureau of the Census, Fourteenth Census, 1920, for the City of St. Louis, Microfilm Roll T625_956, p. 12–A, Enumeration District 338. A list of the residents of Father Dunne's Home is also found in the United States Bureau of the Census, Fifteenth Census, 1930, for the City of St. Louis, Microfilm Roll 1238, p. 1–A, Enumeration District 676.

31. List of residents of Father Dunne's Home, 1920 Census; *St. Louis Globe-Democrat,* March 17, 1939.

32. Gormley, *History of Father Dunne's News Boys' Home,* 87; United States Bureau of the Census, Thirteenth Census, 1910, for the City of St. Louis, Microfilm Roll T624_820, p. 11–B, Enumeration District 321; list of residents of Father Dunne's Home, 1920 Census.

33. United States Bureau of the Census, Fourteenth Census, 1920, for Rockwood, Pa., Microfilm Roll T625_1655, p. 4–B, Enumeration District 192; United States Bureau of the Census, Fifteenth Census, 1930, for the City of St. Louis, Microfilm Roll 1233, p. 18–B, Enumeration District 453; list of residents of Father Dunne's Home, 1930 Census.

34. Sharon Kinney Hanson, daughter of Raymond T. Kinney (1915–1999), telephone interview with the author, August 30, 2007.

35. Gormley, *History of Father Dunne's News Boys' Home,* 91, 120; United States Bureau of the Census, Thirteenth Census, 1910, for the City of St. Louis, Microfilm Roll T624_812, p. 14–B, Enumeration District 54; United States Bureau of the Census, Fourteenth Census, 1920, for the City of St. Louis, Microfilm Roll T625_950, p. 5–B, Enumeration District 118.

36. *St. Louis Globe-Democrat,* March 17, 1939. Gormley, *History of Father Dunne's News Boys' Home,* p. 158, listed the graduates of Father Dunne's who died in World War I as Andrew McAllister, Francis McGrath, Francis Bannon, Roy E. Brem, and Michael Euge.

37. Primm, *Lion of the Valley,* 441–42; *St. Louis Post-Dispatch,* August 3, 1931. For a discussion of segregation in St. Louis, see Lawrence O. Christensen, "Race Relations in St. Louis, 1865–1916." Christensen maintains that St. Louis was less

racially segregated than many southern cities.

38. *St. Louis Globe-Democrat,* March 17, 1939; clipping from the *St. Louis Post-Dispatch,* February ? [1940], on file at Father Dunne's Newsboys' Home.

39. Clipping from the *St. Louis Post-Dispatch,* February ? [1940], on file at Father Dunne's Home.

40. *St. Louis Post-Dispatch,* April 14, 1950, and undated clippings on file at Newsboys' Home. At the time of this research, the Newsboys' Home was located in Florissant, Missouri. It has since been closed.

41. Sharon Kinney Hanson interview, August 30, 2007.

42. Ibid.

CHAPTER SEVEN: CITY ON THE SKIDS

1. The Records of the Bureau for Men (1925–1982) are housed in the Western Historical Manuscripts Collection at the University of Missouri–St. Louis. The finding aid to this collection provides an excellent overview of the bureau and its work. These records will be cited as the Bureau for Men Records.

2. Wallace, *Skid Row,* 13–17, 18.

3. Harvey A. Siegel and James A. Inciardi, "The Demise of Skid Row," 39–40.

4. Wallace, *Skid Row,* 18, 125–38.

5. Sandweiss, "Construction and Community," 196, 200; Sandweiss, *St. Louis,* 190–93; Primm, *Lion of the Valley,* 390–93.

6. Primm, *Lion of the Valley,* 396–98.

7. *St. Louis Post-Dispatch,* May 8, 1910.

8. Frank Tobias Higbee, *Indispensable Outcasts: Hobo Workers and the Community in the American Midwest, 1880–1930,* 5, 10; *St. Louis Post-Dispatch,* May 8, 1910; Minehan, *Boy and Girl Tramps of America,* xiv–xv. Higbee has studied the subject of hoboes and found that the origins of the word *hobo* are obscure. Some people believe it came from the Latin *homo bonus,* or "good man." Others say it is a shortened form of "hoe boy," or agricultural worker. Another theory is that it was a version of the railroad workers' greeting "Hello, boy."

9. Higbee, *Indispensable Outcasts,* 102; *St. Louis Post-Dispatch,* May 8, 1910.

10. *St. Louis Post-Dispatch,* May 8, 1910.

11. Robert S. Wilson, *Community Planning for Homeless Men and Boys: The Experience of Sixteen Cities in the Winter of 1930–31,* 69–70; Bureau for Men Records, descriptive material in finding aid.

12. *St. Louis Globe-Democrat,* February 20, 1908.

13. Ibid., February 21, 1908.

14. *St. Louis Post-Dispatch,* January 28, 1911.

15. *St. Louis Globe-Democrat,* February 20, 1908; United States Bureau of the Census, Thirteenth Census, 1910, for the City of St. Louis, Microfilm Roll T624_817, p. 2–B, Enumeration District 211.

16. Mormino, *Immigrants on the Hill,* 138; Ed Reid, *The Grim Reapers: The Anatomy of Organized Crime in America,* 72; *St. Louis Star-Chronicle,* November 21, 1927.

17. Giovanni Schiavo, *The Italians in Missouri,* 59–66; Mormino, *Immigrants on the Hill,* 56–67; Primm, *Lion of the Valley,* 417–18.

18. Schiavo, *Italians in Missouri,* 59–66; Mormino, *Immigrants on the Hill,* 56–67;

Primm, *Lion of the Valley,* 417–18.

   19. Berra, *Yogi,* 37; Garagiola, *Baseball Is a Funny Game,* 14.

   20. Primm, *Lion of the Valley,* 418; Mormino, *Immigrants on the Hill,* 135–36.

   21. Scott H. Decker, Jeffrey J. Rojek, and Eric P. Baumer, "A Century-or-More of Homicide in St. Louis," in Brady Baybeck and E. Terrence Jones, eds., *St. Louis Metromorphosis: Past Trends and Future Directions,* 264–65.

   22. *St. Louis Globe-Democrat,* January 2, 1924; *St. Louis Post-Dispatch,* December 29, 1921, August 16, 1963, and March 30, 1965; Mormino, *Immigrants on the Hill,* 137–40; Frederic M. Thrasher, *The Gang: A Study of 1,313 Gangs in Chicago,* 118–19.

   23. Bureau for Men Records, Folder 80; Henrietta Additon, "Delinquency Prevention Measures in St. Louis," December 1935, on file in the Bureau for Men Records, Folder 85. According to Additon, of a total of 2,707 juvenile delinquency cases in St. Louis in 1930, 2,328 (86 percent) involved boys.

   24. Bureau for Homeless Men, "Analysis of 100 Cases of Homeless Boys, April 25, 1930," Bureau for Men Records, Folder 84.

   25. Ibid.; Isaac Gurman, "Case Work with Homeless Men and Boys," 32–34. Gurman was a caseworker and later an administrator for the Bureau for Men. He wrote a master's thesis entitled "An Analysis of the Techniques Employed in the Professional Care of Homeless Men at St. Louis during the Depression Years, and a Suggested Plan of Treatment" in 1935.

   26. Bureau for Men Records, Folder 83.

   27. Primm, *Lion of the Valley,* 441; Bureau for Men Records, Folder 6.

   28. Berry, *Autobiography,* 2–3, 20, 39, 49–72.

   29. A. E. Hotchner, *The Boyhood Memoirs of A. E. Hotchner: King of the Hill and Looking for Miracles,* 160–268.

   30. Primm, *Lion of the Valley,* 455–56.

   31. Martin G. Towey, "Hooverville: St. Louis Had the Largest," 4–11.

   32. Primm, *Lion of the Valley,* 458–59; Ron Fagerstrom, *Mill Creek Valley: A Soul of St. Louis,* 11; Eugene J. Meehan, *The Quality of Federal Policymaking: Programmed Failure in Public Housing,* 16, 58–59.

   33. Charles Hoch and Robert A. Slayton, *New Homeless and Old: Community and the Skid Row Hotel,* 172–75.

   34. Ann Douglas, "Punching a Hole in the Big Lie: The Achievement of William S. Burroughs."

   35. William S. Burroughs, "St. Louis Return," 264–66.

CHAPTER EIGHT: YOUNG MEN AND CRIMINAL GANGS

   1. Frederic M. Thrasher, "What Is a Gang?" 4–7.

   2. Whyte, *Street Corner Society,* 140–45.

   3. Ibid., 111.

   4. *St. Louis Globe-Democrat,* September 21, 1923.

   5. David A. Ruth, *Inventing the Public Enemy: The Gangster in American Culture, 1918–1934,* 50–53.

   6. Mormino, *Immigrants on the Hill,* 137–39; Waugh, *Egan's Rats,* 119.

   7. Katharine Darst, "St. Louis in the Twenties: The Girls Kept Their Shoes On," 52; Ruth, *Inventing the Public Enemy,* 45–47.

8. *St. Louis Post-Dispatch,* August 16, 1963, April 6, 1921, and September 10, 1923.

9. Ibid., December 29, 1921, and August 16, 1963.

10. Ibid., December 29, 1921; Waugh, *Egan's Rats,* 140.

11. *St. Louis Post-Dispatch,* December 29, 1921; Mormino, *Immigrants on the Hill,* 139; Waugh, *Egan's Rats,* 142–43.

12. Waugh, *Egan's Rats,* 129; *St. Louis Post-Dispatch,* September 17, 1923; United States Bureau of the Census, Thirteenth Census, 1910, for the City of St. Louis, Microfilm Roll T624_817, p. 7–A, Enumeration District 32; United States Bureau of the Census, Fourteenth Census, 1920, for the City of St. Louis, Microfilm Roll T625_955, Enumeration District 300. James Hennessy appeared in the records of the Juvenile Court on February 14, 1909.

13. Case Number 145, April 20, 1920, Circuit Court of the City of St. Louis, on file at the Missouri State Archives–St. Louis.

14. *St. Louis Post-Dispatch,* December 29, 1921, August 16, 1963, and March 30, 1965; Mormino, *Immigrants on the Hill,* 137–40; Thrasher, *The Gang,* 118–19; *St. Louis Post-Dispatch,* September 10, 1923; *St. Louis Globe-Democrat,* January 2, 1924.

15. *St. Louis Post-Dispatch,* September 10 and 13, 1923.

16. Ibid., September 10, 1923.

17. Ibid., September 10 and 13, 1923.

18. Ibid., September 14, 1923.

19. Ibid., September 13, 1923.

20. Ibid., September 13 and 17, 1923; *St. Louis Globe-Democrat,* September 17, 1923.

21. Waugh, *Egan's Rats,* 129–30; *St. Louis Post-Dispatch,* September 18, 1923; *St. Louis Globe-Democrat,* September 17, 1923.

22. *St. Louis Post-Dispatch,* September 18, 1923; *St. Louis Globe-Democrat,* September 17, 1923.

23. *St. Louis Globe-Democrat,* September 17, 1923.

24. Waugh, *Egan's Rats,* 202–3.

25. *St. Louis Globe-Democrat,* January 2, 1924; Mormino, *Immigrants on the Hill,* 139.

26. *St. Louis Post-Dispatch,* September 11, 1927; Waugh, *Egan's Rats,* 128; *St. Louis Post-Dispatch,* September 9, 1927.

27. *St. Louis Post-Dispatch,* September 9, 1927.

28. Ibid., September 11, 1927; *St. Louis Globe-Democrat,* November 28, 1927.

29. Ibid.

30. Ibid., November 20, 1927.

31. Ibid.

32. Ibid.

33. Ibid.; United States Bureau of the Census, Fifteenth Census, 1930, for Jefferson City, Cole County, Mo., Microfilm Roll T626_1184, Enumeration District 6; Waugh, *Egan's Rats,* 129.

34. *St. Louis Globe-Democrat,* November 26, 1927.

35. Ibid.

36. United States Bureau of the Census, Fourteenth Census, 1920, for the City of St. Louis, Microfilm Roll T625_949, p. 7–A, Enumeration District 140; United States Bureau of the Census, Fifteenth Census, 1930, for the City of St. Louis,

Microfilm Roll 1230, p. 7–B, Enumeration District 380.

37. *St. Louis Globe-Democrat,* November 27, 1927.

38. *St. Louis Post-Dispatch,* November 22, 1930; Waugh, *Egan's Rats,* 212.

39. *St. Louis Post-Dispatch,* November 22, 1930.

40. Whyte, *Street Corner Society,* 111; Mormino, *Immigrants on the Hill,* 140.

41. Whyte, *Street Corner Society,* 255–59.

CHAPTER NINE: A NEW DEAL FOR HOMELESS YOUTH

1. Lewis L. Lorwin's *Youth Work Programs: Problems and Policies* describes the New Deal philosophy and discusses specific programs, including the Civilian Conservation Corps (CCC) and the National Youth Administration (NYA).

2. *St. Louis Post-Dispatch,* October 17, 1933. Strangely enough, the luckless James Riordan had been involved in a previous accident, in April 1933, when he and a companion slid into a sand pit. Riordan was able to pull himself out, but his young friend, Neil Y. Muench, died.

3. Errol Lincoln Uys, *Riding the Rails: Teenagers on the Move during the Great Depression,* 11–13; *St. Louis Post-Dispatch,* January 1, 1933; Nels Anderson, *Men on the Move,* 66.

4. Department of Delinquency and Its Prevention, St. Louis Community Council, "Report of Committee on Migrant Boys," September 20, 1933, Bureau for Men Records, Folder 310.

5. Uys, *Riding the Rails,* 32–33, 104–5.

6. *St. Louis Post-Dispatch,* October 19, 1933.

7. Anderson, *Men on the Move,* 93–98.

8. Wilson, *Community Planning for Homeless Men and Boys,* 71–77.

9. Ibid., 73–75.

10. *New York Times,* November 19, 1933; "Men of St. Louis: A Monthly Bulletin of Information Regarding Resident Non-Family Men," vol. 1, no. 1 (June 1935), on file in Bureau for Men Records, Folder 12. Dempsey died in 1936. His obituary appeared in the *St. Louis Post-Dispatch* on April 6, 1936.

11. Minehan, *Boy and Girl Tramps,* 253–60.

12. Ibid., 67–70.

13. Ibid., 80–91.

14. Ibid., 54–63.

15. Nels Anderson, *On Hobos and Homelessness,* 43.

16. Uys, *Riding the Rails,* 34, 180–84.

17. Department of Delinquency and Its Prevention, "Report of Committee on Migrant Boys."

18. Ibid.

19. Minehan, *Boy and Girl Tramps,* 169.

20. Anderson, *On Hobos and Homelessness,* 109–15.

21. Uys, *Riding the Rails,* 17; editorial, *New York Times,* August 4, 1933.

22. Kingsley Davis, *Youth in the Depression,* 8.

23. Ibid., 12–24.

24. *St. Louis Post-Dispatch,* January 1, 1933.

25. Ibid.

26. Ibid., January 4, 1933.

27. Ibid.; United States Bureau of the Census, Fourteenth Census, 1920, for the City of St. Louis, Microfilm Roll T625_960. p. 7–A, Enumeration District 473; United States Bureau of the Census, Fifteenth Census, 1930, for the City of St. Louis, Microfilm Roll 1241, p. 10–A, Enumeration District 581.

28. *St. Louis Post-Dispatch,* January 4, 1933.

29. Ibid.

30. Case Number 55, filed April 27, 1933, Judgment, January 12, 1934, Circuit Court of the City of St. Louis, Division 12, records on file at the Missouri State Archives–St. Louis.

31. Case Number 54, April Term 1933, Circuit Court of the City of St. Louis, Division 12.

32. United States Bureau of the Census, Fifteenth Census, 1930, for the City of St. Louis, Microfilm Roll 1245, p. 9–B, Enumeration District 226, and Microfilm Roll 1241, p. 10–A, Enumeration District 581.

33. Reiman, *New Deal and American Youth,* 24–25.

34. Perry H. Merrill, *Roosevelt's Forest Army: A History of the Civilian Conservation Corps, 1933–1942,* 2–11, 144–45.

35. Ibid., 11–14.

36. Ibid.

37. Holland and Hill, *Youth in the CCC,* 58–90.

38. Ibid., 126–32.

39. Archie Moore, *Any Boy Can,* 121–26; excerpted in Gerald Early, ed., *Ain't But a Place: An Anthology of African American Writings about St. Louis,* 87–88.

40. Ibid., 126–28.

41. Bureau for Men Records, Folder 311–A; Davis, *Youth in the Depression,* 31–33.

42. Bureau for Men Records, Folders 6, 12, 17.

43. Reiman, *New Deal and American Youth,* 121, 186–88; Davis, *Youth in the Depression,* 41–43; Lorwin, *Youth Work Programs,* 3.

44. Bonnie Stepenoff, "The New Deal's Camp Sherwood Forest: An Incubator of Democracy," 52–55.

45. Ibid., 56–57.

46. Ibid., 57–58.

47. Ibid., 58.

48. Ibid., 58–59.

49. National Archives and Records Administration, Record Group 64, U.S. World War II Army Enlistment Records, 1938–1946, database online accessed through Ancestry.com (microfilm, Provo, Utah: Generations Network, 2005).

50. See Despotis, Korte, and Lary, *Victory through Valor,* and Bennett, *When Dreams Came True.*

CHAPTER TEN: YOUTH AND THE CHANGING CITY STREETS

1. Bennett, *When Dreams Came True,* 302. Liston's story has been told often in print.

2. Auble, *History of St. Louis Gangsters,* 88–89; Tosches, *The Devil and Sonny Liston,* 37–40; Young, *Sonny Liston,* 52–56.

3. Auble, *History of St. Louis Gangsters,* 89–99.

4. Young, *Sonny Liston,* 2–3; Tosches, *The Devil and Sonny Liston,* 201–2, 240–41.

5. Turner, "On Boyhood and Public Swimming," 216; Wallace, *Skid Row,* 22–23.

6. Primm, *Lion of the Valley,* 458–60.

7. Meehan, *Quality of Federal Policymaking,* 58–59.

8. *New York Times,* September 26, 1951.

9. Ibid., July 22, 1952. Benjamin Fine, education editor of the *New York Times,* wrote a book about the problem entitled *1,000,000 Delinquents* (1955).

10. Richard S. Kirkendall, *A History of Missouri,* 5:257.

11. *St. Louis Post-Dispatch,* July 21 and July 22, 1955.

12. Ibid., July 23, 1955.

13. Ibid., July 27, 1955.

14. Ibid., July 30, 1955.

15. Ibid., December 22, 1959.

16. Ibid., December 23, 1959.

17. Selwyn K. Troen and Glenn E. Holt, eds., *St. Louis,* 202–6; Kirkendall, *History of Missouri,* 5:294; Mary Kimbrough and Margaret W. Dagen, *Victory without Violence: The First Ten Years of the St. Louis Committee of Racial Equality (CORE), 1947–1957,* 41–43; Sue Dubman, *Poverty in St. Louis,* 61.

18. Primm, *Lion of the Valley,* 467.

19. Troen and Holt, *St. Louis,* 202–6; Kimbrough and Dagen, *Victory without Violence,* 41–43; Primm, *Lion of the Valley,* 476.

20. Meehan, *Quality of Federal Policymaking,* 66–68.

21. Ibid., 68.

22. Primm, *Lion of the Valley,* 485.

23. Fagerstrom, *Mill Creek Valley,* 22.

24. Troen and Holt, *St. Louis,* 202–6; Primm, *Lion of the Valley,* 468.

25. Bonita H. Valien, *The St. Louis Story: A Study of Desegregation,* 17.

26. Ibid., 11–12.

27. Ibid., 14–15.

28. Ibid., 19, 21.

29. Ibid., 37–39.

30. Troen and Holt, *St. Louis,* 202–6; Kenneth B. Clark, *Dark Ghetto: Dilemmas of Social Power,* 23–27.

31. Meehan, *Quality of Federal Policymaking,* 45, 66–72; Lee Rainwater, *Behind Ghetto Walls: Black Families in a Federal Slum,* 10.

32. Rainwater, *Behind Ghetto Walls,* 10–11, 101–3.

33. See Scott H. Decker and Barrik Van Winkle, *Life in the Gang.*

34. Rainwater, *Behind Ghetto Walls,* 282–83, 286–92.

35. Ibid., 167. It is worth noting here that in the half century between 1950 and 2000, the percentage of households headed by married couples in St. Louis decreased from 78 percent to 26 percent. In St. Louis County, the number of households of married couples declined from 90 percent to 51 percent. This was a national trend; however, it was much more pronounced in the central city. See Lois Pierce, "Family and Household Types, 1950 to 2000: Where Have All the Cleavers Gone?" in Baybeck and Jones, eds., *St. Louis Metromorphosis,* 235–56.

36. Walter B. Miller, "Lower Class Culture as a Generating Milieu of Gang Delinquency," 262–63.

37. Ibid., 263–64.
38. Ibid., 264–65.
39. Rainwater, *Behind Ghetto Walls*, 288–89.
40. Young, *Sonny Liston*, 50.

EPILOGUE

1. William Pollack, *Real Boys: Rescuing Our Sons from the Myths of Boyhood*, 44–46.
2. Ibid., 340–41.

BOOKS, ARTICLES, DISSERTATIONS, AND THESES

Abrams, Douglas E. *A Very Special Place in Life: The History of Juvenile Justice in Missouri.* Jefferson City: Missouri Juvenile Justice Association, 2003.

Addams, Jane. *The Spirit of Youth and the City Streets.* Urbana: University of Illinois Press, 1972.

Anderson, Nels. *Men on the Move.* New York: Da Capo Press, 1974, reprint of 1940 edition.

————. *On Hobos and Homelessness,* ed. Raffaele Rauty. Chicago: University of Chicago Press, 1998.

Atherton, Lewis. *The Cattle Kings.* Bloomington: Indiana University Press, 1961.

Auble, John. *A History of St. Louis Gangsters.* St. Louis: National Criminal Research Society, 2000.

Baker, James F. "The St. Louis and Suburban Streetcar Strike of 1900." *Missouri Historical Review* 101, no. 4 (July 2007): 226–36.

Bartholomew, Harland. *Problems of St. Louis.* St. Louis: Nixon-Jones, 1917.

Baybeck, Brady, and E. Terrence Jones, eds. *St. Louis Metromorphosis: Past Trends and Future Directions.* St. Louis: Missouri Historical Society Press, 2004.

Beaumont, Gustave de, and Alexis de Tocqueville. *On the Penitentiary System in the United States and Its Application in France.* Carbondale: Southern Illinois University Press, 1964, reprint of 1833 edition.

Bennett, Michael J. *When Dreams Came True: The GI Bill and the Making of Modern America.* Washington, D.C.: Brassey's, 1996.

Berra, Yogi, and Ed Fitzgerald. *Yogi: The Autobiography of a Professional Baseball Player.* Garden City, N.Y.: Doubleday, 1961.

Berry, Chuck. *Autobiography.* London: Faber and Faber, 1988.

Brown, Thomas J. *Dorothea Dix: New England Reformer.* Cambridge, Mass.: Harvard University Press, 1998.

Burbank, David. *Reign of the Rabble: The St. Louis General Strike of 1877.* New York: Augustus M. Kelly, 1966.

Burroughs, William S. Prologue to *Junky,* reprinted in *Word Virus: The William S. Burroughs Reader,* ed. James Grauerholz and Ira Silverberg. New York: Grove Press, 1998.

———. "St. Louis Return," from *The Burroughs File,* reprinted in *Word Virus: The William S. Burroughs Reader,* ed. James Grauerholz and Ira Silverberg. New York: Grove Press, 1998.

Christensen, Lawrence O. "Race Relations in St. Louis, 1865–1916." *Missouri Historical Review* 78, no. 2 (January 1984): 123–36.

Clark, Kenneth B. *Dark Ghetto: Dilemmas of Social Power.* New York: Harper and Row, 1965.

Corbett, Katharine T. *In Her Place: A Guide to St. Louis Women's History.* St. Louis: Missouri Historical Society Press, 1999.

Curzon, Julian. *The Great Cyclone at St. Louis and East St. Louis, May 27, 1896.* Carbondale: Southern Illinois University Press, 1997.

Dacus, J. A., and James W. Buel. *A Tour of St. Louis; or, The Inside Life of a Great City.* St. Louis, 1878.

Darst, Katharine. "St. Louis in the Twenties: The Girls Kept Their Shoes On." *Missouri Historical Society Bulletin* 14, no. 1 (October 1957): 45–47.

Davis, Kingsley. "Adolescence and the Social Structure." In *Adolescents in Wartime,* ed. James H. S. Bossard and Eleanor S. Boll, 8–16. New York: Arno Press, 1974, reprint of 1944 edition.

———. *Youth in the Depression.* Chicago: University of Chicago Press, 1935.

Decker, Scott H., and Barrik Van Winkle. *Life in the Gang.* Cambridge, Eng.: Cambridge University Press, 1996.

DePastino, Todd. *Citizen Hobo: How a Century of Homelessness Shaped America.* Chicago: University of Chicago Press, 2003.

Despotis, George J., Donald E. Korte, and Matthew Lary, eds. *Victory through Valor: A Collection of World War II Memories.* St. Louis: Reedy Press, 2008.

Deutsch, Albert. *Our Rejected Children.* Boston: Little, Brown, 1950.

Dickens, Charles. *American Notes: A Journey.* New York: Fromm International Publishing Corporation, 1985.

———. *Oliver Twist.* Mineola, N.Y.: Dover Publishing, 2002.

Douglas, Ann. "Punching a Hole in the Big Lie: The Achievement of William S. Burroughs." In *Word Virus: The William S. Burroughs Reader,* ed. James Grauerholz and Ira Silverberg, xv–xix. New York: Grove Press, 1998.

Downs, Susan Whitelaw, and Michael W. Sherraden. "The Orphan Asylum in the Nineteenth Century." *Social Service Review* 57, no. 2 (June 1983): 272–90.

Doyle, Sir Arthur Conan. *The Celebrated Cases of Sherlock Holmes.* London: Longmeadow Press, 1981.

Dreiser, Theodore. *A Book about Myself.* New York: Boni and Liveright, 1922.

Dubman, Sue. *Poverty in St. Louis.* St. Louis: Center of Community and Metropolitan Studies, University of Missouri–St. Louis, 1973.

Early, Gerald, ed. *Ain't But a Place: An Anthology of African American Writings about St. Louis.* St. Louis: Missouri Historical Society Press, 1998.

Edson, D. L. "Neglected and Dependent Children in Missouri." In the *10th Biennial Report of the State Board of Charities and Corrections of Missouri, 1915–1916,* 201–7. Jefferson City, Mo.: Hugh Stephens Printing Co., 1916.

Ehrlich, Walter. *Zion in the Valley: The Jewish Community of St. Louis.* Vol. 2, *The Twentieth Century.* Columbia: University of Missouri Press, 2002.

Eliot, Charlotte C. *William Greenleaf Eliot: Minister, Educator, Philanthropist.* Boston: Houghton Mifflin, 1904.

Faden, Regina M. "The German St. Vincent Orphan Home: The Institution and Its Role in the Immigrant German Catholic Community of St. Louis, 1850–1900." Ph.D. diss., Saint Louis University, 2000.

Fagerstrom, Ron. *Mill Creek Valley: A Soul of St. Louis.* St. Louis: privately printed, 2000.

Faherty, William Barnaby. *St. Louis German Catholics.* St. Louis: Reedy Press, 2004.

Father Dunne's Newsboys' Home *Bulletin,* Winter 1981. Father Dunne's Newsboys' Home, Florissant, Mo.

Fighting Father Dunne. RKO Pictures, 1948. Videotape by Turner Home Entertainment.

Fine, Benjamin. *1,000,000 Delinquents.* Cleveland: World, 1955.

Fisher, Linda A. "A Summer of Terror: Cholera in St. Louis, 1849." *Missouri Historical Review* 99, no. 3 (April 2005): 189–211.

Foley, William E., and C. David Rice. *The First Chouteaus: River Barons of Early St. Louis.* Urbana: University of Illinois Press, 1983.

Folks, Homer. *The Care of Destitute, Neglected, and Delinquent Children.* New York: Arno Press, 1971, reprint of 1900 edition.

Garagiola, Joe. *Baseball Is a Funny Game.* Philadelphia: Lippincott, 1960.

Gerteis, Louis S. *Civil War St. Louis.* Lawrence: University Press of Kansas, 2001.

Gilfoyle, Timothy J. *A Pickpocket's Tale*. New York: Norton, 2006.

————. "Street-rats and Gutter-snipes: Child Pickpockets and Street Culture in New York City." *Journal of Social History* 37, no. 4: 853–82.

Gormley, J. W. *History of Father Dunne's News Boys' Home and Protectorate*. St. Louis: Father Dunne's Newsboys' Home, [1927?].

Greenstone, J. David. "Dorothea Dix and Jane Addams: From Transcendentalism to Pragmatism in American Social Reform." *Social Service Review* 53, no. 4 (1979): 527–59.

Greenwood, Peggy Thomson. "Beyond the Orphanage." *St. Louis Genealogical Society Quarterly* 24, no. 4 (Winter 1991): 103–7.

————. "The House of Refuge." *St. Louis Genealogical Society Quarterly* 25, no. 2 (Summer 1992): 45.

Guinn, Lisa G. "Building Useful Women from the Depths of Poverty: A Social History of the Girls' Industrial Home and School in St. Louis, Missouri, 1853–1935." Ph.D. diss., Oklahoma State University, 2003.

————. "Building Useful Women from the Depths of Poverty: The Founding and Establishment of the Girls' Industrial Home and School in St. Louis, 1853–1916." *Missouri Historical Review* 100, no. 3 (April 2006): 125–40.

Gurman, Isaac. "An Analysis of the Techniques Employed in the Professional Care of Homeless Men at St. Louis during the Depression Years, and a Suggested Plan of Treatment." Master's thesis, Saint Louis University, 1935.

————. "Case Work with Homeless Men and Boys." St. Louis: Bureau for Homeless Men, 1936.

Higbee, Frank Tobias. *Indispensable Outcasts: Hobo Workers and the Community in the American Midwest, 1880–1930*. Urbana: University of Illinois Press, 2003.

Hoch, Charles, and Robert A. Slayton. *New Homeless and Old: Community and the Skid Row Hotel*. Philadelphia: Temple University Press, 1989.

Holland, Antonio F. "African-Americans in Henry Shaw's St. Louis." In *St. Louis in the Century of Henry Shaw*, ed. Eric Sandweiss, 51–78. St. Louis: Missouri Historical Society Press, 2002.

Holland, Kenneth, and Frank Ernest Hill. *Youth in the CCC*. New York: Arno Press, 1974, reprint of 1942 edition.

Holt, Marilyn Irvin. *The Orphan Trains: Placing Out in America*. Lincoln: University of Nebraska Press, 1992.

Hotchner, A. E. *The Boyhood Memoirs of A. E. Hotchner: King of the Hill and*

Looking for Miracles. St. Louis: Missouri Historical Society Press, 2007.

Hugo, Victor. *Les Miserables.* Philadelphia: George Barrie, 1983.

Hunt, Marion. "Women and Child Saving: St. Louis Children's Hospital, 1879–1979." Pt. 1. *Missouri Historical Society Bulletin* 36, no. 2 (1980): 65–79.

Hurley, Andrew, ed. *Common Fields: An Environmental History of St. Louis.* St. Louis: Missouri Historical Society Press, 1997.

Hyde, William, and Howard L. Conard. *Encyclopedia of the History of St. Louis.* Vol. 2. New York: Southern History Company, 1899.

Johnson, Palmer O., and Oswald L. Harvey. *The National Youth Administration.* Washington, D.C.: Government Printing Office, 1938.

Jonquet, Eugene Maurice. "A History of Bellefontaine Farms from 1853 to 1938." Master's thesis, Washington University, St. Louis, 1938.

Kamphoefner, Walter. "Learning from the Majority-Minority City: Immigration in Nineteenth Century St. Louis." In *St. Louis in the Century of Henry Shaw,* ed. Eric Sandweiss, 79–102. St. Louis: Missouri Historical Society Press, 2002.

Kelley, Ora Aurilla. "The Newsboy Problem in St. Louis." Master's thesis, Washington University School of Social Economy, St. Louis, 1912.

Kimbrough, Mary. *He Who Helps a Child: The Children's Home Society of Missouri: Its First 100 Years.* St. Louis: Patrice Press, 1991.

———. *125 Years of Caring: A History of Family and Children's Services of Greater St. Louis, 1860–1985.* St. Louis: The Service, 1985.

Kimbrough, Mary, and Margaret W. Dagen. *Victory without Violence: The First Ten Years of the St. Louis Committee of Racial Equality (CORE), 1947–1957.* Columbia: University of Missouri Press, 2000.

Kingsley, Sidney. *Dead End: A Play in Three Acts.* New York: Random House, 1936.

Kirkendall, Richard S. *A History of Missouri.* Vol. 5, *1919–1953.* Columbia: University of Missouri Press, 1986.

Koenig, Evelyn Roberts. "The History of the Episcopal Home for Children in St. Louis, 1843–1935." Ph.D. diss., Washington University, St. Louis, 1935.

Kusmer, Kenneth L. *Down and Out, On the Road: The Homeless in American History.* New York: Oxford University Press, 2002.

Landau, Gaylord E. "A History of the St. Louis Board of Children's Guardians in Relation to the Care of Dependent and Neglected Children from 1912–1938." Ph.D. diss., Washington University, St. Louis, 1939.

Ling, Huping. *Chinese St. Louis: From Enclave to Cultural Community*. Philadelphia: Temple University Press, 2004.

Lorwin, Lewis L. *Youth Work Programs: Problems and Policies*. Washington, D.C.: American Council on Education, 1941.

Mayhew, Henry. *London Labor and the London Poor*. New York: Dover, 1968.

McAuliffe, Harold J. *Father Tim*. Milwaukee: Bruce, 1944.

McGerr, Michael. *A Fierce Discontent: The Rise and Fall of the Progressive Movement in America, 1870–1920*. New York: Oxford University Press, 2003.

McGuire, John M. "A Morning in the Cave." *St. Louis Post-Dispatch Magazine*, Sunday, July 28, 1996, 7–9.

McLear, Patrick E. "The St. Louis Cholera Epidemic of 1849." *Missouri Historical Review* 63, no. 2 (January 1969): 171–81.

Meehan, Eugene J. *The Quality of Federal Policymaking: Programmed Failure in Public Housing*. Columbia: University of Missouri Press, 1979.

Merrill, Perry H. *Roosevelt's Forest Army: A History of the Civilian Conservation Corps, 1933–1942*. Montpelier, Vt.: Author, 1981.

Miller, Walter B. "Lower Class Culture as a Generating Milieu of Gang Delinquency." In *Classics of Criminology*, 3rd ed., ed. Joseph E. Jacoby. Long Grove, Ill.: Waveland Press, 2004.

Minehan, Thomas. *Boy and Girl Tramps of America*. Seattle: University of Washington Press, 1976, reprint of 1934 edition.

Moore, Archie. *Any Boy Can: The Archie Moore Story*. Englewood Cliffs, N.J.: Prentice-Hall, 1971.

Mormino, Gary Ross. *Immigrants on the Hill: Italian-Americans in St. Louis, 1882–1982*. Columbia: University of Missouri Press, 2002.

Morris, Ann N. "The History of the St. Louis Protestant Orphan Asylum." Pt. 1. *Missouri Historical Society Bulletin* 36, no. 2 (January 1980): 80–91.

Nasaw, David. *Children of the City: At Work and at Play*. Garden City, N.Y.: Doubleday, 1985.

Olds, Edward. *Trends in Child Dependency in St. Louis, 1860–1944*. St. Louis: Social Planning Council of St. Louis and St. Louis County, 1946.

Pickett, Robert S. *House of Refuge: Origins of Juvenile Reform in New York State, 1815–1857*. Syracuse, N.Y.: Syracuse University Press, 1969.

Pierce, B. K. *A Half Century with Juvenile Delinquents; or, The New York House of Refuge and Its Times*. New York: D. Appleton, 1869.

Pike, E. Royston. *Human Documents of the Victorian Golden Age, 1850–1873*. London: Allen and Unwin, 1967.

Piott, Steven L. "Modernization and the Anti-Monopoly Issue: The St.

Louis Transit Strike of 1900." *Missouri Historical Society Bulletin* 35 (October 1987): 8–15.

Pisciotta, Alexander W. "Treatment on Trial: The Rhetoric and Reality of the New York House of Refuge, 1837–1935." *American Journal of Legal History* 29, no. 2 (1985): 151–81.

Pollack, William. *Real Boys: Rescuing Our Sons from the Myths of Boyhood.* New York: Henry Holt, 1999.

Primm, James Neal. *Lion of the Valley: St. Louis, Missouri, 1764–1980.* 3rd ed. St. Louis: Missouri Historical Society Press, 1998.

Puffer, J. Adams. *The Boy and His Gang.* Boston: Houghton Mifflin, 1912.

Putzel, Max. *The Man in the Mirror: William Marion Reedy and His Magazine.* Columbia: University of Missouri Press, 1998.

Rainwater, Lee. *Behind Ghetto Walls: Black Families in a Federal Slum.* Chicago: Aldine, 1970.

Ray, Jo Colay. *These Little Ones: The History of the Missouri Baptist Children's Home.* Missouri Baptist Children's Home, 1986.

Reid, Ed. *The Grim Reapers: The Anatomy of Organized Crime in America.* Chicago: Henry Regnery, 1969.

Reiman, Richard A. *The New Deal and American Youth: Ideas and Ideals in a Depression Decade.* Athens: University of Georgia Press, 1992.

Review of Famous Crimes Solved by St. Louis Policemen. St. Louis: Moinster Printing, n.d.

Romanofsky, Peter. "The Public Is Aroused: The Missouri Children's Code Commission, 1915–1919." *Missouri Historical Review* 68, no. 2 (January 1974): 204–22.

Rothensteiner, John. *History of the Archdiocese of St. Louis.* Vol. 2. St. Louis, 1928.

Rother, Hubert, and Charlotte Rother. *Lost Caves of St. Louis: A History of the City's Forgotten Caves.* St. Louis: Virginia Publishing, 1996.

Rumbold, Charlotte. *Housing Conditions in St. Louis: Report of the Housing Committee of the Civic League of St. Louis.* St. Louis: Civic League, 1908.

Ruth, David A. *Inventing the Public Enemy: The Gangster in American Culture, 1918–1934.* Chicago: University of Chicago Press, 1996.

Ryan, Christine V. "Work of the Board of Children's Guardians with Delinquent Boys at Bellefontaine Farms." Master's thesis, Saint Louis University, 1937.

Sandweiss, Eric. "Construction and Community in South St. Louis, 1850–1910." Ph.D. diss., University of California–Berkeley, 1991.

———. *St. Louis: The Evolution of an American Urban Landscape.* Philadelphia: Temple University Press, 2001.

Scharnhorst, Gary. *Horatio Alger, Jr.* Boston: Twayne Publishers, 1980.

Schiavo, Giovanni. *The Italians in Missouri.* New York: Arno Press, 1975, reprint of 1929 edition.

Settle, William A., Jr. *Jesse James Was His Name; or, Fact and Fiction concerning the Career of the Notorious James Brothers of Missouri.* Columbia: University of Missouri Press, 1967.

Siegel, Harvey, and James A. Inciardi. "The Demise of Skid Row." *Society* 19, no. 2 (January 1982): 39–45.

Skinner, Mary, and Alice Scott Nutt. "Adolescents Away from Home." In *Adolescents in Wartime,* ed. James H. S. Bossard and Eleanor S. Boll, 51–59. New York: Arno Press, 1974, reprint of 1944 edition.

Spencer, Thomas. *The St. Louis Veiled Prophet Celebration: Power on Parade, 1877–1995.* Columbia: University of Missouri Press, 2000.

Stepenoff, Bonnie. "The New Deal's Camp Sherwood Forest: An Incubator of Democracy." *Gateway Heritage* 11, no. 3 (Winter 1990–1991): 52–59.

"Summer Beer Gardens of St. Louis." Pt. 1. *Missouri Historical Society Bulletin* 9, no. 4 (July 1933): 391–92.

Teeters, Negley K. "The Early Days of the Philadelphia House of Refuge." *Pennsylvania History* 27, no. 2 (April 1960): 49–65.

Thrasher, Frederic M. *The Gang: A Study of 1,313 Gangs in Chicago.* Abridged ed. Chicago: University of Chicago Press, 1963.

———. "What Is a Gang?" Reprinted in *Classics of Criminology,* ed. Joseph E. Jacoby. Long Grove, Ill.: Waveland Press, 2004.

Thurston, Henry W. *The Dependent Child: A Story of Changing Aims and Methods in the Care of Dependent Children.* New York: Columbia University Press, 1930.

Tosches, Nick. *The Devil and Sonny Liston.* Boston: Little, Brown, 2000.

Towey, Martin G. "Hooverville: St. Louis Had the Largest." *Gateway Heritage* 1, no. 2 (Fall 1980): 2–11.

Troen, Selwyn K., and Glenn E. Holt, eds. *St. Louis.* New York: New Viewpoints, 1977.

Turner, Jeffrey. "On Boyhood and Public Swimming: Sidney Kingsley's *Dead End* and Representations of Underclass Street Kids in American Cultural Production." In *The American Child: A Cultural Studies Reader,* ed. Caroline F. Levander and Carol J. Singley, 208–25. New Brunswick, N.J.: Rutgers University Press, 2003.

Twain, Mark. *The Adventures of Huckleberry Finn.* New York: Modern Library, 2001.

———. *The Adventures of Tom Sawyer.* In *The Works of Mark Twain.* Vol.

4, ed. John C. Gerber, Paul Baender, and Terry Firkins. Berkeley: University of California Press, 1980.

————. *Life on the Mississippi.* New York: Dover, 2000.

Uys, Errol Lincoln. *Riding the Rails: Teenagers on the Move during the Great Depression.* New York: Routledge, 2003.

Valien, Bonita H. *The St. Louis Story: A Study of Desegregation.* New York: Anti-Defamation League of B'Nai B'rith, 1956.

Vollmar, Helen D., and Joseph E. Vollmar, Jr. "Caves, Tunnels and Other Holes under St. Louis." *Gateway Heritage* 8, no. 2 (Fall 1987): 1–7.

Wagner, Gillian. *Barnardo.* London: Weidenfeld and Nicolson, 1979.

Wallace, Samuel E. *Skid Row as a Way of Life.* Totowa, N.J.: Bedminster Press, 1965.

Waugh, Daniel. *Egan's Rats: The Untold Story of the Prohibition-Era Gang That Ruled St. Louis.* Nashville: Cumberland House, 2007.

White, Frederick. "History of St. Joseph's Home for Boys." Master's thesis, Saint Louis University, 1949.

Whyte, William Foote. *Street Corner Society: The Social Structure of an Italian Slum.* Chicago: University of Chicago Press, 1943.

Wilson, Robert S. *Community Planning for Homeless Men and Boys: The Experience of Sixteen Cities in the Winter of 1930–31.* New York: Welfare Association of America, 1931.

Winget, Martha Osborn. "History of the St. Louis Protestant Orphans' Home, 1834–1870." Master's thesis, Washington University, St. Louis, 1943.

Wright, John A. *Discovering African-American St. Louis: A Guide to Historic Sites.* St. Louis: Missouri Historical Society Press, 1994.

Young, A. S. *Sonny Liston: The Champ Nobody Wanted.* Chicago: Johnson, 1963.

Young, Andrew D. *The St. Louis Streetcar Story.* Glendale, Calif.: Interurban Press, 1988.

Young, Diana M. "The St. Louis Streetcar Strike of 1900." *Gateway Heritage* 11 (Summer 1991): 4–17.

MANUSCRIPT COLLECTIONS, ORAL SOURCES, AND PUBLIC RECORDS

Breckenridge, William Clark. Papers. Missouri Historical Society, St. Louis.

Bureau for Men (1925–1982). Records, 1920–1981. Western Historical Manuscripts Collection, University of Missouri–St. Louis.

Children's Aid Society, St. Louis. *Report,* 1887. Missouri Historical Society, St. Louis.

Hanson, Sharon Kinney. Telephone interview with the author, August 30, 2007.

Missouri State Board of Health, Bureau of Vital Statistics. Death Certificate Number 10553. Missouri State Archives.

National Archives and Records Administration. World War II Army Enlistment Records, 1938–1946. Online database. Provo, Utah: The Generations Network, Inc., 2005.

St. Louis, City of, Circuit Court. Case File Number 125, December Term, 1897. Missouri State Archives–St. Louis.

St. Louis, City of, Circuit Court. Case File Number 145. Missouri State Archives–St. Louis.

St. Louis, City of, Circuit Court. Division Twelve, Case Number 54, April Term 1933. Missouri State Archives–St. Louis.

St. Louis, City of, Circuit Court. Division Twelve, Case Number 55, filed April 27, 1933, Judgment, January 12, 1934. Missouri State Archives–St. Louis.

St. Louis, City of, Circuit Court for Criminal Cases. Division Nine. Record Book, January 4, 1897–February 5, 1898. Missouri State Archives–St. Louis.

St. Louis, City of, Court of Criminal Correction. Microfilmed Criminal Cases, C46920, Case Number 26. Missouri State Archives–St. Louis.

St. Louis, City of, Criminal Court Issues Book, 1872. Missouri State Archives–St. Louis.

St. Louis, City of, Juvenile Court. Probation Officer's Report, Appendix to the House and Senate Journals of the 44th Missouri General Assembly. Jefferson City, Mo.: Hugh Stephens Printing Company, 1907.

St. Louis House of Refuge. Journal of Commitments, July 25, 1854–January 28, 1899. Missouri Historical Society, St. Louis.

St. Louis House of Refuge. Proceedings of the Board of Managers, August 6, 1860. Missouri Historical Society, St. Louis.